Forum Umwelt-, Agrar- und Klimaschutzrecht

Edited by
Prof. Dr. Ines Härtel

Volume 8

Ines Härtel/Roman Budzinowski (eds.)

Food Security, Food Safety, Food Quality

Current Developments and Challenges in
European Union Law

HART
PUBLISHING

Nomos

Supported by

**VIADRINA CENTER
B/ORDERS IN
MOTION**

Proofread by
Donald R. Black

The Deutsche Nationalbibliothek lists this publication in the
Deutsche Nationalbibliografie; detailed bibliographic data
are available on the Internet at http://dnb.d-nb.de

ISBN: HB (Nomos)   978-3-8487-2939-5
         ePDF (Nomos)   978-3-8452-7333-4

British Library Cataloguing-in-Publication Data
A catalogue record for this book is available from the British Library.

ISBN: HB (Hart)   978-1-50991-131-8

Library of Congress Cataloging-in-Publication Data
Härtel, Ines / Budzinowski, Roman
Food Security, Food Safety, Food Quality
Current Developments and Challenges in European Union Law
Ines Härtel / Roman Budzinowski (eds.)
281 p.

ISBN   978-1-50991-131-8   (hardcover Hart)

1. Edition 2016
© Nomos Verlagsgesellschaft, Baden-Baden, Germany 2016. Printed and bound in Germany.

Foreword

The adequate and secure supply of food was and is still a central problem of the people. Foods are existential resources for life and of extremely high importance. Therefore, the agricultural production, the refinement of agricultural products to the culinary refinement were always framed in legal, economic, social and political control systems. Today too little attention is paid to the cultivation of plants, the containment of wild animals and the development of agricultural technology, but these issues are very notable innovations of mankind. Food security was also supported by scientific evidences in the last 150 years. Since the Green Revolution, the precarious situation in food production has been overcome and food security has been made step by step – "having enough to eat" is changing more and more to the question "How do I become sated?". It is not only the quantity but also the quality of food products at affordable prices which we see as a normal case today. Especially the historical perspective illustrates clearly the change: Food shortage was replaced by abundance of food in Europe, eating became more convenient, selection became larger, you can find a variety of cultural food styles. Today we do not only hear of and read about the variety of conventional foods, but also of convenience food, fast food, paleo food, superfood, spiritual food, organic and vegan food and many other hypes and trends which indicate that foods have also become a life style meaning. However, the media hype must not cover that the production, processing and refinement of agricultural products are results of extensive and varied work. The "well-laid table" has many prerequisites. Health, quality and safety of foods, which play an important role in the food sector today, are benefits that need to be renewed permanently. Framings and requirements specifications for production (and trade) of food goods are largely legally codified especially in the European context in decades of genesis under changing socioeconomic and political conditions. Today the European Union has highly complex control systems in the field of agricultural production, food security, food safety and food quality, which include with different emphases all Member States due to regional-national features. Thus, the European Agricultural and Food Law ensures a high, internationally recognized standard of food goods, but also requires a constant development.

In this anthology, the complex relationships and specifics of the food industry of the European Union were discussed from the perspective of law. In presentation, analysis and discussions, important topics were taken up, for example the Right to Food, the development of the agricultural production and the Common Agricultural Policy (Greening, EU state aid law), contractual relations and value chains in the food sector, organic farming, food labeling and health claims, pesticides, patenting, GMO`s, the role of institutions such the EFSA and the responsibility of the trade. The idea for the anthology was created within the German-Polish law colloquium of the European University Viadrina Frankfurt (Oder) and the Adam Mickiewicz University in Poznań that focussed on current developments in Agricultural and Food Law and was ran by the two editors. The legal framework, key issues and future developments of food security, food safety and quality of food goods in the European context are the horizon of the contributions with a view of problem discussions and solutions.

Roman Budzinowski   Ines Härtel

Table of Content

Contributors

Editors

Härtel, Ines, Prof. Dr. jur., Vice President of European University Viadrina Frankfurt (Oder), Chair of Public Law, Administrative, European, Environmental, Agricultural and Food Economic Law, Faculty of Law / Adjunct Professor at China Agricultural University of Beijing, China

Budzinowski, Roman, Prof. Dr. jur., Dean of the Faculty of Law and Administration, Adam Mickiewicz University in Poznań, Head of Chair of Agricultural Law / President of the Polish Society for Agricultural Law; Vice President of the Comité Européen de Droit Rural

Contributors

Zielinski, Adam, Scientific Assistant, Department of Polish and European Agricultural Law, The Institute of Law Studies of the Polish Academy of Sciences

Leśkiewicz, Katarzyna, Dr. jur., Assistant Professor, Chair of Agricultural Law, Faculty of Law and Administration, Adam Mickiewicz University in Poznań

Thomas, Christian, Lawyer at Hoffmann, Liebs, Fritsch & Partner and PhD-Student, Chair of Public Law, Administrative, European, Environmental, Agricultural and Food Economic Law, Faculty of Law, European University Viadrina Frankfurt (Oder)

Flaskühler, Christina Agnetha, Scientific Assistant and PhD-Student, Chair of Public Law, Administrative, European, Environmental, Agricultural and Food Economic Law, Faculty of Law, European University Viadrina Frankfurt (Oder)

Szymecka-Wesołowska, Agnieszka, Dr. jur., Food Lawyer in the Food Law Centre and Lecturer at Kozminski University in Warsaw

Monien, Johanna, Dr. jur., EAM GmbH & Co KG, Lecturer, Faculty of Law, European University Viadrina Frankfurt (Oder)

Różański, Krzysztof, PhD-Student, Chair of Agricultural Law, Faculty of Law and Administration, Adam Mickiewicz University in Poznań,

Sokołowski, Łukasz Mikołaj, PhD-Student, Chair of Agricultural Law, Faculty of Law and Administration, Adam Mickiewicz University in Poznań

Olbrisch, Mathias, Scientific Assistant and PhD-Student, Chair of Public Law, Administrative, European, Environmental, Agricultural and Food Economic Law, Faculty of Law, European University Viadrina Frankfurt (Oder)

Brandauer, Daniel, Law Student, European University Viadrina Frankfurt (Oder)

Stoepker Johan Fried, Law Student, European University Viadrina Frankfurt (Oder)

Hindahl, Jan, Law Student, European University Viadrina Frankfurt (Oder)

Lipińska, Izabela, Dr. jur., Head of Economic and Agriculture Law Unit, Management and Law Department, Faculty of Economics and Social Sciences, Poznań University of Life Sciences

Mayer, Anne-Kristin, Academic Advisor of the Administrative Department, Ministry of Science, Research and Cultural Affairs, Health Campus Brandenburg and PhD-Student, Chair of Public Law, Administrative, European, Environmental, Agricultural and Food Economic Law, Faculty of Law, European University Viadrina Frankfurt (Oder)

Kapała, Anna, Dr. jur., Lecturer, Chair of Economic Policy and Law in the Institute of Economic and Social Sciences, Faculty of Natural Sciences and Technology, University of Environmental and Life Sciences in Wrocław

Suchoń, Aneta, Dr. jur., Assistant Professor, Chair of Agricultural Law, Faculty of Law and Administration, Adam Mickiewicz University in Poznań.

Schmelz, Hanna, Scientific Assistant and PhD-Student, Chair of Public Law, Administrative, European, Environmental, Agricultural and Food Economic Law, Faculty of Law, European University Viadrina Frankfurt (Oder)

Aust, Elisa, Scientific Assistant and PhD-Student, Chair of Public Law, Administrative, European, Environmental, Agricultural and Food Economic Law, Faculty of Law, European University Viadrina Frankfurt (Oder)

Wilhelm, Malte, PhD-Student, Chair of Public Law, Administrative, European, Environmental, Agricultural and Food Economic Law, Faculty of Law, European University Viadrina Frankfurt (Oder)

First Chapter:
Legal Framework, Structures and Developments

§ 1 The Right to Food – normative references in the multi-level system

Ines Härtel

A. Disparity of problems for world food

The Bible states: Man does not live by bread alone – but that indeed means first of all by bread. He must eat to ensure his existence. Food is thus the primary means for living. This appears, at first glance, to be simple and self-evident. And yet the production (and consumption) of food goods is the important result of diverse, interwoven historical, economic, socio-cultural and legal developments. At present, food goods are, above all, hemmed in to a high and complex degree by a differentiated legal regulation structure in the area of production, by the value chain (mainly processing, trading) to distribution, and by specific requirements such as, for example, food safety.

This applies not only for the European Union and her Member States, but worldwide – also where governmental, cultural, geographical, climatic and other peculiarities play an important role respectively. There arises, in the course of the current globalization, against this backdrop of such complex developments, and the growing world population (around 9 thousand-million in 2050) combined with a longer lifespan, the increasingly important question on the relationship between law and food goods. This means taking into view both the phenomenon of food scarcity as well as the phenomenon of food abundance with their different consequences. Naturally, it involves a large bandwidth of problems with the corresponding complex issues, which require a structured identification of the problems and the normative points of reference in order to solve the problems. In view of the high complexity, it is meaningful, in a simplified model, to distinguish between two worlds[1]: the world of food scarcity and the world of food

---

1 This simplified idea of two world models must for a proper reference – in following Frege, Peirce, Popper, Kantorowicz and Radbruch – be differentiated by experience and must prevail in the tangible world of objects in the conscious world and in the spiritual form, as they relate to each other in practice.

abundance; for both worlds there are a number of interlaced references and transitional stages. The world of food scarcity is characterized by 795 million people who currently suffer from hunger and malnutrition (above all, in so-called developing countries)[2], while in 2013 it was still 842 million people. This number shows – against the backdrop of the UN millennium goal at the time – in comparison to previous decades with over a thousand-million hungering, that successes are to be noted in the war against hunger.

On the other hand, in view of the high number of people still affected, the worldwide hunger problem continues and needs further problem solving measures. Hunger, as a fundamental shortcoming in human existence, should never, as a matter of principle, be acceptable. Beyond the quantity perspective (absolute number of hungry people), the concept of hunger, and the related supply need, has to be grasp and expanded to cover quality aspects. Malnutrition due to lack of possibility to feed oneself adequately to secure life means inadequate nutrition in the sense of so-called "hidden hunger". It has to be stated that such an inadequate diet exists for some two thousand million people. These people suffer from an under supply in the form of a lack of vitamins, minerals and other substances (micro-nutrient deficiencies). It is about providing both sufficient and adequate foodstuff. So, the levels of quality and quantity must also be taken into view.[3] Added to this is the complication that the problem of qualitative lack or under supply – albeit put in slightly different contexts – can also arise in the world of food abundance, which is basically characterized by sufficient, healthy food.

Characteristic of the world of food abundance is a very wide variety of food goods in quantity and quality. This correlates to a wide diversity of diet styles, which in the Western welfare states, above all, express greater individualisation, social status and a values-related lifestyle in an experience-oriented multi-option society.

There is such an abundant supply of food as never before in human history for the broad social strata of society. The positive effects are greater

---

2 FAO / IFAD / WFP, 'The State of Food Insecurity in the World – Meeting the 2015 international hunger targets: taking stock of uneven progress' (FAO Report 2015) <http://www.fao.org/3/a-i4646 e.pdf> accessed 13 January 2016.

3 German Federal Ministry of Food and Agriculture, 'Welternährung: Verbesserung der Ernährung weltweit' (2016) <https://www.bmel.de/DE/Landwirtschaft/Welternaehrung/_Texte/VerbesserungDerErnaehrung.html> accessed 13 January 2016.

health, higher vitality in old age and longer life expectancies. A new problem has arisen in the world of food abundance due to a physically less active life: 1.4 thousand million are overweight or indeed adipose – and this not only in industrial countries, but increasingly in countries with an expanding middle class like China, Brazil, India and smaller south Asian states, but also African countries south of the Sahara. Moreover, highlighting the disparity of the problems between the two worlds of food scarcity and food abundance, is that a waste of food can be noted[4]: in the world of food abundance by (too early) waste disposal, in the world of food scarcity by the spoilage of crop yield in a proportionally high percentage. In view of such developments, a sustainable handling of life resources is required for the security of world food. The inter-relationship between the agricultural/food industry and the environmental resources (soil, water, air, climate) must be addressed. Natural resources are utilized through the agri-food economy to achieve higher productivity, while simultaneously burdening the ecology. Agriculture, as the basis for food security, depends upon an intact ecological system.

For both worlds – that of food abundance as well as that of food scarcity – it is important to ask about the legal foundation. The first point of reference to be mentioned legally is the "The Human Right to Food". Such a human right to food requires guaranteeing world food and food security in all parts of the world globally, while especially engaging simultaneously against hunger in respect of quantity and quality. The normative references of the law on food must be found with their specific factors linked to law in the multi-level system, i.e. at global supra-national and national levels. It must be differentiated here between the Right to Food as such, and the instruments for realising this right.

---

4 See, in particular, here, Bärbel Dieckmann / Iris Schöninger, 'Hunger satt – Wege aus der Welternährungskrise' in Ines Härtel (ed), *Nachhaltigkeit, Energiewende, Klimawandel, Welternährung: Politische und rechtliche Herausforderungen des 21. Jahrhunderts* (Forum Umwelt-, Agrar- und Klimaschutzrecht, vol 1, Nomos 2014) § 31, 725; Ulrich Koester, 'Wegwerfen von Lebensmitteln – ineffizient und unmoralisch angesichts des Hungers in der Welt?' ibid § 32, 741.

B. The Right to Food in a global perspective

The most recent (legal-political) response of the world community to the global challenges of securing the Right to Food can be found in particular in "The 2030 Agenda for Sustainable Development", which was adopted on 25th September 2015 at the UN Summit in New York and which replaced the UN Millennium Development Goals. From a total of 17 Sustainable Development Goals (SDG), in the relevant Goals 2, the Right to Food was formulated as follows: "End hunger, achieve food security and improved nutrition and promote sustainable agriculture". The following sub-goals are to be achieved by 2030 (in accordance with 2.1 to 2.4):

2.1 end hunger and ensure access by all people, in particular the poor and people in vulnerable situations, including infants, to safe, nutritious and sufficient food all year round.

2.2 end all forms of malnutrition, including achieving, by 2025, the internationally agreed targets on stunting and wasting in children under 4 years of age, and address the nutritional needs of adolescent girls, pregnant and lactating women and older persons.

2.3 double the agricultural productivity and incomes of small-scale food producers, (…)

2.4 ensure sustainable food production systems and implement resilient agricultural practices that increase productivity and production, that help maintain ecosystems, that strengthen capacity for adaptation to climate change, extreme weather, drought, flooding and other disasters and that progressively improve land and soil quality.

According to 2.5 "by 2020 maintain the genetic diversity of seeds, cultivated plants and farmed and domesticated animals and their related wild species, including through soundly managed and diversified seed and plant banks at the national, regional and international levels, and promote access to and fair and equitable sharing of benefits arising from the utilization of genetic resources and associated traditional knowledge, as internationally agreed".

The communiqué of the leaders of the G20 Summit in Antalya (15 to 16 November 2015) also takes up reference to the Agenda 2030 and contains an action plan for food security and sustainable nutrition systems. The manner in which food is produced, consumed, and sold, should be sustainable economically, socially and ecologically within the meaning a three-dimensional approach (cf. Number 20, Communiqué). In addition to

SDG 2, the G20 obligate themselves to reduce food loss and food waste worldwide. A practical approach referring to the issue of the food goods problematic of the two worlds was, at least, made by the inclusion of the food waste problem in the communiqué. Concretisations can be found in the communique of the G20 in the "Agriculture Ministers Communique" of 7-8 May 2015 regarding the food security complexity and in the "Implementation Plan of the G20 Food Security and Nutrition Framework". Although these current declarations represent only Soft Law, they are path-finding for the implementation of the Right to Food in political and practical respects.

The human right to food was already adopted universally in International Law in the Universal Declaration of Human Rights (UDHR) of 10 December 1948.[5] It is not settled whether it has binding legal force as customary international law.[6] Under Article 25 (1) UDHR "Everyone has the right to a standard of living adequate for the health and well-being of himself and of his family, including food,...". Moreover, enshrined in Article 11 of the International Covenant on Economic, Social and Cultural Rights (ICESCR), which the UN General Assembly adopted in 1966 and which over 160 countries have already ratified, is the human right to adequate food. The Federal Republic of Germany ratified the ICESCR in 1973, and has been bound by it through international law since its entry into force in 1976[7,] whereby the treaty has the effect of ordinary federal law within Germany pursuant to Article 59 paragraph 2 of the Basic Law.[8] The Right to Food is also a principle in other special international treaties, e.g. in the Convention on the Elimination of All Forms of Discrimination against

---

5 UNGA Res 217 A (III) (10 December 1948) UN Doc A/RES/217 A (III).
6 Karl Doehring, *Völkerrecht* (2nd edn, C.F. Müller 2004) 428; Frithjof Ehm, 'Lebensmittel und Völkerrecht in Deutschland' (2013) ZLR 395, 398. For the range of views concerning the question of the legally binding effect of the UDHR see for example Marcel Kau in Wolfgang Graf Vitzthum (ed), *Völkerrecht* (6th edn, De Gruyter 2013) 203 recital 235 and 420; Martin Nettesheim, 'Die Allgemeine Erklärung der Menschenrechte und ihre Rechtsnatur' in Detlef Merten / Hans-Jürgen Papier (eds), *Handbuch der Grundrechte in Deutschland und Europa*, vol VI/2 (C.F. Müller 2009) § 173, 191 recital 38 ff.
7 German Federal Law Gazette 1976 II, 'Bekanntmachung über das Inkrafttreten des Internationalen Pakts über wirtschaftliche, soziale und kulturelle Rechte' (9 March 1976) 428.
8 See Frithjof Ehm, 'Lebensmittel und Völkerrecht in Deutschland' (2013) ZLR 395, 398.

Women[9], in the Convention on the Rights of the Child,[10] and in the Convention on the Rights of Persons with Disabilities[11]. It remains to be clarified legally to what extent the Right to Food can also be derived from the Right to Life pursuant to Article 6 sentence 1 of the International Covenant on Civil and Political Rights, and what such a deriving would mean. Another question concerns the relationship of the Right to Food pursuant to Article 11 ICESCR to the human right to water[12], which is recognized by the UN Resolution of 28 July 2010. The focus here is on the human right to *adequate food* pursuant to Article 11 section 1 of the ICESCR, which reads as follows:

"1. The States Parties to the present Covenant recognize the right of everyone to an adequate standard of living for himself and his family, including *adequate food* ... The States Parties will take appropriate steps to ensure the realization of this right, recognizing to this effect the essential importance of international co-operation based on free consent.
2. The States Parties to the present Covenant, recognizing the fundamental *right of everyone to be free from hunger*, shall take, individually and through

---

9 Art 12 (2) UN-Frauenrechtskonvention vom 18. Dezember 1979, German Federal Law Gazette 1985 II, 'Gesetz zu dem Übereinkommen vom 18. Dezember 1979 zur Beseitigung jeder Form von Diskriminierung der Frau' (25 April 1985) 647 ff.; Convention on the Elimination of all Forms of Discrimination against Women (adopted 18 December 1979, entered into force 3 September 1981) UNGA Res 34/180 A/34/46, 193 (CEDAW).
10 Art 24 (2) lit c), e) and art 27 (3) UN-Kinderrechtskonvention vom 20. Dezember 1989, German Federal Law Gazette 1992 II, 'Bekanntmachung über den Geltungsbereich des Übereinkommens über die Rechte des Kindes' (28 October 1992) 121 ff.; Convention on the Rights of the Child (adopted 20 November 1989, entered into force 2 September 1990) UNGA Res 44/25 (CRC).
11 Art 25 sentence 3 lit f) and art 28 (1) UN-Behindertenrechtskonvention vom 13. Dezember 2006, German Federal Law Gazette 2008 II, 'Gesetz zu dem Übereinkommen der Vereinten Nationen vom 13. Dezember 2006 über die Rechte von Menschen mit Behinderungen sowie zu dem Fakultativprotokoll vom 13. Dezember 2006 zum Übereinkommen der Vereinten Nationen über die Rechte von Menschen mit Behinderungen' (21 December 2008) 1419 ff.; Convention on the Rights of Persons with Disabilities (adopted 13 December 2006, entered into force 3 May 2008) UNGA A/RES/61/106 (CRPD).
12 Barbara Schmitz, '1. Subsistenzrechte – 1.5 Wasser' in Arnd Pollmann / Georg Lohmann (eds), *Menschenrechte: Ein interdisziplinäres Handbuch* (J.B. Metzler 2012) 238, 239 f.; see also Silke R. Laskowski, *Das Menschenrecht auf Wasser* (Mohr Siebeck 2010); Jessica Stubenrauch, 'Ein Menschenrecht auf Wasser' (2010) ZUR 521.

international co-operation, the measures, including specific programmes, which are needed ..."

It is distinguished between the right to adequate food and the right to freedom from hunger on account of the different formulations in Article 11 paragraph 1 and paragraph 2, ICESCR[13]. But the distinction is in practice increasingly less important[14]. Original semantic differences between "freedom from", "sufficient" and "adequate" are discarded in favour of a comprehensive understanding. General Comment 12 of the UN Committee on Economic, Social and Cultural Rights (CESCR)[15] of 1999[16], now serves for a more detailed definition of the scope of the right to adequate food and the related state obligations.

According to General Comment 12, the Right to Food is ensured if food is available[17], and contains no harmful substances[18], and is acceptable within a given culture[19], if it is available in sufficient quantity and quality in order to satisfy individual needs, and access to food is guaranteed in a sustainable way. This applies to the (global) population living now as well

---

13 Barbara Schmitz, '1. Subsistenzrechte – 1.2 Ernährung' in Arnd Pollmann / Georg Lohmann (eds), *Menschenrechte: Ein interdisziplinäres Handbuch* (J.B. Metzler 2012) 234, 235.

14 Katharina Engbruch, *Das Menschenrecht auf einen angemessenen Lebensstandard* (Peter Lang 2008) 163 (the distinction has no practical effect on the particular application of the Right to Food or to the reviewing of the national reports).

15 The Committee on Economic, Social and Cultural Rights (CESCR) monitors the compliance with the UN Covenant on Economic, Social and Cultural Rights (ICESCR).

16 Cf United Nations, Economic and Social Council, General Comment no 12 'The right to adequate food (art 11)' (12 May 1999) E/C.12/1999/5 <http://www.refworld.org/pdfid/4538838c11.pdf> accessed 13 January 2016.

17 '12. *Availability* refers to the possibilities either for feeding oneself directly from productive land or other natural resources, or for well-functioning distribution, processing and market systems that can move food from the site of production to where it is needed in accordance with demand'.

18 '10. *Free from adverse substances* sets requirements for food safety and for a range of protective measures by both public and private means to prevent contamination of foodstuffs through adulteration and/or through bad environmental hygiene or inappropriate handling at different stages throughout the food chain; care must also be taken to identify and avoid or destroy naturally occurring toxins'.

19 '11. *Cultural or consumer acceptability* implies the need also to take into account, as far as possible, perceived non nutrient-based values attached to food and food consumption and informed consumer concerns regarding the nature of accessible food supplies'.

as to future generations. At the core are the principle of accessibility, the principle of availability and the principle of sustainability.[20] The European Parliament adopted in its resolution of 18 December 2011[21] that the Right to Food security "... is achieved when all people, at all times, have physical and economic access to suitable, adequate and nutritious food to meet their dietary needs and preferences for an active and healthy life;"

According to General Comment 12 of the ICESCR, there is an obligation, in view of the Right to Food, for the States to respect, protect and guarantee the right. Firstly, the states must respect a standing right of access to food, i.e. cease activities which rob people of their standing right of access to food (obligation to respect). Secondly, the states must protect access to food from the assaults of third persons, be it through legislative or police measures (obligation to protect). Thirdly, they must guarantee access to food, if such is not present (obligation to provide).[22] If states are not in the position to fulfil their obligation to provide, they should accept international help.[23] A series of remarkable and important legal forms, which, in reference to the regulatory object, like governmental and non-governmental regulatory addressees, and attributable, above all, to Soft Law, have established themselves at the world level next to explicitly legally binding regulations, in trans-national global measure, due to particular constitutive and institutional conditions. The voluntary guidelines of the UN Food and Agriculture Organization (FAO) of 2004 and 2012 are particularly important, in this respect, for the further concretization and implementation of the Right to Food. Even if they are not legally binding (in the sense of Hard Law), they fulfil a series of ground-breaking functions. They promote problem awareness, make orientation possible, serve

---

20 United Nations, Economic and Social Council, General Comment no 12 'The right to adequate food (art 11)' 12 May 1999, E/C.12/1999/5 <http://www.refworld.org/pdfid/4538838c11.pdf> accessed 13 January 2016.
21 European Parliament, 'Resolution of 18 January 2011 on recognition of agriculture as a strategic sector in the context of food security (2010/2112(INI))' [2012] OJ C 136 E/02, R. 4.
22 This concept of duties can be found in a similar manner in the respect/protect/remedy approach of the UN Guidelines on Business and Human Rights (Human Rights Council (UNHRC) 'UN Guiding Principles on Business and Human Rights') UN Doc A/HRC/17/31.
23 The duties of the state, see United Nations, Economic and Social Council, General Comment no 15 (s.o.); overall see <http://www.bpb.de/internationales/weltweit/178491/menschenrecht-auf-nahrung> accessed 13 January 2016.

as an action guide, as a help to interpretation, and, in the long run, are pathfinders for setting legally binding standards.[24] The "Voluntary Guidelines to support the progressive realization of the right to adequate food in the context of national food security"[25] of 2004 contain an operational framework for the implementation of the Right to Food. These practical operating instructions for governments and civil society relate to the creating of national strategies, the securing of access to resources (land, water, seed), sustainability, the strengthening of women's rights, transparency, participation, the establishing of food safety and consumer protection, responding to disasters, as well as, to the establishment of monitoring and benchmarks. They also show the international framework, for example, in relation to food aid, and in promoting commerce and investment.[26]

The "Voluntary Guidelines on the Responsible Governance of Tenure of Land, Fisheries and Forests in the Context of National Food Security"[27] of 2012[28], take up the need for food safety with a view toward rights to land and natural resources as well as to their sustainable management. The

---

24 Frithjof Ehm, 'Lebensmittel und Völkerrecht in Deutschland' (2013) ZLR 395, 400; Johanna Monien, 'Die "Freiwilligen Leitlinien für die verantwortungsvolle Verwaltung von Boden- und Landnutzungsrechten, Fischgründen und Wäldern im Kontext nationaler Ernährungssicherung" der Vereinten Nationen in rechtlicher Perspektive' in Ines Härtel, *Nachhaltigkeit, Energiewende, Klimawandel, Welternährung: Politische und rechtliche Herausforderungen des 21. Jahrhunderts* (Forum Umwelt-, Agrar- und Klimaschutzrecht, vol 1, Nomos 2014) § 34, 789 – meaning, advantage and disadvantage of Soft Law.

25 FAO, 'Voluntary Guidelines to support the progressive realization of the right to adequate food in the context of national food security' (2012); see FAO, 'Zwischenstaatliche Arbeitsgruppe zur Erarbeitung eines Rahmenwerks freiwilliger Leitlinien zur Unterstützung der schrittweisen Verwirklichung des Rechts auf angemessene Nahrung im Rahmen der nationalen Ernährungssicherheit' (Report 2004) <http://www.bmel.de/SharedDocs/Downloads/Landwirtschaft/Welternaehrung/Leitlinien-RechtaufNahrung.pdf?__blob=publicationFile> accessed 13 January 2016.

26 See Amnesty International, 'Keine Rechte zweiter Klasse – wirtschaftliche, soziale und kulturelle Rechte' (2010) <http://www.amnesty.de/files/Brosch%C3%BCre_WSK-Rechte_DS.pdf> accessed 13 January 2016.

27 FAO, 'Voluntary Guidelines on the Responsible Governance of Tenure of Land, Fisheries and Forests in the Context of National Food Security' (2012) <http://www.fao.org/docrep/016/i2801e/i2801 e.pdf> accessed 13 January 2016.

28 124 member states of the Committee on World Food Security of the United Nations (CFS) decided unanimously these guidelines on 11 May 2012.

voluntary guidelines contain minimum standards for recognition, transfer and administration of ownership, possessory and use rights to land, fishing grounds and forests, regulations for expropriation by compulsory purchase, issues of compensation, and agricultural reform measures including land redistribution schemes as well as to procedural norms and standards of good governmental leadership for land administration from price setting and evaluation to land administration.[29] In particular, they deal with the problematical result where land investment appears in a series of cases in the form of "Landgrabbing".[30] Here, food will still be produced, but at the same time, above all, from the perspective of the non-governmental organisations, food security and/or land rights of the indigenous population are at risk or even destroyed.[31]

With regard to the global effectiveness of the Right to Food, not only are questions about practical implementation in the states raised, but also questions about the justiciability and legal standing to sue over the Right to Food: which groups of people will be allowed to sue for which injuries of law before which courts? How far do the obligations of states reach – are they limited to the territory of each state or do they in fact apply extraterritorially? Can the Right to Food be enforced, or sued for, against private persons like (trans-national) companies? These questions, which are meanwhile being discussed more than previously in legal publications[32], require a further deeper analysis in future – also against the back-

---

29 See the summary of the German Federal Ministry of Food and Agriculture, 'Welternährung: Das Menschenrecht auf Nahrung und die Freiwilligen Leitlinien der FAO' (2015) <https://www.bmel.de/DE/Landwirtschaft/Welternaehrung/_Texte/RechtAufNahrung-LeitlinienFAO.html> accessed 13 January 2016.

30 Asit Datta, *Armutszeugnis* (dtv 2013) 92 ff.; Fred Pearce, *Land Grabbing: der globale Kampf um Grund und Boden* (5th edn, Verlag Antje Kunstmann 2012).

31 For more details, see, for example, Jochen von Bernstorff, ' "Land Grabbing" und Menschenrechte: die FAO Voluntary Guidelines on the Responsible Governance of Tenure' (2012) 11 INEF 7 ff., 29 ff. <http://www.humanrights-business.org/files/landgrabbing_final_1.pdf> accessed 14 January 2016; Bettina Rudloff, 'Kein schöner Land' (SWP-Studie 2012) <https://www.swp-berlin.org/fileadmin/contents/products/studien/2012_S19_rff.pdf> accessed 14 January 2016.

32 For the fundamentals in a special context, see, for example, Ibrahim Kanalan, *Die universelle Durchsetzung des Rechts auf Nahrung gegen transnationale Unternehmen* (Mohr Siebeck 2015); Steffen Kommer, *Menschenrechte wider den Hunger. Das Recht auf Nahrung zwischen Wissenschaft, Politik und globalen Märkten* (Forum Umwelt-, Agrar- und Klimaschutzrecht, vol 7, Nomos forthcom-

drop of continued developments in legal practice and legal reference in the national, European and global multi-level system.

C. The Right to Food in EU-Law

The law of the European Union does not itself expressly regulate a right to food. There is, however, an international law obligation in the EU for the human right to food. A direct obligation arises for the EU specifically due to its accession to the Convention on the Rights of Persons with Disabilities in 2010, which contains the Right to Food.[33] Moreover, there is, in general, an indirect international law obligation for the EU for the Right to Food pursuant to Article 11 of the International Covenant on Economic, Social and Cultural Rights (ICESCR) via Article 6 (1) of the Treaty on European Union in conjunction with Article 53 of the Charter of Fundamental Rights of the European Union (CFR).[34]

Pursuant to Article 53 CFR, nothing in the Charter shall be interpreted as restricting or adversely affecting human rights and fundamental freedoms "as recognised, in their respective fields of application, by Union law and international law and by international agreements to which the Union, the Community or all the Member States are party". All Member States have ratified the ICESCR so that the safeguarding provision in Article 53 CFR has application effect.[35]

---

ing 2016) § 4, § 8 A. III; see in general Anne Peters, *Jenseits der Menschenrechte – Die Rechtsstellung des Individuums im Völkerrecht* (Mohr Siebeck 2014).

33 United Nations Treaty Collection, Chapter IV: Human Rights, no 15 'Convention on the Rights of Persons with Disabilities' <https://treaties.un.org/Pages/ViewDetails.aspx?src=IND&mtdsg_no=IV-15&chapter=4&lang=en> accessed 14 January 2016; UN Convention on the Rights of Persons with Disabilities (adopted 13 December 2006, entered into force 3 May 2008) UNGA A/RES/61/106 (CRPD) art 28.

34 See Silke R. Laskowski, *Das Menschenrecht auf Wasser* (Mohr Siebeck 2010) 897; Andreas Fischer-Lescano, 'Austeritätspolitik und Menschenrechte, Rechtspflichten der Unionsorgane beim Abschluss von Memoranda of Understanding' (Rechtsgutachten im Auftrag der Kammer für Arbeiter/innen und Angestellte für Wien, Zentrum für europäische Rechtspolitik Fachbereich Rechtswissenschaft, Universität Bremen 2013) 13 ff.

35 Eibe Riedel in Jürgen Meyer (ed), *Charta der Grundrechte der Europäischen Union, Kommentar* (4th edn, Nomos 2014) title IV: Solidarität, Vorbemerkungen, recital 34; Steffen Kommer, *Menschenrechte wider den Hunger. Das Recht auf*

It has not yet been conclusively clarified whether a direct binding effect exists on the EU due to the ICESCR. The UN Economic and Social Council is of the opinion that international organisations are themselves bound by the ICESCR.[36] Such a direct binding effect on the EU could be grounded upon universal customary law application of human rights. Assuming that the Right to Food is qualified for application, then international organisations, and thus also the EU, are bound by this.[37] In addition, there is also an extraterritorial application of the Right to Food for the EU, i.e. the obligation to respect law in third countries. This can be derived from Article 21 (1) TEU (The Treaty on European Union) (and Article 205 TFEU) (The treaty on the Functioning of the European Union), whereby the EU in its activity at the international level is guided by the universal applicability of human rights.[38]

A Right to Food is not expressly written in the EU-CFR as it is also not in the Constitutions of the Member States. However, a Right to Food could derive implicitly from the EU-CFR. It must first be examined what dogmatic fundamental right connection might come into question for the Right to Food. Two aspects can basically be distinguished regarding the direction and content of the protective sphere of the Right to Food, modelled on the universal human right to food: 1. ensuring sufficient, adequate, safe food (basic security, protection against hunger) and, 2. food safety (protection against food harmful to health). Both aspects are interconnected inasmuch as food security simultaneously extends to guaranteeing safe food. There must be a distinction made between the two aspects of food security and food safety for deviating dogmatically from the protection of fundamental rights. These two aspects of the Right to Food

---

Nahrung zwischen Wissenschaft, Politik und globalen Märkten (Forum Umwelt-, Agrar- und Klimaschutzrecht, vol 7, Nomos forthcoming 2016) § 4, § 8 A II. 3.a.

36 UN Committee on Economic, Social and Cultural Rights (CESR), General Comment no 8 'The relationship between economic sanctions and respect for economic, social and cultural rights' (1997) UN Doc E/C.12/1997/8 recital 11; CESR, General Comment no 15 'The Right to Water (art 11 and 12 of the Covenant)' (2003) UN Doc E/C.12/2002/11 recital 38; CESR, General Comment no 19 'The right to social security (art 9 of the Covenant)' (2008) UN Doc E/C.12/GC/19 recital 38.

37 Steffen Kommer, *Menschenrechte wider den Hunger. Das Recht auf Nahrung zwischen Wissenschaft, Politik und globalen Märkten* (Forum Umwelt-, Agrar- und Klimaschutzrecht, vol 7, Nomos forthcoming 2016) § 8 A II. 2.

38 Ibid § 8 A. II. 3.

could find protection in the right to life (Article 2 (1) CFR) as well as in the right to physical integrity (Article 3 (1) CFR). In regards to interpreting these rights, a modelling based upon the interpretation of the same identical Basic Rights in the Basic Law must be considered, since in this respect, during the formulation of the Basic Rights, the Convention (presided over by Roman Herzog, former President of the Constitutional Court, and Federal President in Germany) borrowed from the CFR at the time. Therefore, the right to life and the right to physical integrity within the meaning of the UN CFR as identical basic rights pursuant to Article 2 paragraph 2 sentence 1 of the Basic Law, which are primarily subjective rights, do indeed protect against intrusions by governmental authority.[39] From the perspective of a defence for the above mentioned aspects of food, they, as a rule, hardly have any practical relevance. In any case, they could attain an objective legal content. This could exist in the obligation of governmental (Union) power to protect life and physical integrity. While the ECJ has already recognised EU obligations to protect in the area of fundamental freedoms regarding an obligation to protect, a judicature is yet lacking in regards to the obligation to protect under fundamental rights of the Union. But, the complicated relationship of the EU to its Member States must be taken into account for a dogmatic foundation of any possible protection obligations of the EU. An obligation to protect, however, will only come into consideration, if there is law-making power competence for each legal act proposed. This makes clear the area of applicability of the fundamental rights charter pursuant to Article 51 (1) CFR, which has to respect the limits of the Union's responsibility pursuant to primary law.[40] The need to clarify thus remains, whether a basic right obligation of the Union to protect its Union citizens is only present in the case of an exclusive competence of the Union, or whether other grounds could be decisive. The EU disposes of a series of powers to decree legal acts, which serve to realise the Right to Food. The first one to highlight here, is the

---

39 Christian Starck in Hermann von Mangoldt / Friedrich Klein / Christian Starck (eds), *Kommentar zum Grundgesetz*, vol 1 (6th edn, Vahlen 2010) art 2 (2) recital 190; Friedhelm Hufen, *Staatsrecht II - Grundrechte* (4th edn, C.H. Beck 2014) § 13 recital 9.

40 See Dirk Ehlers, 'Allgemeine Lehren der Unionsgrundrechte' in Dirk Ehlers (ed), *Europäische Grundrechte und Grundfreiheiten* (4th edn, De Gruyter 2015) § 14, 513 ff.; for the competences of the Union refer to Ines Härtel, 'Die Zuständigkeiten der Union' in Matthias Niedobitek (ed), *Europarecht – Grundlagen der Union* (De Gruyter 2014) § 6, 503.

legal competence power over agriculture that the Union shares with its Member States (cf. Article 4 (2) (d) TFEU).[41] The goals of the Common Agricultural Policy (CAP), pursuant to Article 39 (1) TFEU, stand in direct connection to the Right to Food. Pointing, above all, to this are the goals of security of availability and of supplying to the consumer at reasonable prices (Article 39 (1) (d) TFEU). And, the necessity of resource protection for sustainable agriculture as the basis for food security finds its safeguarding in primary law within the section clause for environmental protection (Article 11 TFEU). The Right to Food is also supported by primary law by the section clause for consumer protection (Article 12 TFEU) as well as for human health protection (Article 168 no. 1 TFEU).

Secondary law of the EU for Common Agricultural Policy (in regards to agricultural production) shows an extensive inventory of legal norms, which in totality is assignable to the Right to Food. It must be differentiated fundamentally between the first and second pillars in regard to the regulatory instruments of the CAP. Measures of agricultural market policy belong to the first pillar, in particular, to common agricultural market regulation and to direct income payments to the farmers. The second pillar encompasses the promotion of rural development. The ecological sustainability of agriculture was strengthened, in particular, with the last reform of the CAP. In addition to Cross Compliance[42], which was already introduced years ago, Greening is now included.[43] The farm operator must fulfil additional agro-ecological requirements under Greening, to receive agricultural subsidies, which go beyond the special law for Cross Compliance.

---

41 The legal basis for Union acts is contained in art 43 (2) TFEU.

42 'Cross-compliance is a mechanism that links direct payments to compliance by farmers with basic standards concerning the environment, food safety, animal and plant health and animal welfare, as well as the requirement of maintaining land in good agricultural and environmental condition'; European Commission, 'Landwirtschaft und ländliche Entwicklung: Cross-Compliance – Erfüllung von Umweltschutzauflagen' (2016) <http://ec.europa.eu/agriculture/envir/cross-compliance/index_en.htm> accessed 13 January 2016.

43 Regulation (EU) 1307/2013 of the European Parliament and of the Council of 17 December 2013 establishing rules for direct payments to farmers under support schemes within the framework of the Common Agricultural Policy and repealing Council Regulation (EC) 637/2008 and Council Regulation 73/2009 [2013] OJ L 347/608, art 43 ff.

Furthermore, the CAP has also developed a legal harmonisation policy which can be labelled quasi as a third pillar. The legal harmonisation extends, for example, to the areas of plant protection, animal breeding, animal protection, animal feed, and the veterinary field, but, also to food security and quality security in agriculture. The regulation of ecological farming and the geographically protected origin information, in turn, belong, among other matters, also to quality policy.[44]

There is a secondary law conglomerate in the two (three) pillars of the CAP in the form of law-making acts (of the European Parliament and of the Council), delegated legal and implementing acts of the EU Commission[45] - above all, in the form of regulations, but also in Soft Law of the Commission (e.g. shaping the guidelines). Joining the great number of regulations in this area are a series of further directives with reference to agriculture (e.g. Nitrates Directive, Water Framework Directive, Sewage Sludge Directive, Birds Directive, Habitats Directive).

Article 114 no. 1 TFEU represents a central legal basis of the harmonisation competence for decreeing legal acts to guarantee food security. In the areas of health, security, and environmental protection and consumer protection, the Union's law-making power must proceed from a high level of protection and take into account all new developments based on scientific facts (Article 114 no. 3 TFEU). The Union law-maker has already introduced a differentiated tiered approach (risk evaluation, risk management, risk communication including governmental information/consumer warnings for hazardous foods). The principle of traceability from farm to fork and vice versa applies.

The EU is challenged in various ways in foreign policy in regard to the Right to Food. On the one hand, the EU desires to make a contribution in the war against world hunger. Therefore, food security forms a central priority in development cooperation (Article 208 to 211 TFEU) and humanitarian aid (Article 214 TFEU). The policy of the EU is not restricted to food aid, but supports broadly laid out regional, national and global strate-

---

44 Reinhard Priebe in Eberhard Grabitz / Meinhard Hilf / Martin Nettesheim (eds), *Das Recht der Europäischen Union: EUV/AEUV* (C.H. Beck 2015) TFEU, 57 a.d. 2015, art 40 recital 142 ff.; Carsten Bittner in Jürgen Schwarze (ed), *EU-Kommentar* (3rd edn, Nomos 2012) TFEU, art 38 recital 50 ff.
45 See Ines Härtel, 'Gesetzgebungsordnung der Europäischen Union' in Armin Hatje / Peter-Christian Müller-Graff (eds), *Enzyklopädie Europarecht*, vol 1 (Nomos 2014) § 11, 62312,0 recital 1 ff.

gies of food security.[46] Beyond this, the EU desires, within the framework of international trade policy (in particular, based upon the export power, Article 207 TFEU), to work towards the improvement of food safety, and, at least, keep food safety at the EU entry level, also when concluding bilateral treaties, as, for example, with the U.S.A. (TTIP).

D. The Right to Food in the Basic Law

The Right to Food has been expressly enshrined in the constitutions of 29 states[47], however, among these are not a single Member State of the EU. The universal human right to food has internal validity[48] and also creates for public authority extraterritorial validity abroad.[49]

It was discussed at the creation of the German Basic Law, following the draft of the Universal Declaration of Human Rights, to attach the following provision to the then existing draft of Article 3 Basic Law: "In no case may the minimum amount necessary for food, clothing and shelter be denied"[50]. Even if this right was not ultimately expressly adopted, an implied recognition of an individual basic right to adequate food to secure life is mandated by the need for protection. This basic right derives from the basic right to life and physical integrity pursuant to Article 2 paragraph 2 sentence 1 of the Basic Law, indeed due to its legal-objective content. The

---

46 Ines Härtel, 'Vom Klimawandel bis zur Welternährung – zentrale Weltprobleme, Rechtsintegration und Zukunftsgesellschaft' in Ines Härtel (ed), *Nachhaltigkeit, Energiewende, Klimawandel, Welternährung: politische und rechtliche Herausforderungen des 21. Jahrhunderts* (Forum Umwelt-, Agrar- und Klimaschutzrecht, vol 1, Nomos 2014) § 1, 13, 43.

47 The wording of the constituions can be accessed at <http://faolex.fao.org/> accessed 20 January 2016.

48 For reviewing the discussion whether validity has its grounds under art 25 sentence 1 or 2 Basic Law (GG) or under art 59 (2) GG, see Ines Härtel, 'Ein (Menschen-)Recht auf Nahrung?' in Max-Emanuel Geis / Markus Winkler / Christian Bickenbach (eds), *Von der Kultur der Verfassung, Festschrift für Friedhelm Hufen* (C.H. Beck 2015) 23 with further references.

49 Anne Peters, *Jenseits der Menschenrechte* (Mohr Siebeck 2014) 221 ff., 421 ff.

50 Anlage zum stenographischen Bericht der 9. Sitzung am 6. Mai 1949, Schriftlicher Bericht des Abgeordneten Dr. von Mangoldt über den Abschnitt I. Die Grundrechte, Parlamentarischer Rat, Bonn 1948/1949, p. 12 can be accessed at <http://www.gewaltenteilung.de/gewaltenteilung-in-deutschland/1147.html> accessed 20 January 2016.

obligation of public authority to protect life and physical integrity results from this.

The scope of protection in Article 2 paragraph 2 sentence 1 of the Basic Law extends in a dual manner to the governmental obligation to protect basic security with food and food security as a part of an existential infrastructure (caring for existence). The collective is addressed with individual rights within the individual sphere, including the right to seek legal redress, by its obligations to protect which extend to measures to secure sufficient and adequate food in caring for the population. The obligations to protect refer to risk prevention, and also to risk precaution.[51] But here, the state cannot be obligated to prevent every single last risk. In regards to basic security with food, there is, on the one hand, the obligation for the state, pursuant to Article 2 paragraph 2 sentence 1, to take precautions, respecting grave supply and food shortages, to provide for possible emergencies (natural catastrophes, animal epidemics, serious accidents, or terrorist attacks). The legislator has fulfilled this obligation in that he has passed corresponding laws: Food Security Law (for political/military emergencies) and Food Supply Law (for supply emergencies in peacetime). Accordingly, there are national crisis inventories/state emergency stockpiles (federal grain reserve and civil emergency reserve). In part, under § 14 of the Civil Disaster Relief Law (ZSKG) and the Federal/State Joint Crises Management Exercises (LÜKEX). And in part, the governmental obligation to protect extends to the prevention of hunger in the needy individual in respect to basic security for food. In particular, food poverty can arise due to unemployment. Here, the governmental obligation can, in an individual case, compress into the claim of an individual person. A claim arises from the right to life under Article 1 paragraph 2 sentence 1, Basic Law, "to be protected ... against hunger, when the public authority becomes attributably cognisant, and the possibilities to act are present".[52] "Claims for securing a minimum existence that do not directly serve to support life" are incidentally derived from Article 1, paragraph 1, Basic Law, in conjunction with the social principle pursuant to Article 20

---

51 See Philip Kunig in Ingo von Münch / Philip Kunig (eds), *Grundgesetz-Kommentar*, vol 1 (6th edn, C.H. Beck 2012) art 2 recital 67 f.
52 Udo Di Fabio in Theodor Maunz / Günter Dürig (eds), *Grundgesetz-Kommentar* (C.H. Beck 2015) 75 a.d. 2015, art 2 (2) sentence 1 recital 45.

paragraph 1 Basic Law.[53] The livelihood necessary for guaranteeing a minimum existence, in particular for food, is encompassed by ordinary law (see§ 27 a Social Law, Book No. XII in conjunction with § 20 paragraph 1 Social Book No. II). A further special case for the governmental obligation for food security is that of forced feeding during a hunger strike in the public sphere.

The second dimension of the governmental obligation to protect refers to food safety. The basic right under Article 2 paragraph 2 sentence 1, Basic Law, is also "particularly important ... as constitutional basis for health-related consumer protection"[54]. In following EU law, the German law-maker already introduced a differentiated tiered approach regarding food security. The right to physical integrity includes the "right to self-determination for food".[55] For this reason, the legislator must standardise certain labelling obligations for food. This refers to the "marketing of foods that are treated with chemical additives, that are radiated radioactively, or that are genetically altered". "The ingestion of chemical substances impairs, namely, always then when it does not ensue voluntarily."[56]

Both dimensions of the Right to Food, rather of the right to adequate food - the life-sustaining basic security of food and food safety - can also be understood within the meaning of unwritten constitutional law. In this sense, the Right to Food is not expressly enshrined in the Basic Law in

---

53 Ibid; for the fundamental right to a decent minimum standard of living see BVerfGE 125, 175 (Federal Constitutional Court) – Leitsatz. Sceptical in terms of the derivation of this fundamental right, Heinrich Lang in Volker Epping / Christian Hillgruber (eds), *Beck'scher Online-Kommentar GG* (26th edn, C.H. Beck 2014) art 2 recital 81. One concludes the claim of livelihood, so of survival, from art 2 (2) GG. According to him, the claim to ensuring one's livelihood, thus the right to live is established in art 2 (2) GG.

54 Friedhelm Hufen, *Staatsrecht II - Grundrechte* (4th edn, C.H. Beck 2014) § 13 recital 4.

55 Dietrich Murswiek in Michael Sachs, *Grundgesetz Kommentar* (7th edn, C.H. Beck 2014) art 2 recital 204; Christian Starck in Hermann von Mangoldt / Friedrich Klein / Christian Starck (eds), *Kommentar zum Grundgesetz*, vol 1 (6th edn, Verlag Franz Vahlen 2010) art 2 (2) recital 233; Cathrin Correll in Erhard Denninger / Wolfgang Hoffmann-Riem / Hans P. Schneider / Ekkehart Stein (eds), *Kommentar zum Grundgesetz für die Bundesrepublik Deutschland (AK-GG)* (3rd edn, Hermann Luchterhand Verlag 2001) art 2 (2) recital 112 ff.

56 Dietrich Murswiek in Michael Sachs (ed), *Grundgesetz Kommentar* (7th edn, C.H. Beck 2014) art 2 recital 204.

writing, but still "applies legally as though it were so enshrined"[57] and therefore possesses normative validity. In regards to this, the Constitutional court of Baden (*Badische Staatsgerichtshof*) held early on that it here involves "the human right to food, which exists inherently as an unwritten basic right not abolish-able by any legal act"[58].

Due to the development of international law, processes of "constitutional changes without changes in the constitutional text"[59], "which are not expressed as norms in the constitutional text", must be considered generally and, in regards to the basic right to food, also beyond the principle of commitment to international law[60].

E. Conclusion

The law forms a central reference point, next to economic, political and social influence factors, in order to realise the goal of sustainable food security worldwide. The human right to food can be used as a fundamental norm for further legal formations. There are multilevel differentiated starting points at the levels of national, European and global law. The requirements for the obligations to observe, protect, fulfil or guarantee are found in specific legal forms which encompass both forms of Hard Law as well as Soft Law.

Here, however, the problems of the two worlds of food abundance and food scarcity, with their different models, have to be considered differently, even if the goal of supplying adequate and sufficient food applies to both. In future, other problems must also be taken into account that will also challenge the right. This includes the growing world population, climate change, scarcer resources, and unequal distribution. A quantitative and qualitative increase in the production of food will only be possible by observing the planet's limits, even if made through further advances in science and technology. From this perspective, the "war against hunger (se-

---

57 Heinrich Amadeus Wolff, *Ungeschriebenes Verfassungsrecht unter dem Grundgesetz* (Mohr Siebeck 2000) 4 with further references to literature, the Right to Food is mentioned particularly in his list of unwritten Constitutional rights (p. 5).

58 VerwRspr 1 (1949), no 81, 249, 251 (Baden State Court).

59 Horst Dreier, 'Kontexte des Grundgesetzes' (1999) DVBl 667, 678.

60 Ibid, Dreier refers in this context for example to changes by the supranational European Union Law.

curing existence) and the war for food security" will stand intensified in the focus of the law at all three levels. Sufficient and adequate food, and safe food, remain the goal of all humankind. Both worlds are obligated to find problem solutions that are legally binding.

They remain inter-linked by giving and taking direction from each other in a normative regard for the human right to food.

§ 2 Food-related challenges of the Common Agricultural Policy in the context of the development of agricultural law

Roman Budzinowski

A. Introduction

The title of this work, at least at first glance, seems obvious. After all, looking back, "food-related challenges" constituted an important justification of legislative intervention in agricultural matters and determined the development of agricultural law and its direction. It might seem under the conditions of the contemporary market, the characteristic feature of which, at least in Europe, is accessibility of food at a reasonable price, that these challenges should be losing in importance, or at least not growing in significance. However, what we are observing is exactly the opposite. Food-related challenges are becoming more important not only in agricultural policy (here: the Common Agricultural Policy) but also in legal regulations.

The discussion on the present form of the Common Agricultural Policy, initiated during the CAP Health Check in 2008, resulted in a number of EU documents which spelt out the challenges, objectives and tools for their achievement, of which the main document is the Communication of the European Commission presented on 18 November 2010 "The CAP towards 2020: Meeting the food, natural resources and territorial challenges of the future"[1]. A reference to this document can be found in the EU's legal acts establishing the legal framework of the Common Agricultural Policy for the years 2014-2020. It may thus be said that the above "challenges of the future" have been responsible for the content of the tools or instruments for which those legal acts provided. They may, and should, constitute a point of reference in the formulating of a new regulation of the

---

1 European Commission, 'Communication of the European Commission to the European Parliament, the Council, the European Economic and Social Committee and the Committee of the Regions of 18 November 2010 - The CAP 2020: Meeting the food, natural resources and territorial challenges of the future' COM (2010) 672 final.

European Union law as well as the laws of individual Member states. Furthermore, having regard to the relationship between politics and law, it is justified to conclude that food-related challenges of the Common Agricultural Policy are also reflected in law.

The remarks formulated herein point to the importance of the research subject undertaken in this work. Of predominant importance is the meaning of this subject from the point of view of law. It is, after all, the legislator who must resolve the difficult problems connected with food, having regard to the challenges of the future. It is not accidental that in the Communication of the European Commission quoted above, the challenges referred to in the title of this paper were mentioned first. And yet, arguments supporting the application of law must also be taken into account. Competent bodies should apply the law in a way allowing efficient implementation of the premises that underlie their statutory solutions. Finally, the importance of the research topic from the point of view of the development of agricultural law cannot be overlooked, as it has been noted in the title of this work.

Challenges of the CAP regarding food, analysed in the context of the development of agricultural law, have not as yet been the subject of a separate paper, although many issues have already been highlighted. These "challenges of the future" are the background theme of the whole monograph by J.S. Zegar on the contemporary challenges facing agriculture[2]. They have also been reflected in many articles, especially on the Common Agricultural Policy[3], agricultural law[4] and food law[5].

---

2 Roman Budzinowski, 'Prawo rolne wobec współczesnych wyzwań' (2014) 2 (15) Przegląd Prawa Rolnego 11 (and literature quoted therein).
3 Compare eg Claude Blumann, 'La politique agricole commune face aux nouveaux défis planétaires et européens' (2013) 416 Revue de Droit rural; Kamila Błażejewska, 'Klimatyczne wyzwania Wspólnej Polityki Rolnej po 2013 r.' (2011) 1 (8) Przegląd Prawa Rolnego 135.
4 Mariarita D'Addezio, 'Sicurezza e coordinemento delle esigenze alimentari con quelle energetiche: nuove problematiche per il diritto agrario' (2011) 3 Agricoltura - Istituzioni – Mercati 11; see also eg Ines Härtel, 'Agrarrecht im Paradigmenwechsel: Grüne Gentechnik, Lebensmittelsicherheit und Umweltschutz' in Christian Calliess / Ines Härtel / Barbara Veit (eds), *Neue Haftungsrisiken in der Landwirtschaft: Gentechnik, Lebensmittel- und Futtermittelrecht, Umweltschadensrecht* (Schriften zum Agrar, Umwelt- und Verbraucherschutzrecht, vol 55, Nomos 2007) 21; Ines Härtel, 'Chapter 7 – Agricultural Law' in Matthias Ruffert (ed), *Europäisches*

The aim of this discussion is to articulate the challenges of the Common Agricultural Policy and to determine the consequences of their implementation insofar as the development of agricultural law is concerned. Due to the broad range of the research subject on the one hand, and the limitations enforced by the size of this paper on the other, this work is rather synoptic, and legal acts referred to in this paper are but a few examples only. In consequence, this paper is a mere attempt to present some reflections on the contemporary paradigm of the development of the CAP and the development of agricultural law. There are two assumptions that underlie the discussion in this paper. One is that the close relationships between agriculture (agricultural production) and food, or the provision of food determine the equally close relationships between agricultural law and food law. The other assumption is that without agriculture (agricultural production) there would be no further stages leading to achieving society's expectations[6].

Our discussion will focus on the challenges of the contemporary world analysed from a historical perspective[7]. Such approach will make it possible to show the role that this discussion played in the development of agricultural law and legislation, and will help to establish the current paradigm of the shaping the agricultural policy and agricultural law.

Sektorales Wirtschaftsrecht (Enzyklopädie Europarecht, vol 5, Nomos 2013); Ines Härtel, 'Chapter 1 – Begriff und Bedeutung des Agrarrechts' in Ines Härtel (ed), *Handbuch des Fachanwalts Agrarrecht* (Luchterhand 2012) 2.

5 See eg Daniel Gadbin, 'Faut-il consacrer en Europe un droit a l'alimentation' (2013) 410 Revue de Droit rural 2; Mariarita D'Addezio, *Agricoltura e contemperamento delle esigenze enrgetiche ed alimentari* (Atti dell'incontro di studi, Giuffrè 2012) 9; Ines Härtel, 'Vom Klimawandel bis zur Welternährung – zentrale Weltprobleme, Rechtsintegration und Zukunftsgesellschaft' in Ines Härtel (ed), *Nachhaltigkeit, Energiewende, Klimawandel, Welternährung: Politische und rechtliche Herausforderungen des 21. Jahrhunderts* (Forum Umwelt-, Agrar- und Klimaschutzrecht, vol 1, Nomos 2014) § 1, 13, 39 ff.

6 Such thought has been formulated by Luigi Costato, 'Du droit rural au droit agroalimentaire et au droit alimentaire' (2008) 3 Rivista di Diritto Agrario 317, 326.

7 This was my assumption when writing 'Prawo rolne wobec współczesnych wyzwań' (2014) 2 (15) Przegląd Prawa Rolnego 11, 13 f.

B. Food-related challenges and the development of agriculture and legislation

Satisfying food demands has always been a 'natural' challenge that agriculture has been faced with, although the manner of meeting those demands was changing over time depending on the development of agriculture itself, as well as on other sectors of economy, factors of agricultural production and their accessibility, on technological advancements, external markets and the like. It may even be said that after successful elimination of certain barriers (restrictions) that hindered proper satisfaction of the challenge, new barriers would appear at subsequent stages of development, and all those barriers together influenced the shape of the agricultural policy and the choice of legal instruments necessary for its implementation. Thus, they have been worthwhile, if only in a simplified analysis, in the context of particular stages of agriculture in which they occurred[8].

Pre-industrial agriculture was developing over many thousands of years and went through many different models, from the gathering stage, through natural and traditional farming. Its predominant objective was to satisfy hunger and ensure living conditions, and was based on the use of land on which animals would also be bred. Such models of agriculture underwent different stages of development, but during the times of the dominance of an agricultural society, the agricultural produce obtained from land was basically used by its producer. Even in those far away times different aspects of agriculture were subject to legal regulation, albeit not comparable to agricultural law as we know it today. Within the primarily agricultural society, legal regulation of various aspects of agriculture was basically part of the civil law framework.

Some substantial changes occurred at the next stage known as industrial agriculture (frequently called conventional). Its beginnings date back to some 150 years ago[9]. Industrialisation, and extensive use of technological advancements in particular, had gradually led to a huge growth of agricultural production, the effect of which was full satisfaction of food demand,

---

8 For more about the differentiation of the three stages of agriculture, ie pre-industrial, industrial and post-industrial see: Roman Budzinowski, 'Prawo rolne wobec współczesnych wyzwań' (2014) 2 (15) Przegląd Prawa Rolnego 11 (and the literature quoted therein).

9 For more, see: Józef Stanisław Zegar, *Współczesne wyzwania rolnictwa* (Wydawnictwo Naukowe PWN 2012) 36 ff.

and resulting from it growth in population. It is noteworthy though, that at a certain stage of the development of a capitalist system, distinct differences between agriculture, industry and trade emerged and natural production was gradually replaced by production for the market needs resulting from the development of towns and industry. It was then, when the natural weaknesses of agriculture vis a vis other branches of economy became apparent, giving rise to an idea of a state protection system, that there developed what we today understand as an agricultural policy. Such is also the feature of the genesis of agricultural law from today's point of view, the regulation of which, differently to its treatment of industry or trade, was for many years largely protectionist towards those who worked on land.

Despite the fact that in wealthy countries industrial agriculture was capable of producing abundance of low-price food, multiple negative consequence of its development became to be felt at many different levels. Agriculture became tied to business environment, mainly to agro-business but has never gained a dominant position in the latter. Moreover, big industrial and trading corporations which operate globally can considerably influence the organisation of demand, the prices, and, consequently, the supply of agricultural products (food). In this context, the words of Antonio Jannarelli, who when describing different stages of agricultural development referred to the transition from the battle against hunger (freedom from hunger) to the battle aimed at a division of wealth (distribution of resources) in food supply chains,[10] can be understood better. Agriculture was not the winning party, though.

At a certain stage, the growth in agricultural production came across a barrier of demand, in consequence of which the price for agricultural products had to go down, ultimately failing to provide farmers with satisfactory income, despite their more specialised and more efficient production. At the same time, industrial agriculture turned to other factors of production, not necessarily strictly agricultural, mainly agricultural chemistry, and those factors exercised a negative impact on the environment, leading to soil, air and water pollution, or threatening the biodiversity of the environment. The area of cultivated agricultural land diminished. Finally, industrial agriculture distorted the vitality of rural areas by reducing their

---

10 Antonio Jannarelli, 'Il divenire del diritto agrario italiano ed europeo tra sviluppi tecnologici e sostenibilità' (2012) 2 Rivista di Diritto Agrario 21.

population, while the pursuit to increase production at lower cost has become a threat to healthy food.

From the very beginning, industrial agriculture was accompanied by intensive public intervention in quite extensive forms. At times of inadequate food supply, this intervention aimed to increase agricultural production, ensure access to land and protection of farmers. That intervention
was strong and intense after the First World War, and even stronger after
the Second World War, when it took the form of a struggle to ensure food
supplies. Also, the first decades of the functioning of the Common Agricultural Policy were characterised, basically, by a pro-production trend.
As it turned out, though, this policy failed to ensure an adequate increase
in farmers' incomes, and even created a number of adverse phenomena in
the market, affecting the environment, the safety of agricultural products,
and their quality. Thus, also due to the international conditions and circumstances, the mono-functional (production-focused) agriculture was
abandoned for the sake of a multifunctional agriculture serving different
functions for the society. The Community's agricultural policy has thus resulted in a wider scope of agricultural regulation which included issues
such as environmental protection, food safety, food quality, or the development of rural areas.

As can be seen, the evolution of the CAP and its adaptation to the
changing economic, environmental, political and international conditions
was a response to new challenges emerging, among other things, in consequence of negative effects of the reforms in agriculture already implemented. The conditions underlying those changes had an external and an
internal source. They were always part of a discussion on the future of the
Common Agricultural Policy and its desired shape as well as a search for a
different model other than the industrial model of agriculture, that was
needed if the food demand was to be satisfied, but one that would not impair the environment, but rather ensure food safety, animal welfare, vitality of rural areas, and restrict the use of natural resources. And so the criticism of industrial agriculture gave rise to the idea of sustainable agriculture[11], which, besides sustainable development in agriculture, seeks to
maintain its multifunctional character and ensure vitality of rural areas.
Such a model constitutes an alternative to further development of industri-

---

11 For more on the sustainable agriculture model, its justification and shape, see
Józef Stanisław Zegar, *Współczesne wyzwania rolnictwa* (Wydawnictwo Naukowe
PWN 2012) 59 ff.

al agriculture. Needless to say, implementation of a sustainable agriculture model is an extremely big challenge not only for the agricultural policy, but for agricultural law as well.

C. Meeting the food, natural resources and territorial challenges– a new paradigm of the Common Agricultural Policy and agricultural law

If we attempted to identify the challenges facing the European Union today, we would arrive at their quite extensive and still open-ended catalogue. After all, difficult and hard to solve problems exist in all areas that are subject to EU policies, and may all be regarded as challenges for the future. They are reflected in a number of EU documents and legislative acts, including the Communication of the European Commission of 2 February 2011: "Tackling the challenges in commodity markets and on raw materials"[12]. The Communication of the European Commission of 18 November 2010 "The CAP towards 2020: Meeting the food, natural resources and territorial challenges of the future", mentioned above, refers to three challenges of the CAP that determine the paradigm of the development of agricultural policy and agricultural law in a given financial period. At least two questions may be asked here: (i) to what extent is this paradigm new, and (ii) does the meeting of food challenges, natural resources and territorial aspects create a closed list of the CAP problems which the European Union is now to resolve?

Food-related challenges have accompanied the Common Agricultural Policy since the very beginning which can be seen in some of the early treaty provisions articulated as different forms of its goals (currently encapsulated in Article 39 TEU). Security of supplies and consumer prices are but two examples. However, when satisfying these challenges, necessary solutions addressing other problems must also to be taken into account, such as, inter alia, liquidation of the agricultural surplus, environment protection in agriculture, development of rural areas, food quality and food safety, etc. These, and other challenges, formulated in the current CAP have their origin, partly, in the past experiences.

---

12 European Commission, 'Communication of the European Commission to the European Parliament, the European Council, the Economic and Social Committee and the Committee of the Regions of 2 February 2011 - Tackling the changes in the commodity markets and on raw materials' COM (2011) 25 final.

The recent changes in the external and internal conditions and environment of the CAP have added a new dimension to food challenges. Now, satisfaction of those challenges requires new tools and legal instruments, or at least a major revision of the existing ones. These challenges have determined a new paradigm for the development of agricultural policy and agricultural law. Thus the dilemma whether to continue to support the development of agriculture, by limiting or restricting agricultural production with respect for the environment and food safety, or whether to support the development of agriculture by further development of agricultural production, with respect for the environment and food safety, is no longer there. The choice of the latter option in a situation of a growing food demand and limits in its supply, is today obvious[13].

The formulation of contemporary challenges contained in the CAP is very general and may include very many items; therefore it is justified to treat it as exhaustive. This, however, does not mean that there do not exist other challenges connected with certain concrete problems of today's reality. And indeed, within the catalogue of so-called environmental challenges, alongside climatic challenges, the other challenges that are mentioned include protection of biological diversity, rational water management, or protection of soil against erosion. They articulate the threegeneral challenges facing the CAP already mentioned above. The answer to which of those is the most important seems obvious.

Without the fear of making a mistake, it should be said that the basic challenge is food, although regard is also to be had to natural resources and territorial aspects. These last two indicate the manner in which food-related challenges are to be met, and such a solution is socially accepted and legitimises public intervention in agricultural matters. It is not accidental that the Communication of the European Commission of 18 November 2010 includes a statement, otherwise quite obvious, that the main task of agriculture is to supply food.[14], whereas the assurance of

---

13 Many years ago Luigi Costato supported a choice of a pro-production direction, with respect to the environment protection and food security, Luigi Costato, 'Attività agricole, sicurezza alimentare e tutela del territorio' (2008) 4 Rivista di Diritto Agrario 451.

14 European Commission, 'Communication of the European Commission to the European Parliament, the Council, the European Economic and Social Committee and the Committee of the Regions of 18 November 2010 - The CAP 2020: Meeting the food, natural resources and territorial challenges of the future' COM (2010) 672 final, 5.

food security and food safety[15], as well as ensuring a high nutritious value of agricultural products should continue to constitute the fundamental raison d'etre of the CAP; moreover, 'second-tier' public values such as natural environment, land management or animal welfare, albeit also among the CAP's objectives, are but complementary to the 'first-tier' public values and should not replace them[16].

Regarding food security, it must be noted that an increased demand for agricultural products is a consequence of an increase in the world population as well as an increased demand for agricultural raw materials from non-food sectors. The latter is also responsible for the declining, or limited market supply of foodstuffs due to their altered purpose which is no longer food (e.g. for energy purposes). There exist many other factors that limit the supply of food products, such as, for example, a smaller size of the area under agricultural cultivation, soil erosion, water deficit, negative impact of climate change, fall in agricultural income, limited use of pesticides or insecticides, and the like. Despite the fact that an increased supply is a result of a technological advancement and the use of genetic engineering and biotechnology, it may jeopardise food safety and therefore requires caution. As experience thus far has shown, an absolute pursuit to ensure food security may, as a consequence, lead to a threat to food safety[17]. Thus the European Union's answer to advancing globalisation is the support of the "agricultural quality market". It extends to products which are characteristic of certain particular features connected with the manner of their production, the tradition, or the particular territory. Thus, they may be an instrument used for fighting competition and serving to protect the European market.

---

15 For more, see Katarzyna Leśkiewicz, 'Bezpieczeństwo żywnościowe i bezpieczeństwo żywności – aspekty prawne' (2012) 1 (10) Przegląd Prawa Rolnego 179.

16 See European Parliament, 'Resolution of the European Parliament of 8 July 2010 on the future of the common agricultural policy after 2013' P7_TA(2010)0286 final draft, point 6.

17 Eg Jerzy Małysz, 'Ekonomiczna interpretacja bezpieczeństwa żywnościowego' in Stanisław Kowalczyk (ed), *Bezpieczeństwo żywności w erze globalizacji* (Oficyna Wydawnicza SGH 2009) 79.

D. Conclusions

The above discussion allows us to formulate the following general reflections:

Firstly, a challenge that agriculture, agricultural policy and agricultural law have always faced is to satisfy society's food expectations. The manner in which this task, or challenge, was addressed differed over times, being contingent upon the developments in agriculture and other sectors of the economy, the accessibility of factors of agricultural production, the implementation of technological advancements, or the opening up to the external market. Elimination of one type of barrier (or limitation) that hindered satisfaction of a given challenge, entailed the emergence of other barriers in subsequent stages of development. All these together influenced the decisions for solutions undertaken in the agricultural policy and determined the choice of necessary legal instruments. It is not surprising that the Common Agricultural Policy today must take into account and address both food-related challenges as well as natural resources and territorial aspects.

Secondly, the food challenge must be regarded as fundamental, while the other two determine the manner of the realisation of the first. Such satisfaction of food expectations and needs is accepted socially and also legitimises public intervention in agricultural matters, and justifies special treatment given to food supply in the economic policy and arising from such differences when it comes to the legal regulation. The Common Agricultural Policy today should ensure food security and food safety, and should support the quality of agricultural products as regards the natural resources and territorial aspects requirements.

Thirdly, satisfying the society's food needs has substantially determined the development of legal regulations pertaining to agriculture, even if the methods and tools used for their implementation differed and varied over time. The EU (formerly Community) agricultural law has also undergone changes in consequence of the "reforms of reforms" of the Common Agricultural Policy. This law, since its inception and even if only in embryonic form, has been food law related to agriculture[18]. Elements of food law can also be found in a number of legal acts constituting the legal

---

18 Luigi Costato, 'Du droit rural au droit agroalimentaire et au droit alimentaire' (2008) 3 Rivista di Diritto Agrario 317, 318.

framework of the Common Agricultural Policy for the years 2014-2020. Thus it might be claimed that European Union agricultural law is also, partly, agro-food law.

Second Chapter:
Common Goods, Technological Developments, Food Safety

§ 3 The role of the European Food Safety Authority in shaping the safety and quality of food

Adam Zielinski

A. Introduction

The fragmented and disorderly development of food law, along with preparations for the enlargement of the European Union coincided with major food crises. Information about the presence of dioxins in feed for animals and the spread of BSE[1] were widely commented on by press and consumers. In response to these problems, the European Commission issued the Green Paper (1997) and White Paper (2000) – two important documents for the integration of food law. Another milestone is Regulation (EC) 178/2002 of the European Parliament and of the Council from 28 January 2002 laying down the general principles and requirements of food law, establishing the European Food Safety Authority and laying down procedures in matters of food safety (hereinafter "Regulation 178/2002").

> "The establishment of a European Food Safety Authority, hereinafter referred to as "the Authority", should reinforce the present system of scientific and technical support which is no longer able to respond to increasing demands on it."[2]

The role of the European Food Safety Authority in shaping food safety, as a priority objective of the institution, was noticed and presented in the doctrine[3]. However, the meaning of EFSA cannot be reduced only to the

---

1 Małgorzata Korzycka-Iwanow, 'Prawo żywnościowe – nowa dziedzina prawa' in Małgorzata Korzycka-Iwanow (ed), *Studia z prawa żywnościowego* (LIBER 2006).

2 Regulation (EC) 178/2002 of the European Parliament and of the Council of 28 January 2002 laying down the general principles and requirements of food law, establishing the European Food Safety Authority and laying down procedures in matters of food safety (General Food Law) [2002] OJ L 31/1, Preamble.

3 Ie Paweł Wojciechowski, *Wspólnotowy model urzędowej kontroli żywności* (Wolters Kluwer Poland 2008) 261; Kazimiera Ćwiek-Ludwicka / Hanna Półtorak / Marzena Pawlicka, 'Rola EFSA w systemie zarządzania ryzykiem w odniesieniu do materiałów i wyrobów przeznaczonych do kontaktu z żywnością' (2009) 60 (4) Yearbook National Institute of Hygiene 311; James Lawless, 'EFSA under pres-

important area of assessing the risk of a direct threat to life. For example, on 27 May 2015 the Authority published a report on the health consequences of eating habits associated with the daily intake of caffeine[4]. Nowadays, scientific risk assessment goes beyond the common perception of imminent danger understood as a disease which shows symptoms immediately after food consumption.

The purpose of this publication is trying to determine the impact of the European Food Safety Authority on shaping the concepts of food safety and quality in European food law.

In the following the history and nature of the legal entity EFSA will be outlined.

The European Food Safety Authority (referred to as 'EFSA' or 'the Authority') is a key body of the European Union (EU). The EFSA is an entity independent from the European Commission, the European Parliament and the Member States, nevertheless it is financed with the EU budget. EU legislation directly determines the EFSA as "the Authority". At the same time, the Authority has no power to issue legally binding administrative decisions or legislative acts.

The mission of the EFSA is to provide scientific opinions and advice to support EU legislation and policies in all fields which have a direct or indirect impact on the safety of food and feed products, as well as related issues in the area of animal health and welfare and plant health. The Authority acts as a compulsory link in the consultation process for the European Commission, European Parliament and, in the area of implementing EFSA recommendations, the Member States. Article 22 (2) and (3) of Regulation (EC) 178/2002 state the following:

"2. The Authority shall provide scientific advice and scientific and technical support for the Community's legislation and policies in all fields which have a direct or indirect impact on food and feed safety. It shall provide independent information on all matters within these fields and communicate on risks.
3. The Authority shall contribute to a high level of protection of human life and health, and in this respect take account of animal health and welfare,

---

sure: Emerging Risks, Emergencies and Crises' in Alberto Alemanno / Simone Gabi (eds), *Foundations of Food Law Policy: Ten Years of the European Food Safety Authority* (Ashgate Publishing 2014).
4 EFSA, 'Scientific Opinion on the safety of caffeine' (2015) 13(5):4102 EFSA Journal <http://www.efsa.europa.eu/sites/default/files/scientific_output/files/main_documents/4102.pdf> accessed 7 September 2015.

plant health and the environment, in the context of the operation of the internal market."[5]

The main fields of action of the EFSA correspond to three objectives of food law: reduce, eliminate or avoid health risks. Functions focus on hazard analysis, assessment, management and communication to provide a systematic methodology for the determination of effective, proportional and rightly targeted measures or other actions to protect human health.

There is a direct correlation between consumer confidence in food safety and the trust shown in regard to foodstuffs. The EFSA supports the implementation of free trade principles such as wholesome food in a non-discriminatory manner, following the practice of fair and ethical trading.[6]

A part of the EFSA structure consists of an Advisory Forum, the Scientific Committee, Scientific Panels and the Executive Officer. These positions are filled by open competition. This arrangement and the nature of the Advisory Forum's work should guarantee independence of test results and recommendations presented. The Forum consists of representatives of all Member States.

In order to coordinate cooperation at the national level and also to create a national network of institutions related to risk assessment in food law, the Authority decided to set up Focal Points in Member States (pursuant to Article 36 of Regulation 178/2002).

The ongoing development of EFSA's research work becomes visible when looking at the number of published papers, (174 in 2006, 658 in 2011). Furthermore, the annual budget has risen from 3.3 million € in 2002 to 76.96 million € in 2011.

It should be also noticed that, especially in the early years of the Authority's work, serious critical opinions were published on the practical functioning of the EFSA. Particular attention was paid to the non-fulfilment of the original objectives, particularly the ideal of an independent expert role[7].

---

5 Regulation (EC) 178/2002 of the European Parliament and of the Council of 28 January 2002 laying down the general principles and requirements of food law, establishing the European Food Safety Authority and laying down procedures in matters of food safety (General Food Law) [2002] OJ L 31/1, art 22.

6 Ibid Preamble.

7 Klara Kanska, 'Wolves in the Clothing of Sheep, The case of the European Food Safety Authority' (2004) 24 European Law Review 711.

B. The concepts of "safety" and "quality" of food

The evolution of the EU food law proceeded in accordance with the principle "from quantity to quality".[8] According to the market assessment, changes in the past few years have led to a state in which an average consumer has no problem with the availability of foodstuffs. Saturation of the food market has led to rising expectations of citizens in regard to individual characteristics of the product, such as packaging, labels and production methods. Another important aspect is the scientific progress and the need to provide proper monitoring of its products. In the end, the main concern is, after all, safety – each foodstuff available on the EU market must be safe, i.e. not harmful to health or unsuitable for human consumption[9].

The legislator aimed at implementing equilibrium between the interests of consumers, free movement of agricultural products and the environment. The creation of particular European food quality systems became one of the important steps of progressive development of the Common Agriculture Policy. Among them we may enumerate examples[10]:

- traditional specialties guaranteed[11],
- protected designations of origin and protected geographical indications[12],
- optional quality terms[13],
- organic production[14].

---

8 John McInerney, 'The production of food: from quantity to quality' (2002) 61.02 Proceedings of the Nutrition Society 273.
9 Regulation (EC) 178/2002 of the European Parliament and of the Council of 28 January 2002 laying down the general principles and requirements of food law, establishing the European Food Safety Authority and laying down procedures in matters of food safety (General Food Law) [2002] OJ L 31/1, art 14.
10 Katarzyna Leśkiewicz, *System jakości produktów rolnictwa ekologicznego. Aspekty prawne* (Iuris 2011) 38 f.
11 Regulation (EU) 1151/2012 of the European Parliament and of the Council of 21 November 2012 on quality schemes for agricultural products and foodstuffs [2012] OJ L 343/1, Title II.
12 Ibid Title III.
13 Ibid Title IV.
14 Council Regulation (EC) 834/2007 of 28 June 2007 on organic production and labelling of organic products and repealing Regulation (EEC) 2092/91 [2007] OJ L 189/1.

The normative acts establishing the above schemes show the concept of "high quality"[15]. Moreover, each of the food products placed on the market must meet "minimum standards" of quality. These assumptions lead to a conclusion in terms of legal logic that the set of "food quality" is a part of a broader set of "food safety". Food products that then meet the "minimum standards" and certain features can be attributed to a particular set of higher quality foods, which was created by EU law in order to meet the desires of consumers or to provide better protection of the environment.

In European legislation there is no definition of "food quality". Meanwhile, the Polish legislator decided to introduce a separate regime for commercial quality agri-food products on the basis of which the producer may be controlled separately from the supervisory duties regarding food safety. The roots of this solution can be found in regulations from the previous century (before the Polish accession to the European Union), which concerned the standardisation of food products. The new solution is based on a national definition of food quality, understood as features of agri-food products regarding organoleptic, physico-chemical and microbiological parameters in terms of production technology, size or weight and the requirements arising from the process of production, packaging, presentation and marking not covered by the requirements of sanitary, veterinary or phytosanitary regulations[16].

In Poland, the authority responsible for quality control of food is the Quality Inspection of Agricultural and Food (Polish abbreviation: IJHARS), which performs its work independently of individual institutions established to manage the risk to life and health of the consumer. IJHARS is responsible for: creating opinions on the granting of the quality label, trainings, and issuing quality certificates after the evaluation of the products made at the request of entrepreneurs.

The ongoing EU integration and the idea of a common market require effective rules of food quality on the basis of European law only. The next step should be to harmonise the control of food quality and to further integrate scientific papers related to this issue, perhaps with the leading role of the EFSA.

---

15 Ie Council Regulation (EC) 834/2007 of 28 June 2007 on organic production and labelling of organic products and repealing Regulation (EEC) 2092/91 [2007] OJ L 189/1, art 3.

16 Polish Act of 21 December 2000 on Commercial Quality of Agricultural and Food Products (Official Journal No 5, item 44 with amendments), art 3 (5).

C. EFSA in procedure of risk analysis

Regulation 178/2002[17] defines the term "risk" as a function of the probability of an adverse health effect and the severity of that effect, consequential to a hazard. The more likely it is to occur, and with higher severity effects on human life, the greater the risk. The role of the Authority is to give scientific advice with the utmost care in order to identify risks in the food chain. Risk analysis means a process consisting of three interconnected components: risk assessment, risk management and risk communication. The EFSA is the most important risk assessor in the European Union.

I. EFSA as an opportunity for the effective implementation of the precautionary principle in the Common Agricultural Policy

The precautionary principle is one of the EU's priorities in the field of environmental protection. It is recognised to be one of the main rules concerning the protection of public health in the context of the Common Agricultural Policy.[18] Against the background of this priority, food safety should also consider the long-term effects of a particular product on consumers health, including the welfare of future generations. Moreover, this principle highlighted the significance of probable cumulative toxic effects[19] and led to a new scientific approach which focuses on dangerous concentrations of active substances. However, Member States cannot impose protective restrictions on an entrepreneur on the basis of presumptions not justified scientifically[20]. Recommendations, data, scientific outputs and risk assessments presented by the EFSA may provide sufficient

---

17 Regulation (EC) 178/2002 of the European Parliament and of the Council of 28 January 2002 laying down the general principles and requirements of food law, establishing the European Food Safety Authority and laying down procedures in matters of food safety (General Food Law) [2002] OJ L 31/1, art 3 (9).

18 Alina Jurcewicz, *Traktatowe podstawy unijnego prawa rolnego w świetle orzecznictwa. Zagadnienia wybrane* (Wolters Kluwer Polska 2012) 76.

19 Regulation (EC) 178/2002 of the European Parliament and of the Council of 28 January 2002 laying down the general principles and requirements of food law, establishing the European Food Safety Authority and laying down procedures in matters of food safety (General Food Law) [2002] OJ L 31/1.

20 Alina Jurcewicz, *Traktatowe podstawy unijnego prawa rolnego w świetle orzecznictwa. Zagadnienia wybrane* (Wolters Kluwer Polska 2012) 77.

evidence to take protective measures due to the high probability of a risk to public health. The Authority is also responsible for scientific work, which indirectly affects food safety.

In March 2015, EFSA published a report on food quality concerning pesticide residues in food. According to the provided data, 2.6% of the samples exceeded permitted levels of chemicals which derived from plant protection products[21]. At the same time the report directly shows that there is a tool for informing consumers about current threats and unsafe food. The EFSA has done research which may be useful for risk managers - the European Commission and Member States – in order to create more effective national monitoring programs or to guarantee a more effective application of the law by national authorities.

II. EFSA as initiator changes in legal standards specific food quality schemes

Following an assessment carried out by the Authority concerning rosemary extract, this substance has been approved as an antioxidant and added to the list of products in Annex VIII to Regulation (EC) 889/2008, approved for use as a food additive in the organic farming. Particularly noteworthy is the fact that the EFSA studies were explicitly mentioned in the European Commission's implementing regulation as the reason for the establishment of standards in the act establishing the principles of the system of quality organic production[22].

The Authority presented the results concerning the content of pesticides in food by including specific information about the difference between "conventional" and organic food. The results clearly indicated the lower

---

21 5,7% imported food, 1,4% food produced in EU, Iceland and Norway, see more, EFSA, 'Scientific Report of EFSA - The 2013 European Union report on pesticide residues in food' (2015) 13(3):4038 EFSA Journal 68 ff. <http://www.efsa.europa.eu/sites/default/files/scientific_output/files/main_documents/4038.pdf> accessed 7 September 2015.

22 Commission Implementing Regulation (EU) 344/2011 of 8 April 2011 amending Regulation (EC) 889/2008 laying down detailed rules for the implementation of Council Regulation (EC) 834/2007 on organic production and labelling of organic products with regard to organic production, labelling and control [2011] OJ L 96/15.

levels of pesticides in agricultural products labelled as organic[23]. The criterion of food division into "conventional" and organic shows EFSA's research-based interest in shaping a higher quality system for particular foods.

According to a survey of Belgian consumers, the public perception of food products seems to be more focused on a smaller concentration of impurities, which, for example, is ahead of a priority for nutritional value of food[24]. The Authority undertakes scientific trials to verify the effective functioning of the higher quality system of food production in relation to specific consumers expectations. Among other things, the EFSA conducted far-reaching research on the public health consequences of various systems of rearing hens[25]. The results have shown higher levels of dioxins and of dioxin-like PCBs for eggs produced in free-range systems (including organic farming) than for eggs produced in cage systems. This scientific output also concerns quality of the egg as a final product for a consumer.

III. EFSA as a verifier of nutrition and health claims on foods

Food promoted with claims may be perceived by consumers as having a nutritional, physiological or other health advantage over similar or other products to which such nutrients and other substances are not added. This may encourage consumers to make choices, which directly influence their total intake of individual nutrients or other substances in a way that is inconsistent with scientific advice.

---

23 EFSA, 'Scientific Report of EFSA - The 2009 European Union report on pesticide residues in food' (2011) 9(11):2430 EFSA Journal <http://www.efsa.europa.eu/sites/default/files/scientific_output/files/main_documents/2430.pdf> accessed 11 January 2016.

24 Christine Hoefkens / Wim Verbeke / Joris Aertsens / Koen Mondelaers / John Van Camp, 'The nutritional and toxicological value of organic vegetables: Consumer perception versus scientific evidence' (2009) 111 (10) British Food Journal 1062.

25 Scientific Panel on Animal Health and Welfare (AHAW), 'Opinion of the Scientific Panel on Animal Health and Welfare on a request from the Commission related to the welfare aspects of various systems of keeping laying hens' (2005) 197 EFSA Journal <http://www.efsa.europa.eu/sites/default/files/scientific_output/files/main_documents/197.pdf> accessed 3 June 2016.

In 2006, the EFSA received another area of responsibility – verification of marketed foods according to their labels and marketing information, including the nutritional and health claim. The European Commission makes the decision in this area, but with the approval of the Authority. The EFSA verifies the wording of health claims for compliance with scientific data and the requirements of the EU law[26]. In addition, the EFSA at the request of a Member State and the European Commission, may issue an opinion on the further fulfilment of conditions by marking the product in the market.

In the beginning of its functioning, the EFSA issued negative opinions for 80% of the health claims of foods[27].

D. Summary

One of the basic functions of the EFSA is to serve as a bridge between the social and political expectations and the scientific progress. Among the priorities of the Authority, the one to be highlighted is the initiation of exchange and the accumulation of experience, information and research results in European Union. The primary role of the EFSA is to analyse and assess the risk of a direct threat to human life and health relating to the food chain. The intellectual capital, the international composition of its independent position in European Union system also give EFSA the potential to perform three functions:

• objective assessment of the risk of negative indirect impact of food on human health and life,
• scientific impact on the quality systems requirements of specific food products and organic production,
• effective regulation of rotation adapted to the expectations of consumers through credible indications of agricultural products.

It is possible to observe the development of the role that EFSA has had. The institution evolved from European Union helpdesk, which was creat-

---

26 Regulation (EC) 1924/2006 of the European Parliament and of the Council of 20 December 2006 on nutrition and health claims made on foods [2006] OJ L 404/9, art 16.
27 Neil Bowdler, 'EU health food claims law begins to bite' *BBC News* (7 July 2010) <http://www.bbc.com/news/10240263> accessed 10 September 2015.

ed as the scientific response to loud scandals, and research that searched for direct risks to the consumer in food products. Nowadays the Authority is the most important research centre, whose reports were cited in the content of European Union normative acts. Moreover, the EFSA activity was expanded to verification of the health claims in marketing food products and assessing any possible risks of GMOs to human or animal health and their consequences for the environment.

In the face of ongoing development of the research areas, the verification of EFSA's legal status and formal power of the Authority should be considered. The above analysis shows the significant influence of expert opinions regarding the widely understood food safety and quality with impact on legislation in this regard. It seems that, as a result of the growth of competence (i.e. in the field of GMOs, health claims) and organisational development (Focal Points), the Authority goes beyond its original mandate as an independent point of scientific information created in response to public concerns about food crises[28].

Every step of progressive development of the institution recalls a question about the unique position in the Authority in the European Union system. Another publication should be created in response to that problem. It seems that the integration of EU food law would require a more integrated system of institutions, which requires a choice between giving power to the European Commission over the Authority or developing the role of Focal Points in Member States by, among others, giving them the competence of administrative authorities. Implementation of the second proposal would constitute the basis for the unification of quality control of food products and for research work related to the risk in the food chain.

---

28 Ie Marine Friant Perrot / Amandine Garde, 'From BSE to Obesity - EFSA's Growing Role in the EU's Nutrition Policy' in Alberto Alemanno / Simone Gabbi (eds), *Foundations of EU Food Law and Policy: Ten Years of the European Food Safety Authority* (Ashgate Publishing 2014).

§ 4 Legal aspects of the concept of food and of production methods

Katarzyna Leśkiewicz

A. Indroduction

'Agricultural products' according to the Treaty on the Functioning of the European Union means "the products of the soil, of stockfarming and of fisheries and products of first-stage processing directly related to these products"[1]. Just as the concept of agricultural products is a fundamental conceptual category of agricultural law, so also does the food concept belong to the canon of the most important concepts of food law. In turn, food, or used interchangeably in the legislation with the term foodstuff, means "any substance or product, whether processed, partially processed or unprocessed, intended to be, or reasonably expected to be ingested by humans"[2]. Moreover the given term also includes drink, chewing gum and any substance, including water, intentionally incorporated into the food during its manufacture, preparation or treatment. On the other hand the term shall not include feed, live animals, unless they are prepared for placing on the market for human consumption, plants prior to harvesting, medicinal products, cosmetics, tobacco and tobacco products, narcotic or psychotropic substances within the meaning of the United Nations Single Convention on Narcotic Drugs, 1961, and the United Nations Convention on Psychotropic Substances, 1971, residues and contaminants[3].

The Legislator does not limit in any way the method of food preparation or food processing in the definition of food, which means that these possibilities are unlimited. The food market and the offer of food manu-

---

1 Art 38 of the Treaty on the Functioning of the European Union (TFEU).
2 Regulation (EC) 178/2002 of the European Parliament and of the Council of 28 January 2002 laying down the general principles and requirements of food law, establishing the European Food Safety Authority and laying down procedures in matters of food safety [2002] OJ L 31/1, art 2.
3 See Katarzyna Leśkiewicz, 'Pojęcie żywności – aspekty prawne' (2015) 1 Przegląd Prawa Rolnego.

facturers are diverse, they cover a number of categories, types of products, e.g. organic products, genetically modified products, novel food, regional food, but also a number of highly processed products such as candy, chips, or "colored drinks", supplements, measures for particular nutritional uses, etc. The absence of any boundaries to the method of making food results in a situation where various methods and techniques of production can be used in food production. This especially includes cloning[4], nanotechnology[5], production of GMOs and so on. This article attempts to identify possible common elements of these legal concepts of food and agricultural products, including the question of whether the current definition of food can provide health benefits of food products, including modern production techniques.

B. Legal framework

The feature of "naturalness" of food is an advantage for health, which is why nutritionists[6] and doctors of different specialties recommend the consumption of fresh products, the least processed[7]. According to the report of the World Cancer Research Fund published at the end of 2003, falling ill from cancer can be prevented through proper diet and getting rid of excess weight[8]. The question is whether there is a link between the concepts of agricultural and food products under the relevant legislation, since agricultural products in their fresh form can provide human substances required for nutrition. What are therefore the values - health aspects of food within the specified range for the legislator?

---

4 See Katarzyna Leśkiewicz, 'Pojęcie żywności – aspekty prawne' (2015) 1 Przegląd Prawa Rolnego.
5 See Katarzyna Leśkiewicz, 'Prawne aspekty nanotechnologii w produkcji żywności i materiałów przeznaczonych do kontaktu z żywnością' (2013) 2 Przegląd Prawa Rolnego 87.
6 See programme 'Zdrowo jemy, zdrowo rośniemy' <http://zdrowojemy.info/progra m/o-programie> accessed 13 October 2015.
7 Anna Jarosz / Grzegorz Luboiński, 'Dieta antyrakowa - zdrowe odżywianie zapobiega zachorowaniu na raka' (2014) <http://www.poradnikzdrowie.pl/diety/lecznicze /dieta-antyrakowa-zdrowe-odzywianie-zapobiega-zachorowaniu-na-raka_35473.ht ml> accessed 13 October 2015.
8 Ibid.

Regulation No 178/2002 provides "the basis for the assurance of a high level of protection of human health and consumers' interest in relation to food, taking into account in particular the diversity in the supply of food including traditional products, whilst ensuring the effective functioning of the internal market"[9]. For the purposes of accomplishing that objective Regulation lays down "the general principles governing food and feed in general, and food and feed safety in particular, at Community and national level"[10]. The above-cited definition of food has been introduced to Regulation 178/2002 in relation to food safety[11]. In addition, the requirements and procedures necessary to ensure food safety and nutrition in accordance with Regulation 178/2002, the national legislature has regulated in the national (Polish) legal act entitled "law on food safety and nutrition"[12].

Bearing in mind the passage of Regulation 178/2002 *"any substance or product (...) intended to be, or reasonably expected to be ingested by humans"*, it is reasonable to ask how to understand the term "to ingest" as used in the definition. It means *"to enter the food, drink through the mouth into the stomach"*[13]. Consumption of food is not the same as eating or feeding oneself, which mean *to provide live organism with substances necessary for growth and development; feed"*[14]. Therefore, the legislator takes into account in the content of the definition of food solely a technical aspect related to the insertion or introduction of food into the digestive system rather than providing the live organism with substances necessary for life.

Noteworthy is the lack of requirements relating to any qualities of the food, nutritional properties in the content of definition of food[15]. Taking into account consumers expectations that the food be healthy, valuable, of

---

9 Regulation (EC) 178/2002 of the European Parliament and of the Council of 28 January 2002 laying down the general principles and requirements of food law, establishing the European Food Safety Authority and laying down procedures in matters of food safety [2002] OJ L 31/1, art 1 (1).

10 Ibid art 1 (2).

11 Ibid art 2 (1).

12 Law on food safety and nutrition of 25 August 2006, Consolidated text Journal of Laws 2015 Pos 594.

13 <http://sjp.pwn.pl/slowniki/spo%C5%BCywa%C4%87.html> accessed 13 October 2015.

14 <http://sjp.pl/od%C5%BCywia%C4%87> accessed 13 October 2015.

15 See: Albertò Germanò / Eva Rook-Basile, *Definitions of European Food in European Food Law* (Cedam 2012) 93.

good quality and served for nutrition, it should be noted that the definition of food is devoid of these requirements. This means that from a legal point of view, the food can be, and indeed tend to be products which do not value health, necessary for vital functions, which cannot be said, that serve nutrition. The reason for this, it seems, is that the regulation is based on the assumption that the legislature is limited to regulating these issues to a required minimum. In one of the judgments the Regional Administrative Court in Łódź (judgment of 28 February 2013, sign. file III SA / LD 1052-1012[16]) confirmed that *"the definition of foodstuff does not refer to its nutritional value. Therefore, to demonstrate that the product does not meet the definition of foodstuff, authorities should carry out appropriate investigation aimed to prove that the preparation is not intended for human consumption (or such human consumption is not expected), or that it should be one of the categories of products listed in art. 2 point a) -h) of Regulation No 178/2002 (...), which are excluded from the definition of foodstuff"*. The case concerned a product for particular nutritional uses.

Finally, the analysis of the concept of food leads to determine the meaning of the word "substance" used in the definition of food[17]. The substances are involved in chemistry, which raises the association of substances, e.g. with chemical elements from the periodic table. This aspect of the analyzed definition shows basically unlimited content of the concept of food. Whether we are dealing with food within the meaning of Regulation 178/2002 is also decided by destiny of the substance or product intended for human consumption. And here, in principle, it is difficult to identify any criterion by which the possibility for a substance intended for human consumption should be assessed. The legislator did not settle well, who is to decide whether a product or substance may be intended for human consumption, especially if the area is reserved for the legislature or the manufacturers. Some substances in the indicated range are determined by the legislature, for example, on the list of additives[18] which are permitted for use in food production. On the other hand, when it comes to a product as such, it is in the legislation that we find an answer to the question of what specific products can be used for human consumption,

---

16 LEX no 1311275.
17 See the definition in the Polish language dictionary <http://sjp.pl/substancja> accessed 13 October 2015.
18 See Regulation (EC) 1333/2008 of the European Parliament and of the Council of 16 December 2008 on food additives [2008] OJ L 354/16, art 3 (2).

except that the legislature indicates only within the content of the definition of foodstuffs – what they are. Therefore, it seems, in terms of this criterion of intention, that it is ultimately the producers who determine what will happen with food and what they decide to enter the market as food.

It should be added that, in accordance with the Act on the safety of food, only a safe product can be put on the market and that safety determines, and at the same time limits, the possibility of intending the substance or product for human consumption. Looking at the definition of food from the point of view of producers, the assumption made by the legislature that the food can be any substance or product, shows that this element of the definition is a requirement – a warning to producers that they consider what they intend to offer for human consumption.

Examples of specific products that may be regarded as food by Regulation No 178/2002, and that show interesting interpretations of the definition of food are provided by judicial decisions. For example, as foodstuff have been considered, for example, wine yeast, although not intended for human consumption. In its judgment of 29 December 2014 sign. file III SA / LD 1114-1114[19] Regional Administrative Court in Łódź said that wine yeast can be considered food within the meaning of Article 2 of Regulation No 178/2002, as *"they are a product that, even if not intended directly for human consumption, is added to grape, from which house wine is derived. Human consumption of wine yeasts in the final product, which is the house wine you'd expect, even if it is not desirable. House wine is a foodstuff (food) and wine yeast is a substance intentionally added during manufacture"*.

Among the categories of products whose concepts refer to the concept of food even by the fact that the legislature surprisingly even indicates that they are food, supplements may be indicated. According to the law on food safety, dietary supplement *is a "foodstuff, whose purpose is to supplement the normal diet, which is a concentrated source of vitamins or minerals or other substances with a nutritional or other physiological effect, alone or in combination, marketed in a form enabling its dosage, in form of: capsules, tablets, dragees and other similar forms, sachets of powder, ampoules of liquids, drop dispensing bottles and other similar forms of liquids and powders designed to be consumed in small, measured*

---

19 LEX no 1667253.

unit amounts, excluding products which have the properties of a medicinal product within the meaning of pharmaceutical law[20] ".

To this must be added that the form of dietary supplements does not resemble, or cannot be associated with food but with medicinal products. Maybe for this reason the legislature considered that the Act should explicitly indicate that this is a foodstuff? This treatment seems to be superfluous, since these products fall within the concept of food by Regulation No 178/2002. This definition does not present any requirements on the properties, and the food can be any substance.

An aspect that needs highlighting, is a requirement found in the concept of dietary supplements so that they are concentrated sources of vitamins or minerals or other substances with a nutritional or other physiological effect. It is significant that only on the occasion of defining a dietary supplement has the legislator has introduced the requirement that the product have a value brought to man by vitamins, or minerals, or even positively affect the nutrition of people. The legislature abandoned this endeavour while defining the concept of food, because food by definition does not have the nutritional effect.

Another group of foods, which the legislature sets specific requirements for are foods for particular nutritional uses[21]. They must comply with, firstly - the requirement for foods commonly consumed, and secondly – specific requirements for the composition and method of production to ensure that these measures will meet the special dietary needs of final consumers in accordance with its intended purpose. Products with specific nutritional purposes are the only measures for specific groups of consumers, and the categories given are not comprehensive. According to the law on food safety, food for special nutritional purposes is one that due to the special composition or method of preparation is clearly different from foods commonly consumed and, according to the information posted on the packaging is marketed for the purpose of satisfying the specific nutritional needs[22]. The food described above has particular purpose due to certain diseases, health, age of men, which makes it a category of products supporting treatment, diet, human development and so on.

---

20 Law on food safety and nutrition of 25 August 2006, Consolidated text Journal of Laws 2015 Pos 594, art 3 (39).
21 Ibid art 24.
22 Ibid art 3 (43).

Regarding the content of the concept of food, it should be noted that the legislator, as mentioned, does not limit methods or techniques of food production. Therefore, the food could be the products derived from cloned animals. Cloning is a new technique for food production[23]. According to the legislator "cloning" means asexual reproduction of animals with a technique whereby the nucleus of a cell of an individual animal is transferred into an oocyte from which the nucleus has been removed to create genetically identical individual embryos ("embryo clones"), that can subsequently be implanted into surrogate mothers in order to produce populations of genetically identical animals ("animal clone")[24]. The word "cloning" means, firstly, "to artificially lead to creation of a new organism identical with the original, by way of asexual cell division or parental organism" and, secondly, "to copy or reproduce technical device on the basis of somebody else's project" [25].

Australia, Argentina, Brazil, Canada, Japan and United States, confirmed that animals are cloned on their territory[26]. On the territory of the European Union cloning is not used in food production, and the intention of the legislature is to suspend the application of cloning technology for food production and marketing of live animal clones, except clone as part of scientific research or to preserve rare breeds and other motives[27].

Food from animal clones did not live up to the legal regulation devoted exclusively to the issue of animal cloning, or the marketing of food from clones. In preparation, however, are the provisions of two directives cov-

---

23 European Commission, 'Proposal for a Directive of the European Parliament and of the Council of 18 December 2013 on the cloning of animals of the bovine, porcine, ovine, caprine and equine species kept and reproduced for farming purposes COM (2013) 892 final and Proposal for a Council Directive on the placing on the market of food from animal clones COM (2013) 893 final' SWD (2013) 519 final, 520 final.

24 Ibid art 2 lit b).

25 Polish Language Dictionary <http://sjp.pl/klonowanie> accessed 13 October 2015.

26 European Commission, 'Commission tables proposals on animal cloning and novel food' (2013) Memo/13/1170 <http://europa.eu/rapid/press-release_MEMO-13-1170_en.htm> accessed 13 October 2015. The Commission clarifies the concept of animal cloning as follows: cloning means creating animals with genetic material from the cells of another animal.

27 European Commission, 'Proposal for a Directive of the European Parliament and of the Council of 18 December 2013 on the cloning of animals of the bovine, porcine, ovine, caprine and equine species kept and reproduced for farming purposes' COM (2013) 892 final, Justification 1.4.

ering these issues[28]. Cloning may be subject to the provisions of the Regulation on novel foods No 258/1997[29].

The issue of animal cloning raises questions about the potential health risks to animals or people. These questions, among others, are answered i.e. by scientific opinions of the European Food Safety Authority who identified welfare risks arising from the low efficiency of this new production technique[30]. The European Food Safety Authority (EFSA) has confirmed that parent surrogate dams used in cloning suffer in particular from placenta dysfunctions contributing to increased levels of miscarriages. This contributes, amongst other things, to the low efficiency of the technique and the need to implant embryo clones into several dams to obtain one clone[31]. In addition, clone abnormalities and unusually large offspring result in difficult births and neonatal deaths[32]. On the other hand, EFSA repeatedly stated that cloning has no impact on the safety of meat and milk obtained from the clones in comparison with those obtained from regular breeds[33].

The food industry uses engineered nanomaterials. In particular, nanoparticles may enrich food with interesting properties, e.g. salty taste with a low sodium content[34]. In Australia, nanocapsules of tuna fish oil

---

28 European Commission, 'Proposal for a Directive of the European Parliament and of the Council of 18 December 2013 on the cloning of animals of the bovine, porcine, ovine, caprine and equine species kept and reproduced for farming purposes' COM (2013) 892 final, Justification 1.4.; European Food Safety Authority, 'Update on the state of play of Animal Health and Welfare and Environmental Impact of Animals derived from SCNT Cloning and their Offspring, and Food Safety of Products Obtained from those Animals' (2012) 10(7):2794 EFSA Journal Summary, 18; Statements of EFSA 2012 and 2010: <http://www.efsa.europa.eu/en/efsajournal/pub/2794.htm> and <http://www. efsa.europa.eu/en/efsajournal/pub/1784.htm> accessed 19 October 2015.
29 Regulation (EC) 258/97 of the European Parliament and of the Council of 27 January 1997 concerning novel foods and novel food ingredients [1997] OJ L 43/1.
30 European Food Safety Authority, 'Update on the state of play of animal cloning' (2010) 8(9):1784 EFSA Journal <http://www.efsa.europa.eu/sites/default/files/scientific_output/files/main_documents/1784.pdf> accessed 19 October 2015.
31 European Commission, 'Proposal for a Council Directive of 18 December 2013 on the placing on the market of food from animal clones' COM (2013) 893 final (SWD (2013) 519 final).
32 Ibid.
33 Ibid.
34 *Wielka przyszłość nauki o małych rzeczach*, Współczesna żywność 12/2006 <www.eufic.org/article/pl.> accessed 13 October 2015.

omega-3 acid is added to bread, moreover, nanomayonnaise[35] is also recognized. Food packaging may contain nanosensors to detect concentrations of chemical components[36].

Knowledge of manufactured nanoparticles requires improvement, the legislator must have expertise in the field of nanotechnology in regulated areas. The effects of nanoparticles on the human body have not been recognized yet[37]. In particular, the reactions that nanoparticles are subjected to (accumulation of water and food chain) may raise concerns[38]. Hence, research is needed on ensuring safety for human health and the natural environment[39], including in terms of existing legislation. The legislation does not have a single piece of legislation comprehensively regulating issues concerning the use of nanomaterials in these areas. Individual legal solutions are found in various legal acts[40], and many problems in this area

---

35 Małgorzata Idzikowska / Marta Janczura / Tomasz Lepionka / Michał Madej / Edyta Mościcka / Justyna Pyzik / Paulina Siwek / Weronika Szubierajska / Dorota Skrajnowska / Andrzej Tokarz, 'Nanotechnologia w produkcji żywności – kierunki rozwoju, zagrożenia i regulacje prawne' (2012) 4 Bulletin of the Faculty of Pharmacy at the Medical University of Warsaw 28.

36 Ibid.

37 Kuraj Nertila, 'Troppo piccole per preoccuparsene? Le applicazioni delle nanotecnologie in ambito alimentare della normativa europea' (2012) 3 Rivista di Diritto Agrario 514.

38 Małgorzata Idzikowska / Marta Janczura / Tomasz Lepionka / Michał Madej / Edyta Mościcka / Justyna Pyzik / Paulina Siwek / Weronika Szubierajska / Dorota Skrajnowska / Andrzej Tokarz, 'Nanotechnologia w produkcji żywności – kierunki rozwoju, zagrożenia i regulacje prawne' (2012) 4 Bulletin of the Faculty of Pharmacy at the Medical University of Warsaw 23.

39 Cf European Commission, 'Communication from the Commission to the Council, the European Parliament and the European Economic and Social Committee of 29 October 2009 – Nanosciences and Nanotechnologies: An action plan for Europe 2005 – 2009. Second Implementation Report 2007 – 2009' COM (2009) 607 final indicates that, among others, 'Approved a number of methods of characterization of nanoparticles, currently laboratories can use the new reference nanomaterials to improve and demonstrate their abilities in the field of metrology,' and 'in the field of toxicology tests, for which the awards have been given, contribute to increased knowledge of the interactions between nanoparticles and the organism human'.

40 See eg Regulation (EC) 1333/2008 of the European Parliament and of the Council of 16 December 2008 on food additives [2008] OJ L 354/16; Regulation (EC) 1935/2004 of the European Parliament and of the Council of 27 October 2004 on materials and articles intended to come into contact with food and repealing Directives 80/590/EEC and 89/109/EEC [2004] OJ L 338/4; Commission Regulation (EU) 10/2011 of 14 January 2011 on plastic materials and articles intended to

are the subject of *soft law*[41]. Hence the determination of the legal status of the individual case requires analysis of many regulations. Moreover, the law does not always correspond to the practical applications of nanomaterials.

C. Conclusion

Interpretations of the definition of food in the judicial decisions of Polish administrative courts confirm the fact that the authorities sometimes take as a criterion for considering a product to be food – possession of nutritional value by this product, but the nutritional value is not a legal requirement mentioned in the definition of food in Regulation 178/2002. The rulings of administrative courts correct the statements of authorities. From a legal point of view, the food does not have to have any nutritional values, including different formulations and measures that have no nutritional value can be recognized, and are considered food within the meaning of Regulation 178/2002.

The concept of food in Regulation No 178/2002 absorbs the concept of agricultural products within the meaning of the Treaty on the Functioning of the European Union because of its broader scope. Agricultural products are one of many possible groups of products or substances likely to be food. Above all, however, the legislator does not combine the two concepts in the definition of food in Regulation No 178/2002, which means that such food and its ingredients can be substances that have no connection with agriculture. In food law, the well-known saying "from farm to fork", however, does not reflect the relationship of agricultural products and foodstuffs, but only the scope of the legal regulations concerning food safety. Thus, it can be found only in the sphere of application

---

come into contact with food [2011] OJ L 12/1; Regulation (EU) 1169/2011 of the European Parliament and of the Council of 25 October 2011 on the provision of food information to consumers, amending Regulations (EC) 1924/2006 and (EC) 1925/2006 of the European Parliament and of the Council and repealing Commission Directive 87/250/EEC, Council Directive 90/496/EEC, Commission Directive 1999/10/EC, Directive 2000/13/EC of the European Parliament and of the Council, Commission Directives 2002/67/EC and 2008/5/EC and Commission Regulation (EC) 608/2004 [2011] OJ L 304/18.

41 European Commission, 'Recommendation 2011/696/EU of 18 October 2011 on the definition of nanomaterial' [2011] OJ L 275/38.

of food safety, but not in the quality of food, understood as being the added value of something more than safety construed as food safety.

At the level of legal regulation concerning food safety, we can see a breaking of ties between the concepts of food and agricultural products, although the introduction to the legislation of mandatory origin of food, among others, from agriculture (its ingredients of agricultural origin) could be an asset allowing to ensure health benefits of food nutrition. Finally, the unrestricted range of methods and techniques of food production within the concept of food allows manufacturers to use different and not quite explored ways of production, such as cloning and nanotechnology. It is expected that with the development of science and technology it will be possible to use innovative production methods. At the same time, we will probably see even greater disintegration of ties of the food and agricultural product and, increasingly, food product will have no agricultural origin.

§ 5 Requirements for the safety of food commodities

Christian Thomas

A. Introduction

Throughout its life cycle food gets in contact with objects made of different materials. The most direct contact with food is frequently with the directly surrounding packaging. Packaging of foods has a protective and transport function and packaging carries important information. The packaging protects food from environment impact (e.g. light or moisture), from contamination and damage. Therefore, there are also numerous specific requirements for packaging. However, food packaging is indeed an important, but by no means the only food commodity. Food commodities are at the interface between product safety and food law. In the spirit of "good manufacturing practice"[1] for food commodities a transfer of any content or constituent material to food that threatens human health or may cause an unacceptable organoleptic change of the food has to be stopped.

B. Legal framework in the multi-level system

The general requirements for the safety of food commodities are set out in Regulation (EC) 1935/2004. Additionally there are some material specific

---

1 According to Commission Regulation (EC) 2023/2006 of 22 December 2006 on good manufacturing practice for materials and articles intended to come into contact with food [2006] OJ L 384/75, art 3 lit a) ' "good manufacturing practice" refers to those aspects of quality assurance, to ensure that materials and articles are produced and checked in a consistent manner so that their compliance with the rules is guaranteed and they meet the quality standards that are appropriate to their intended use-purpose, and without endangering human health or bring about an face change in the composition of the foodstuffs or a deterioration in their properties'; see Kurt-Dietrich Rathke, *Die Gute Herstellungspraxis zwischen Sein und Sollen* (C.H. Beck 2010).

guidelines on European level.[2] The national legislature has – as probably convenient practice in the meanwhile – chosen a 1:1 implementation of EU law in the Lebensmittel- und Futtermittelgesetzbuch (LFGB) (Food and Feed Code) and further national regulations. However, there are further regulations drafted on national level that are focused in more detail.[3]

I. European Union Law: Regulation (EC) 1935/2004

Food Commodities Regulation (EC) 1935/2004[4] contains the legal basis and the general requirements for the production, labelling and marketing of materials and articles, including active and intelligent food contact materials and articles intended to come into contact with foodstuffs (Article 1 (2) (a)), which are already in contact with food or are intended (Article 1 (2) (b)) or can reasonably be expected to become in contact with food under normal or foreseeable conditions of use, or will transfer their constituents to food (Article 1 (2) (c)). In Article 2 (1) Regulation (EC)

---

2 See Commission Regulation (EU) 10/2011 of 14 January 2011 on plastic materials and articles intended to come into contact with food [2011] OJ L 12/1; Commission Regulation (EC) 282/2008 of 27 March 2008 on recycled plastic materials and articles intended to come into contact with foods and amending Regulation (EC) 2023/2006 [2008] OJ L 86/9; Commission Regulation (EC) 450/2009 of 29 May 2009 on active and intelligent materials and articles intended to come in contact with food [2009] OJ L 135/3 (endurance prolonging or state-sustaining substances, eg moisture or oxygen absorber).
3 At national level, further regulation tendencies within the meaning of health and consumer protection; see German Federal Ministry of Food and Agriculture, draft of the twenty-first regulation, as of 23 January 2015, which provides a positive list of substances that may be used in printing of food commodities and German Federal Ministry of Food and Agriculture, draft of the twenty-second regulation amending the Consumer Goods Ordinance, as of 24 July 2014, the arrangements for the transition from mineral oil from food packaging that have been produced using recycled paper, providing on food.
4 Regulation (EC) 1935/2004 of the European Parliament and of the Council of 27 October 2004 on materials and articles intended to come into contact with food and repealing Directives 80/590/EEC and 89/109/EEC [2004] OJ L 338/4.

1935/2004, there is a wide-ranging reference to the definitions of food base Regulation (EC) 178/2002[5].[6]

1. Food contact as link

A Point of reference is thus, first, that of the materials and articles that (typically) come into contact with food or are intended to do so. A touch always presupposes the direct contact of the material or article with a food. The examples are all used in the preparation of food and beverages and food contact kitchen tools, equipment and containers of all kinds; notably such as pots, pans, utensils, baking accessories or food processors. The commercial and industrial boilers (breweries, butchers), dough pressure instruments, ovens and cooling and freezing equipment, with which food is prepared and which are intended to come into contact with food, as well as extensive transport systems (e.g. line hoses from plastics or rubber, piping of metal or plastics), have to be mentioned.[7] Also wood and bamboo chopsticks and paper umbrellas as well as pieces of cheese ("Party Picker") are excluded. While those that are not intended for human consumption, and easily peelable like sausage casing that is suitable for consumption, and certain plastic wrappers of sausages, are included as well as are non-food consumer goods. This does not apply to the materials covering cheese, prepared meat products or fruit, which form parts of the food and consequently can be consumed.

Examples of items that pursuant to Article 1 (2) (c) Regulation (EC) 1935/2004 under normal or foreseeable conditions of use come into contact with food or transfer their constituents to food, are about measuring tools and scales, weighing and filling machines. Unless there is a direct contact with food, the aforementioned packaging materials have to be seen as independent food commodities; e.g. plastic films, metal foils, cans

---

5 Regulation (EC) 178/2002 of the European Parliament and of the Council of 28 January 2002 laying down the general principles and requirements of food law, establishing the European Food Safety Authority and laying down procedures in matters of food safety [2002] OJ L 31/1.

6 The only exceptions are the autonomously defined terms of 'traceability' and 'marketing'.

7 See in particular with regard to the examples Kurt-Dietrich Rathke in Walter Zipfel / Kurt-Dietrich Rathke (eds), *Kommentar zum Lebensmittelrecht* (C.H. Beck 2015) LFGB, 160 a.d. 2015, § 2 recital 128.

made of metal, glass or plastic bottles and (coated) paper and paper packages. Packaging material that envelops an inner packaging is not covered by the definition, since it is not intended to come into contact with the food.[8] The items that come into contact with the marketing of and during storage of foods, such as transport vehicles, shelves or cabinets, to the extent that the food is loose and not packed, are labelled as food commodities.[9]

2. Intended food contact

Further application requirements are the purpose of the article. According to Article 1 (2) (a) Regulation (EC) 1935/2004 "intended" means when a food material or article comes into contact with food, if there is a possibility that the article may be used for this purpose, even though a different kind of use of the article becomes reality or the items are used on an individual basis for other purposes (general or objective purpose). Decisive is the market perception.[10] Items that are normally intended for a different purpose are also not considered as food commodities, when they are in certain cases (abusively) used as commodities (e.g. thawing of frozen meat in the shower tray).

3. Active and intelligent food contact articles

Active food contact materials and articles are pursuant to Article 2 (2) (a) Regulation (EC) 1935/2004 such materials and articles which are intended to extend the shelf life of packaged food or improve its condition. They are designed so that they can deliver materials to the packaged food or the surrounding environment or to the food. This includes active multi-layer

---

8 For the foregoing and with further examples Kurt-Dietrich Rathke in Walter Zipfel / Kurt-Dietrich Rathke (eds), *Kommentar zum Lebensmittelrecht* (C.H. Beck 2015) LFGB, 160. a.d. 2015, § 2 recital 129.

9 See Alfred Hagen Meyer in Alfred Hagen Meyer / Rudolf Streinz (eds), *Kommentar zum Lebensmittel- und Futtermittelgesetzbuch (LFGB), zur Basis-Verordnung (EG) 178/2002 sowie zur Health Claim Verordnung 1924/2006* (2nd edn, C.H. Beck 2012) LFGB, § 2 recital 189.

10 Kurt-Dietrich Rathke in Walter Zipfel / Kurt-Dietrich Rathke (eds), *Kommentar zum Lebensmittelrecht* (C.H. Beck 2015) LFGB, 160 a.d. 2015, § 2 recital 190.

films or "Controlled Atmosphere" processes by which the carbon dioxide and oxygen content can be adjusted in the package interior to the optimum for a particular food value. Packages may also be made with active perforation or valve technology; the absorbing process is active.[11]

If materials/objects, on the other hand, are used during the manufacturing process where their natural ingredients are released into specific foods (e.g. wooden barrels for wine vats), they are not active or intelligent food contact materials and articles.

Intelligent food contact materials and articles are, pursuant to Article 2 (2) (b) Regulation (EC) 1935/2004, such materials with which the condition of packaged foods or the surrounding environment is monitored. For the purpose of health, the specific characteristics should be, in particular in the microbiological point, where things can be monitored. By using active and intelligent materials and articles which do not change the composition or the organoleptic properties of food, the consumer could, however, be misled; for instance, by masking the spoilage of food by the release of aldehydes (Article 4 (3) Regulation (EC) 1935/2004). The materials have to be provided with an adequate labelling, stating that it is appropriate material (Article 4 (6) Regulation (EC) 1935/2004).

4. Labelling before placing on the market

Food contact materials and articles must be labelled with a specific indication, if they are placed on the market, basically with the words "for food contact". The intended use is shown with the symbol of Annex II and the name and company responsible for marketing of the manufacturer, processor, or the seat of business. In addition, special instructions may be required for safe and proper use. Furthermore, a marking or identification is required for the purpose of re-identification of the material.[12]

---

11 Alfred Hagen Meyer in Alfred Hagen Meyer / Rudolf Streinz (eds), *Kommentar zum Lebensmittel- und Futtermittelgesetzbuch (LFGB), zur Basis-Verordnung (EG) 178/2002 sowie zur Health Claim Verordnung 1924/2006* (2nd edn, C.H. Beck 2012) LFGB, § 2 recital 193.

12 Concrete expression of the general food law principle in Regulation (EC) 1935/2004 of the European Parliament and of the Council of 27 October 2004 on materials and articles intended to come into contact with food and repealing Directives 80/590/EEC and 89/109/EEC [2004] OJ L 338/4, art 17.

II. National requirements

1. Food commodities according to § 2 LFGB

The definition of national § 2 paragraph 6 no. 1 LFGB takes recognition in relation to the scope of Regulation (EC) 1935/2004. The former definition of food commodities from § 5 Lebensmittel- und Bedarfsgegenständegesetz (LMBG) (fomer Food and Feed Code) has been significantly altered. On the one hand, it became more restrictive because as consumer goods or materials are collected as the only objects that come into contact with foodstuffs purposefully or that may come into contact with or that are shedding constituents to food. Items that affect food without contact and without transition to ingredients, no longer fall within the scope. This includes items that affect food without coming into contact with food, in principle, no longer belong to the food commodities. Therefore, microwave ovens, in which only packaged or contained food is heated, or systems with which prepacked foods are checked for foreign substances or other quality criteria, are not regarded as food commodities - at least as long as a contact with food is not reasonably foreseeable. On the other hand, the term was also extended, because it now covers not only objects, but also materials and thus more materials. While substances are consumed, items can only be used.[13]

2. Commodities between LFGB and ProdSG

The LFGB recorded in a catalogue of nine digits, both food consumer goods (no. 1) as well as other commodities, which are characterised in a number of case groups by their purpose and the inherent action options within these on the human body (No. 2-9). In addition to the LFGB, the Produktsicherheitsgesetz (ProdSG) (Product Safety Act) contains provisions on consumer goods. These serve mainly the protection of human health (§§ 30-32) and, unlike the LFBG, also the illusion of protection for content (§ 33). Commodities as defined in § 2 no. 22 ProdSG are products or goods, "which have been produced through a manufacturing process".

---

13 See Kurt-Dietrich Rathke in Walter Zipfel / Kurt-Dietrich Rathke (eds), *Kommentar zum Lebensmittelrecht* (C.H. Beck 2015) LFGB, 160. a.d. 2015, § 2 recital 124.

The right of the consumer regarding goods has therefore been possible to realise even after the entry into force of ProdSG on 1/12/2011 in the tension between LFGB and ProdSG. In accordance with § 1 paragraph 3 sentence 1 no. 4 ProdSG "food, feed, living plants and animals, products of human origin and products of plants and animals relating directly to their future reproduction" do not fall under the scope of ProdSG. The ProdSG, thus, alone relates to the so-called non-food sector. This general scheme corresponds to that of Regulation (EC) 765/2008. Another difference is within respect to the warning of dangers posed by consumer products. So are food commodities. Within the sense of § 2 paragraph 6 no. 1 in the case of serious risks LFGB, not subject to the Community Rapid Information System *RAPEX*, because of the close factual connection with food using the corresponding Quick Information System *RASFF*[14].

Whether it would have required a control of food commodities in § 2 paragraph 6 no. 1 and § 31 paragraph 1 LFGB, which is doubtful, given the mere referral to the LFGB by force of Regulation (EC) 1935/2004. It is striking why the national legislature now prohibits the production on manufacture of Article 3 Regulation (EC) 1935/2004 supplemented by bans on use and on placing onto the market, even though the products, illegally produced, should logically not be placed on the market anyway. Commodities that are not food consumer goods (§ 2 paragraph 6 no. 2-9 LFGB) would, in any case, be better labelled in this way due to the proximity of applicability to the Product Safety Act.[15]

C. Legislative developments and outlook

Concerning the current standard, the *Federal Ministry of Food and Agriculture (BMEL)* provides reasons for consumer health protection and a further need for regulation in the field of food commodities. Against this background, the draft of the so-called "oil Regulation" can be understood.

---

14 This was built on the basis of Regulation (EC) 178/2002 of the European Parliament and of the Council of 28 January 2002 laying down the general principles and requirements of food law, establishing the European Food Safety Authority and laying down procedures in matters of food safety [2002] OJ L 31/1, art 50 ff. and is an improved and enhanced rapid alert system for food and feed.
15 Carsten Schucht in Thomas Klindt (ed), *Kommentar zum Produktsicherheitsgesetz – ProdSG* (2nd edn, C.H. Beck 2015) § 1 recital 63 ff., 104 ff.

It contains provisions concerning the transition from mineral oil and food packaging that have been produced using recycled paper for foods. One main reason for the oil contamination of foods is food packaging made of paper, cardboard or paperboard, especially those made from recycled paper. Because recycled paper contains pulp, which is obtained from waste paper. Recycled paper consists of newspapers, magazines and other graphic papers, as well as packaging papers. For the printing of these papers, printing inks are used, which contain mineral oil. Hence the problem of contamination of packaged food with so-called MOSH (Mineral Oil Saturated Hydrocarbons) and to a lesser extent with MOAH (Mineral Oil Aromatic Hydrocarbons), arises. Mineral oil is derived from petroleum and is a complex mixture which consists mainly of saturated (chain and ring-shaped) and aromatic hydrocarbons. These can be stored in the body and cause damage to the liver. Moreover, partly considerable amounts have been observed on aromatic petroleum hydrocarbons in food. It is not ruled out that among them are substances that can cause severe damage to health even in small quantities. To protect consumers against possible health hazards by the transition of petroleum hydrocarbons from food contact materials and articles which are manufactured using recycled pulp, these should therefore be restricted for food. These should be set to maximum levels of saturated and aromatic petroleum hydrocarbons in food contact materials of recycled paper, paperboard or cardboard. If these values are not respected, products may not be placed on the market. An active processing of the root causes, such as substitution of newspaper inks, to date has not been done.

Also, the present parallel draft "printing inks regulation" aims to protect the consumer against possible health hazards in dealing with printed food commodities. This includes, *inter alia*, a positive list of substances which may be used in such printing.

§ 6 Patents on food – important questions in a world of radical changes

Christina A. Flaskühler

A. Introduction to the principle issues

Patents on animals and plants, and the breeding methods in which they are processed, are a controversial and especially relevant subject for the practice of law at multi-level governance. On the one hand, the proponents of patentability submit that the patentability guarantees the disclosure of important technologies that would otherwise be kept as internal business knowledge, and thus provide an important incentive for technological progress in breeding.[1] The critics and opponents of such patentability suggest that these patents lead to the fact that others will be excluded from the use, reproduction use, selling and processing for a period of 20 years. Furthermore, such patents lead to a risk for the variety of genetic resources within the meaning of biodiversity and finally result in significant problems in terms of food safety and food security[2] because large multinational corporations in the food industry will get the sole exploitation rights.[3] It is clear that in this kind of subject area opposite interests and positions get into conflict. Statistics in 2013 show that the European Patent Office

---

1 See for these arguments for example Pflanzen.Forschung.Ethik, 'Biopatente kontrovers – Pro und Contra' (2014) <http://www.pflanzen-forschung-ethik.de/kontexte/1644.biopatente-pro-contra.html> accessed 2 September 2015.

2 See for questions about food saftey and food security Ines Härtel (ed), *Nachhaltigkeit, Energiewende, Klimawandel, Welternährung: Politische und rechtliche Herausforderungen des 21. Jahrhunderts* (Forum Umwelt-, Agrar- und Klimaschutzrecht, vol 1, Nomos 2014).

3 See for this kind of criticism eg no patents on seeds, 'Patente auf Brokkoli und Tomaten bestätigt – Patente auf konventionell gezüchtete Pflanzen und Tiere auch in Zukunft möglich' <https://no-patents-on-seeds.org/de/information/aktuelles/patente-brokkoli-tomaten-bestaetigt> accessed 2 September 2015.

(EPO)[4] and the German Patent and Trade Mark Office (DPMA)[5] granted a total of 220 patents on crop plants and livestock, 21 of which were classified as worthy of observation[6] (17 in crop plants and 4 in livestock).[7] A significantly higher number of patents have been granted by the EPO, only just one of the patents was granted by the DPMA. But it must be noted that there were only 13 patent applications at the DPMA (the total number of patent applications in 2013 was 507).[8]

B. Currently relevant examples – broccoli and tomato

In recent years, two similar cases in particular have become the focus of interest in this area, which will be discussed in more detail because of their timelines and the recent and now final decision of the Enlarged Board of Appeal. As a first example, the patent which the Plant Bioscience Limited was granted (used by Monsanto subsidiary Seminis) in 2002, the so-called "broccoli patent", has to be mentioned.[9]

On the one hand, it involves a patent granted for a particular variety of broccoli, which has a particularly high proportion of glucosinolates (mustard oils), which presumably act cancer-preventing according to scientific studies, and, on the other hand, at the same time patent for the method by which this component can be increased in broccoli plants. Thus, this patent from 2002 was referring to both: the culturing method as well as the edible broccoli plant, the edible parts and the seeds. To obtain this special

---

4 About the European Patent Office (EPO) <https://www.epo.org/index_de.html> accessed 15 August 2015.
5 About the German Patent and Trade Mark Office (DPMA) <http://www.dpma.de/> accessed 15 August 2015.
6 Granted patents and patent applications are considered worthy of observation, when either there is a possible existence of an exclusion from patentability, that means patent protection is claimed for essentially biological processes or products obtained thereby, or at a Muragenese, that means there is a method in which a spontaneous mutation rate in the genetic material of living things is increased by exposing this material of living genotype-changing (mutagenic) substances or rays.
7 See German Federal Ministry of Justice, 'Biopatentmonitoring 2014'; see also BT-Drucks. 18/2119, 2, 6.
8 BT-Drucks. 18/2119, 2.
9 Decision of the Enlarged Board of Appeal of 9 December 2010, Case Number G 0002/07, Application Number 99915886.8, Publication Number 1069819 *Broccoli/PLANT BIOSCIENCE (Broccoli I)* OJ 2012, 130.

form of broccoli, a "common" broccoli was crossed with a wild variety from Italy. The breeding method used comprises conventional steps as well as genetic markers for identification by the responsible authorities for the genetic material of plants (so-called SMART-Breeding)[10]. Thus, it was a mixed method of genetic marker-assisted selection (MAS) and classical crossbreeding.[11] The agricultural companies Groupe Limagrain Holding AG (French) and Syngenta Participations AG (Swiss) appealed against the patent granted because, in their opinion, the claim refers to "essentially biological processes for the production of plants or animals", which is not patentable on the basis of Article 53 (b) EPC[12], and because not only does the patentee take the method of breeding but also the product itself.

In the opposition procedure, it was decided that the breeding technique claimed is not patentable. In reply, the patentee himself appealed against this decision. The competent Technical Board of Appeal of the EPO referred the case to the Enlarged Board of Appeal[13], which is the highest decision-making body within the EPO, questioning, what exactly does "essentially biological processes for the production of plants or animals" mean.

---

10 SMART-Breeding means 'Selection with Markers and Advanced Reproductive Technologies', see <http://www.pflanzenforschung.de/index.php?cID=8375> accessed 15 August 2015. In this process no foreign genes are introduced into the genetic material of organisms and there are also no genetically modified organisms, but the offspring of crossing partners are examined on the molecular level (THEN) for the presence of specific crossed genes and cultured further in a positive case. If none of the parental lines are genetically modified, the intersection manufactured products (offspring) are not subject to the genetic engineering law. The goal is to breed natural offsprings of two parent lines with specific, desired properties.

11 See Doris Walter, 'Klassische und markergeschütze Zuchtverfahren – Noch kein Patentrezept für Tomaten und Brokkoli' (2010) GRUR-Prax 329.

12 Convention on the Grant of European Patents (European Patent Convention) (EPO) of 5 October 1973 as revised by the Act revising art 63 EPC of 17 December 1991 and the Act revising the EPC of 29 November 2000; current status: 15th edn 2013.

13 The Enlarged Board of Appeal is the highest court within the EPO and it deals with cases referred to it either by one of the technical boards of appeal or by the Legal Board of Appeal or by the President of the European Patent Office for a decision on an important point of law or in order to secure uniform application of the law, see <https://www.epo.org/about-us/boards-of-appeal/faq-boards-of-appeal.ht ml#faq-8> accessed 6 October 2015.

In this context, the "tomato-patent"[14] must also be mentioned. In 2003, the "tomato-patent" was given to the Ministry of Agriculture of the State of Israel which covers a method of breeding tomato plants with low water content and the products resulting from that process.[15] DNA-markers are not used in this technique, instead, the selection of appropriate tomatoes for further breeding was carried out by analyzing the dehydration of the fruit and the wrinkling of the fruit skin.[16] Unilever N.V. (Rotterdam) appealed against that patent to the EPO in 2004, and claimed that the patent does not fulfil several conditions under the EPO and extends to "essentially biological processes for the production of plants or animals" that are excluded from patentability (Article 53 (b) EPC). As a result, the Opposition Division decided to maintain the patent, but in an amended version that no longer covered the breeding method. As a consequence, the patent holder – the Israeli Ministry of Agriculture – appealed against the decision in 2008. The competent Technical Board of Appeal of the EPO again referred the case to the Enlarged Board of Appeal with the question, what does "essentially biological processes for the production of plants or animals" mean within the associated exception to the patentability (Article 4 (1) Directive 98/44/EC[17]; Article 53 (b) EPC).[18]

Due to the comparable issue in the "broccoli patent", the Enlarged Board of Appeal combined both legal proceedings since a separate decision of the "broccoli-patent" did not exist at the time. The Enlarged Board of Appeal confirmed the non-patentability of "essentially biological processes for the production of plants or animals" in a landmark decision of 9 December 2010[19].

---

14 Decision of the Enlarged Board of Appeal of 9 December 2010, Case Number G 0001/08, Application Number 00940724.8, Publication Number 1211926 *Tomatoes/STATE OF ISRAEL (Tomato I)* OJ 2012, 206.
15 Doris Walter, 'Klassische und markergeschütze Zuchtverfahren – Noch kein Patentrezept für Tomaten und Brokkoli' (2010) GRUR-Prax 329.
16 Ibid.
17 Directive 98/44/EC of the European Parliament and of the Council of 6 July 1998 on the legal protection of biotechnological inventions [1998] OJ L 213/13.
18 Preliminary ruling (Vorlageverfahren) G1/108.
19 Decision of the Enlarged Board of Appeal of 9 December 2010, Case Number G 0002/07, Application Number 99915886.8, Publication Number 1069819 *Broccoli/PLANT BIOSCIENCE (Broccoli I)* OJ 2012, 130 and Case Number G 0001/08, Application Number 00940724.8, Publication Number 1211926 *Tomatoes/STATE OF ISRAEL (Tomato I)* OJ 2012, 206.

The question whether plants and parts of the plants created by such breeding methods, are also covered by this exclusion from patentability remained unresolved. This question was referred to the Enlarged Board of Appeal again in the further course of the appeal procedure.

In the following combined decisions "broccoli II" and "tomato II"[20] of 25 March 2015, the Enlarged Board of Appeal determined under which conditions plants, parts of plants and seed are covered by the exclusion from patentability under the EPO, and stated finally that the exclusion from patentability does not apply to plants, parts of plants and seed, which are produced by "essentially biological processes for the production of plants or animals", so that, as a result, their patentability is still possible. The decision will be discussed in the following pages in detail.

C. Legal bases and the application to the cases

The European Patent Convention (EPC) is the legal basis of the decision. It is an entity of international law which is based on the multilateral state treaty signed on the Grant of European Patents of 5 October 1973.[21] Not only members of the European Union but also other European countries could be part of this treaty due to Article 166 EPC.[22] According to Article 52 (1) EPC European patents shall be granted for any inventions, in all fields of technology, given that they are new, involve an inventive step and are susceptible to industrial application.[23]

According to Article 53 (b) EPC, "European patents shall not be granted in respect of plant or animal varieties or essentially biological processes for the production of plants or animals".

---

20 Decision of the Enlarged Board of Appeal of 25 March 2015, Case Number G 0002/13, Appeal Number T 0083/05 *Broccoli/PLANT BIOSCIENCE (Broccoli II)* OJ 2012, 130 and Case Number G 0002/12, Appeal Number T 1242/06 *Tomatoes/ STATE OF ISRAEL (Tomato II)* OJ 2012, 206.

21 Michael Hassemer, *Patentrecht* (Kohlhammer 2011) recital 96; see also Rudolf Kraßer, *Patentrecht* (5th edn, C.H. Beck 2004) § 7, 89.

22 Horst-Peter Götting / Sven Hetmank / Karsten Schwipps, *Patentrecht* (C.H. Beck 2014) recital 38; the European Patent Convention includes not only the EU Member States but also Switzerland, Norway, Croatia, Iceland and Lichtenstein.

23 See with regard to the requirements of patentabillity Klaus-Jürgen Melullis in Georg Benkard (ed), *Europäisches Patentübereinkommen* (2nd edn, C.H. Beck 2012) art 52 recital 35 ff.

But plant varieties can attain plant variety protection under National[24] or Community Law[25]. The terms "plant variety" and "animal variety" are not defined in the EPC.[26] Methods are "essentially biological processes" which go back fully to natural phenomena such as crossing or selection, which mean only methods corresponding to processes in nature.[27] Furthermore, this exclusion includes methods only for breeding, other relevant methods than these are not covered.[28] A breeding method cannot circumvent the patenting exclusion just by the addition of technical steps since the use of them in "essentially biological processes" does not make the plant patentable.[29] The background of this non-patentability is the realisation that the continuous further breeding of varieties and breeds is an essential necessary basis for agriculture and food security, dependent on a constant access to a wide gene pool which should only be limited by patents as little as possible.[30] However, patentability of individual animals

---

24 According to the Sortenschutzgesetz (SortSchG) (Plant Variety Protection Law) in der Fassung der Bekanntmachung vom 19. Dezember 1997 (German Federal Law Gazette 1997 I, 3164), zuletzt geändert durch Artikel 8 des Gesetzes vom 4. April 2016 (German Federal Law Gazette 2016 I, 558).

25 According to Council Regulation (EC) 2100/94 of 27 July 1994 on Community plant variety rights [1994] OJ L 227/1 as amended by Council Regulation (EC) 2506/95 of 25 October 1995 [1995] OJ L 258/3; see also Rudolf Kraßer, *Patentrecht* (5th edn, C.H. Beck 2004) § 14, 201 ff.

26 See with regard to the term 'plant variety' Uwe Fitzner in Uwe Fitzner / Raimund Lutz / Theo Bodewig (eds), *Patentrechtskommentar* (4th edn, Franz Vahlen 2012) art 53 EPÜ recital 33 ff. and the term 'animal variety' Uwe Fitzner in Uwe Fitzner / Raimund Lutz / Theo Bodewig (eds), *Patentrechtskommentar* (4th edn, Franz Vahlen 2012) art 53 EPÜ recital 46 ff.

27 Klaus-Jürgen Melullis in Georg Benkard (ed), *Europäisches Patentübereinkommen* (2nd edn, C.H. Beck 2012) art 53 recital 63 and 89.

28 Ibid art 53 recital 89.

29 Decision of the Enlarged Board of Appeal of 9 December 2010, Case Number G 0002/07, Application Number 99915886.8, Publication Number 1069819 *Broccoli/PLANT BIOSCIENCE (Broccoli I)* OJ 2012, 130 and Case Number G 0001/08, Application Number 00940724.8, Publication Number 1211926 *Tomatoes/STATE OF ISRAEL (Tomato I)* OJ 2012, 206; see also Uwe Fitzner in Uwe Fitzner / Raimund Lutz / Theo Bodewig (eds), *Patentrechtskommentar* (4th edn, Franz-Vahlen 2012) art 53 EPÜ recital 68.

30 German Federal Ministry of Food and Agriculture, 'Biopatente: Keine Patentierung von Tierrassen und Pflanzensorten' (2015) <http://www.bmel.de/DE/Tier/Nutztierhaltung/Biopatente/biopatente_node.htm> accessed 27 July 2015.

and plants is not excluded under the EPC.[31] As a result, patents may be granted for those claims which do not demand any individual plant varieties or animal breeds. A similar regulation can be found in Article 4 (1) Directive 98/44/EC.[32] Article 4 Directive 98/44/EC which says that plant and animal varieties (lit. a) and essentially biological processes for the production of plants or animals (lit. b) shall not be patentable. Article 2 (2) Directive 98/44/EC contains the legal definitions for what "essentially biological processes" means: "A process for the production of plants or animals is essentially biological if it consists entirely of natural phenomena such as crossing or selection".

The Enlarged Board of Appeal determined in the above-described initial case on the basis of a detailed interpretation of Article 53 EPC that the exclusion of patenting of "essentially biological breeding methods" in accordance with Article 53 (b) EPC should be interpreted narrowly. Thus, the patentability does not extend to plants and plant material which have been made with such breeding methods.[33] Plants or plant material (such as parts of plants or fruits) which are obtained through a process which is based on the intersection of plant genomes and subsequent selection are therefore patentable, if they meet the other requirements of the European Patent Convention.[34] That means that the patent claim must be new, involve an inventive step and be susceptible to industrial application (Article 52, 54, 56 EPC) and must not be addressed individually to a particular plant variety (Article 53 (b) EPC). However, a generally worded claim, in

---

31 Klaus-Jürgen Melullis in Georg Benkard (ed), *Europäisches Patentübereinkommen* (2nd edn, C. H. Beck 2012) art 53 recital 70; Jan Busche, 'Die Patentierung biologischer Erfindungen nach Patentgesetz und EPÜ' (1999) GRUR Int. 299, 300; see also Rainer Moufang in Rainer Schulte (ed), *Patentgesetz mit Europäischem Patentübereinkommen* (9 th edn, Carl Heymanns Verlag 2014) § 2 a PatG, art 53 (b) EPÜ recital 43, who is contemplating a possible exclusionary effect also with respect to the produced products.
32 See about the EU Biotechnology Directive eg Geertrui Van Overwalle, 'Legal and Ehtical Aspects of Bio-Patenting. Critical Analysis of the EU Biotechnology Directive' in Christoph Baumgartner / Dietmar Mieth (eds), *Patente am Leben? Ehtische, rechtliche und politische Aspekte der Biopatentierung* (Mentis-Verlag 2003) 145 ff.
33 Decision of the Enlarged Board of Appeal of 25 March 2015, Case Number G 0002/13, Appeal Number T 0083/05 *Broccoli/PLANT BIOSCIENCE (Broccoli II)* OJ 2012, 130 and Case Number G 0002/12, Appeal Number T 1242/06 *Tomatoes/ STATE OF ISRAEL (Tomato II)* 66 ff. OJ 2012, 206.
34 Ibid.

which no particular plant is individually claimed, will be admissible even if it includes (more) plant varieties (G 1/98).

Furthermore, the Enlarged Board of Appeal determined that in formulating a product claim for such a plant, the format of a "product-by-process" claim is permitted.[35] The protected plant can thus be defined by its manufacturing method even if this method is not patentable because it is an "essentially biological breeding method".

D. Criticism of the decision

The board's decision partly provoked severe criticism. The German Plant Breeders' Association (BDP) states, for example, that plant variety rights are undermined by the decision.[36] According to the plant variety law,[37] breeders have the right to use the latest varieties of other breeders for their own growth, including marketing, and thereby building upon inputs of other breeders as an "open-source" system (so-called breeders` privileges, § 10 a paragraph 1 no. 3 Sortenschutzgesetz (German Plant Variety Protection Law), Article 15 (c) Regulation (EC) 2100/94[38]).[39] As a result, a faster breeding process could be possible, involving the entire existing ge-

---

35 Decision of the Enlarged Board of Appeal of 25 March 2015, Case Number G 0002/13, Appeal Number T 0083/05 *Broccoli/PLANT BIOSCIENCE (Broccoli II)* OJ 2012, 130 and Case Number G 0002/12, Appeal Number T 1242/06 *Tomatoes/ STATE OF ISRAEL (Tomato II)* 66 ff. OJ 2012, 206; since the Federal Supreme Court decision 'tetraploid chamomile' are those 'product-by-process' patents allowed also for organic products under national law, Federal Supreme Court, Decision of 30 March 1993 – X ZB 13/90 'Tetraploide Kamille' (1993) GRUR 651.

36 Alfons Deter, 'BDP fordert Korrektur im "Brokkoli-Urteil" ' *topagrar online* (28 April 2015) <http://www.topagrar.com/news/Acker-Agrarwetter-Ackernews-BDP-fordert-Korrektur-im-Brokkoli-Urteil-1765322.html> accessed 15 August 2015; 'BDP übt Kritik an Entscheidung im Brokkoli Fall - Patentrecht wird unangemessen ausgeweitet - Zugang zu genetischer Diversität gefährdet' *na news aktuell* (27 March 2015) <http://www.presseportal.de/pm/100826/2983753> accessed 2 August 2015.

37 See about the plant variety rights Herbert Leßmann / Gert Würtenberger (eds), *Deutsches und Europäisches Sortenschutzrecht* (2nd edn, Nomos 2009).

38 Council Regulation (EC) 2100/94 of 27 July 1994 on Community plant variety rights [1994] OJ L 227/1 as amended by Council Regulation (EC) 2506/95 of 25 October 1995 [1995] OJ L 258/3.

39 Inken Garbe, 'Kapitel 28 - Sortenschutz- und Saatgutverkehrsrecht' in Ines Härtel (ed), *Handbuch des Fachanwalts Agrarrecht* (Luchterhand 2012) recital 41.

netic diversity, which was banned in patent law, so that the recent ruling conditions the preservation of the diversity of an innovative, powerful and diverse landscape which is endangered.[40] According to many people, an unreasonable extension of the patent legal protection has taken place.[41] The Federation of Organic Food (BÖLW) expresses severe criticism as well. In its opinion, the patent on conventionally bred plants serves the interests of multinational seed corporations exclusively, and blocks the development of breeding on the spot.[42] Also, in the field of trade, sharp criticism found expression.[43] The international coalition of "No Patents on Seeds!" published a call to the European level under the slogan "Act now – save the future of our food!", in which they warn that multinational enterprises as Monsanto, get more and more control over the foundation of our food and that acting on the European level is urgently needed. As a result, the criticism focuses on the fear that multinational corporations will get the control over all stages of food production from "Farm to Fork" involving the risks of access to food (World Food) and the safety of food (food safety).

E. Possible solutions

To deal with this problem one needs to took at legal-legislative solutions. Such a narrowed understanding of Article 53 (b) EPC and Article 4 (1) Directive 44/98/EC, as made in the current judgement, will lead to the result that the law "runs empty". This has already been recognised in recent years by politicians, and possible solutions were discussed. Already in

---

40 'Europäisches Patentamt erlaubt Patent auf Brokkoli' *agrarheute* (31 March 2015) <http://www.agrarheute.com/europaeisches-patentamt-erlaubt-patent-auf-brokkoli> accessed 2 May 2015.

41 Instead of many see Greenpeace, 'Der Brokkoli-Fall' (2015) <https://www.greenpeace.de/sites/www.greenpeace.de/files/publications/fs-fall-brokkoli-30032015.pdf> accessed 2 August 2015.

42 'Europäisches Patentamt erlaubt Patent auf Brokkoli' *agrarheute* (31 March 2015) <http://www.agrarheute.com/europaeisches-patentamt-erlaubt-patent-auf-brokkoli> accessed 2 August 2015.

43 Eg Rewe, Handelsunternehmen Tegut; <http://lebensmittelpraxis.de/zentrale-management/12738-round-table-patente-%C3%A2%E2%82%AC%C5%BEwir-brauchen-schutz-und-zugang%C3%A2%E2%82%AC%C5%93.html> accessed 8 November 2015.

2012 the European Parliament demanded that plants and animals derived from conventional breeding cannot be patented and this requirement needs to be legally implemented.[44] Pioneering examples of a change at the European level could be found in the German and the Dutch patent law, which both prohibit such patentability of plants and animals. § 2 a paragraph 1 no. 1 Patentgesetz (German Patent Law)[45] determine that patents shall not be granted for plant varieties and animal varieties or essentially biological processes for the production of plants and animals and the plants and animals obtained exclusively from such processes.[46] The addition of "and the product obtained exclusively from such processes of plants and animals" has been inserted by Article 1 pt. 2 Gesetz zur Novellierung patentrechtlicher Vorschriften und anderer Gesetze des gewerblichen Rechtsschutzes (German Patent Amendment Law)[47] of 19 October 2013 based on a recommendation of the judiciary committee of the German Bundestag.[48] This includes the specific material of their generation, e.g. seeds, animal semen (sperm), ova and embryos.[49] The largely free access to genetic resources is a prerequisite for breeders´ and farmers´ work. Due to the background stated above, the amendment of the German Patent Act, with which the national interpretation possibilities of EU Biopatent Directive are exhausted, is a first important step with a signal to the European patent

---

44 <http://www.europarl.europa.eu/sides/getDoc.do?pubRef=-//EP//TEXT+TA+P7-T
A-2012-0202+0+DOC+XML+V0//DE> accessed 15 August 2015.

45 Patentgesetz (PatG) (German Patent Law) in der Fassung der Bekanntmachung vom 16. Dezember 1980 (German Federal Law Gazette 1981 I, 1), zuletzt geändert durch Artikel 1 des Gesetzes vom 19. Oktober 2013 (German Federal Law Gazette 2013 I, 3830).

46 In Germany the patentability of such processes for the production of plants and animals have been denied even by previous law because of the lack of the required repeatability, without this unique scheme introduced. In application of the principles developed by the Federal Supreme Court in the case 'Rote Traube', see Federal Supreme Court, Decision of 27 March 1969 - X ZB 15/67 *Rote Traube* BGHZ 52, 74, 79 ff.

47 Gesetz zur Novellierung patentrechtlicher Vorschriften und anderer Gesetze des gewerblichen Rechtsschutzes (German Patent Amendement Law), effective from 19 October 2013 (German Federal Law Gazette 2013 I, 3830).

48 Peter Mes in Peter Mes (ed), *Patentgesetz, Gebrauchsmustergesetz* (4th edn, C.H. Beck 2015) § 2 a PatG recital 1; Rainer Moufang in Rainer Schulte (ed), *Patentgesetz mit Europäischem Patentübereinkommen* (9th edn, Carl Heymanns Verlag 2014) § 2 a PatG, art 53 (b) EPÜ recital 43.

49 BT-Drucks. 17/14222 (report of the Committee on Legal Affairs) of 26 June 2013, IV to no 1 (Amendments to § 2 a PatG).

granting practice.[50] In Dutch Law such a scheme can be found in patent law as well. Article 3 paragraph 1 lit. c and d. Dutch Patents Act[51] says „No patent shall be issued for: "plant or animal varieties" (lit. c) and "essentially biological processes consisting entirely of natural phenomena such as hybridisations or selections in order to produce plants or animals and the products obtained thereby" (lit. d).

These two laws represent a legal role model for a change to the European level because, on the one hand, they establish legal transparency and, on the other hand, they recognise the special position and importance of animals and plants, at the same time they can stop possible misuse by multinational corporations.

F. Conclusion

Overall, the decision of the Enlarged Board of Appeal brings to mind that the legal situation on the European level opens the door for an interpretation under which patents on plants and animals are possible which have been created under "essentially biological processes" as shown by the combined "broccoli II" and "tomato II" decision. This situation shows, on the one hand, the inconsistency between German and European law in this legal area, and, on the other hand, an enormous risk for food security and food safety. But certainly, the German and Dutch show legal possibilities on how this problem can be solved.

G. Outlook

Also other countries such as France have a critical opinion on the current development with regard to the patentability of food and in many places people claim that the European level should intervene in its regulatory capacity. It is to be expected because of the strong trends both in the agriculture and in the food sector as well as in the civilian population that im-

---

50 German Federal Ministry of Food and Agriculture, 'Biopatente: Keine Patentierung von Tierrassen und Pflanzensorten' (2015) <http://www.bmel.de/DE/Tier/ Nutztierhaltung/Biopatente/biopatente_node.htm> accessed 20 October 2015.
51 Kingdom Act of 15 December 1994 containing rules in respect of patents (Dutch Patents Act).

provements will be made in this regard to prevent uncertainty and to create a unity between national rules and EU law.

§ 7 Responsibility of the distributor for food labelling – a revolution?

Agnieszka Szymecka-Wesołowska

A. Introduction

The recently introduced Regulation 1169/2011[1] has established a new legal European framework regarding food labelling. It came into force on 13th December 2014. The Regulation introduces many significant changes concerning food labelling, including the division of responsibility between different individual entities present on the food market. In section 21 of the preamble to Regulation 1169/2011, the EU legislator stressed that "In order to prevent a fragmentation of the rules concerning the responsibility of food business operators with respect to food information it is appropriate to clarify the responsibilities of food business operators in this area. That clarification should be in accordance with the responsibilities regarding the consumer referred to in Article 17 of Regulation (EC) 178/2002." The aim expressed in the quoted section of the preamble was implemented by Article 8 of Regulation 1169/2011. In the context of this Regulation, it is worth paying particular attention to the question of responsibility of food distributors.

Until now, various doubts existed as to the scope of responsibility of food distributors for improper labelling. The European Court of Justice was one of the authorities to express its opinion on the matter, *de facto* confirming the possibility to apply the principle of strict responsibility in this regard. Regulation 1169/2011 seems to revolutionise this approach, and therefore opens a path to a completely different manner of regulating

---

1 Regulation (EU) 1169/2011 of the European Parliament and of the Council of 25 October 2011 on the provision of food information to consumers, amending Regulations (EC) 1924/2006 and (EC) 1925/2006 of the European Parliament and of the Council, and repealing Commission Directive 87/250/EEC, Council Directive 90/496/EEC, Commission Directive 1999/10/EC, Directive 2000/13/EC of the European Parliament and of the Council, Commission Directives 2002/67/EC and 2008/5/EC and Commission Regulation (EC) 608/2004 [2011] OJ L 304/18.

legal and commercial relations between individual members of the food business chain, both in domestic and EU trade.

The subject of this article is therefore to present the legal regulations which were in force with regards to the responsibility of food vendors and distributors prior to the introduction of Regulation 1169/2011, as well as to analyse the solutions that were introduced in this regard by the above Regulation.

B. The responsibility of the distributor before and after Regulation 1169/2011

I. Prior to Regulation 1169/2011

Regulation 1169/2011 has replaced the previous Directive 2000/13/EC[2] which did not specify who was responsible for failure to satisfy labelling obligations and, in particular, it did not become clear on how food vendors and distributors should be held responsible. In consequence, general provisions were applied.

Reference has been made to Regulation (EC) 178/2002[3], and in particular to its Article 17 (1) which states: "Food and feed business operators at all stages of production, processing and distribution within the businesses under their control shall ensure that foods or feeds satisfy the requirements of food law which are relevant to their activities and shall verify that such requirements are met."

Based on the above provision it can be said that it makes every food business operator responsible[4]. However, it must be also noted that this provision seems to introduce different kind of requirements depending on the stage of the food chain, as evidenced by the wording "requirements of

---

2 Directive 2000/13/EC of the European Parliament and of the Council of 20 March 2000 on the approximation of the laws of the Member States relating to the labelling, presentation and advertising of foodstuffs [2000] OJ L 109/29.

3 Regulation (EC) 178/2002 of the European Parliament and of the Council of 28 January 2002 laying down the general principles and requirements of food law, establishing the European Food Safety Authority and laying down procedures in matters of food safety [2002] OJ L 31/1.

4 More on this issue see for example, Antonio Sciaudone, 'Responsibilities of food business operators' in Luigi Costato / Ferdinando Albisinni (eds), *European Food Law* (CEDAM 2012) 175.

food law which are relevant to their activities". It could therefore be inferred that food business operators are not obliged to meet all requirements of food law, but only those, that are "relevant", i.e. related to their activities[5]. As noted in the doctrine, differentiation between requirements imposed on individual participants in the food chain seems–to be confirmed in another provision of the same Regulation. Article 19 (2) of Regulation 178/2002 restricts the participation of entities dealing–with retail sales or distribution not related to packaging, labelling, safety or integrity of food to only those actions which "remain within the limits of its respective activities"[6].

A question therefore arises whether meeting requirements concerning food labelling is relevant to the activities of food vendors, and if so, to what extent. This question in particular seems ambiguous with regard to food distributors who trade in packaged food, i.e. "finished" goods that had been produced, packed and labelled by entities working at an earlier stage of the food chain.

The answer to the above question was given by the European Court of Justice (ECJ), in the case mentioned in the introduction to the paper, namely Lidl Italia Srl v. Comune di Arcole (VR) (C-315/05). The case concerned the *Amaro alle erbe* liqueur, imported from Germany and sold by the Lidl chain in Italy; as a result of the tests carried out on the liqueur, it transpired that the alcohol content was lower than declared by the manufacturer on the label. The ECJ determined that it was permissible under national law to hold a distributor responsible for a breach of the labelling provisions in circumstances where the product had been pre-packaged by the producer, even where, as the mere distributor, it simply markets the product as delivered to it by the producer. The Court therefore did not agree with the view held by one of the parties (the distributor) that it could not have known whether the labelling placed on the packaging of the

---

5 In this context, the doctrine states that the legislator established a functional type criteria by introducing responsibility for requirements 'relevant to activities' in Regulation (EC) 178/2002 of the European Parliament and of the Council of 28 January 2002 laying down the general principles and requirements of food law, establishing the European Food Safety Authority and laying down procedures in matters of food safety [2002] OJ L 31/1, art 17 (1); Ilaria Trapè, 'Odpowiedzialność za produkt niebezpieczny podmiotów dystrybuujących żywność' (2008) 2 (4) Przegląd Prawa Rolnego 112.

6 Ibid.

questionable product was correct or not, since it acted only as the interme-
diary between the manufacturer and the consumer.

Furthermore, the Court did not agree with the position of the Advocate
General, who stated that in his opinion the distributor should be held responsible "only if the distributor is in a position to verify that the particu-
lars on the label of the product are substantively accurate", as "the distributor of a product is not usually in a position to supervise the product manufacturing process"[7].

In consequence, by making the distributor responsible, the verdict of
the ECJ introduced a sort of objective responsibility (strict liability),
where determining the fault of the entity distributing food is not necessary
to impose punishment on it. The court concluded the above mostly from
Articles 2, 3 and 12 of Directive 2000/13/EC, also pointing out that this
principle was also confirmed in Article 17 (1) of Regulation 178/2002[8].
Furthermore, the principle of objective responsibility was also confirmed
by the Court (although with regards to a slightly different aspect that does
not refer to labelling) in its recent verdict dated 13th November 2014, reference number C-443/13. In the above decision, the Court confirmed the
responsibility of the distributor of a vacuum sealed fresh boneless turkey
breast that was found to be contaminated with *Salmonella Typhimurium*,
and which had been manufactured and packaged by a third party entity. As
the Court stated: "EU law, in particular Regulation (EC) No 178/2002 of
the European Parliament and of the Council of 28 January 2002 laying
down the general principles and requirements of food law, establishing the
European Food Safety Authority and laying down procedures in matters of
food safety and Regulation No 2073/2005, as amended by Regulation No
1086/2011, must be interpreted as meaning that, in principle, it does not
preclude national law, such as that at issue in the main proceedings, which
imposes a penalty on a food business operator which is active only at the
distribution stage for placing foodstuff on the market, on account of the
failure to comply with the microbiological criterion".

---

7 See Case C-532/03 *Commission v Ireland* [2007] ECR I-11355, Opinion of AG
   Stix-Hackl, paras 61 – 62.
8 For additional information, see eg Barbara Klaus / Alfred Hagen Mayer, 'The Responsibility of the Distributors in the Event of Infringements of Food Law – Case
   involving Lidl Italia: the Judgments of the European Court of Justice and the Giu-
   dice di Pace of Monselice, Italy' (2008) 3 (6) European Food & Feed Law Review
   407.

It is worth noting that a similar legal direction has so far been adopted in other EU Member States, for example, in Poland. With regards to Article 17 (1) of Regulation 178/2002, Polish courts have clearly stressed that this provision "doesn't provide any differentiation as to the obligations of the food business operators" (judgment of Provincial Administrative Court in Warsaw of 4 August 2010, VI SA/Wa 894/10). Polish provisions penalising the introduction of improperly labelled products into commercial circulation automatically extend responsibility to all entities forming the food chain. In particular, this applies to Article 40 a (1) (3) and (4) of the act of 21st December 2000 on the commercial quality of agricultural and food products. Pursuant to Article 40 a (1) (3) of this act: He "Who introduces into circulation agricultural and food products that do not meet the commercial quality specified in provisions of law or declared by the manufacturer on the labelling of these articles, shall be responsible to a financial penalty of up to five times the financial gain that was obtained or which could be obtained by introducing these agricultural and food products into circulation, not lower however than PLN500"; while pursuant to Article 40 a (1) (4): He "Who introduces adulterated agricultural and food products into commercial circulation shall be responsible to a financial penalty of up to 10% of income earned in the financial year preceding the year in which the penalty is imposed, no lower however than PLN1000".

Based on these provisions, courts ruled as a principle that "on all stages – from manufacturing until distribution, all entities participating in the circulation of the product are responsible for meeting the ultimate goal. Each of these entities – the manufacturer, the processor and the distributor are required to comply with procedures concerning food safety. The stage in which the irregularity arose is irrelevant" (judgment of the Provincial Administrative Court dated 17th October 2011, reference number VI SA/Wa 1371/11). In a judgment dated 15th December 2010, reference number VI SA/Wa 1551/10, the Provincial Administrative Court in Warsaw stated also that "Article 40 a (1) (4) of the act of 2000 on the commercial quality of agricultural and food products does not make imposing a penalty dependent on ascertaining that the distributor was at fault for introducing an adulterated product into commercial circulation. Responsibility specified in this provision is of an objective nature and the fact itself of introducing the product into commercial circulation is enough to find an entity responsible.", and furthermore, in a judgment of Provincial Administrative Court in Warsaw dated 4th August 2010, reference number VI SA/Wa 894/10: "This provision [article 40 a (1) (4) of the act on quality] constitutes a simple solution that does not require any additional assumptions or interpretations and that orders competent bodies to impose a penalty on any entities who introduce (regardless of whether they do it knowingly or not) adulterated agricultural and food products into circulation."

These rulings clearly state that if irregularities were found, then official bodies responsible for controlling food were not required to ascertain the degree of fault of the controlled entity (including distributors). It was irrelevant whether and to what extent such entities had a hand in mislabelling products or whether they had a realistic chance to detect the defect, also in situations where the defects were not externally visible and detecting them would require opening the packaging and carrying out tests (e.g. for compliance between the actual content of a given ingredient in the product and the content declared on the label). The degree of the fault of the vendor (e.g. how likely he was to detect the irregularity on his own, among other considerations) did therefore not determine of itself that punishment had to be imposed or not, but it was only taken into account when deciding on the severity of the punishment[9].

II. Under Regulation 1169/2011

Subsequently, it will be examined how the provisions at hand have changed after the implementation of Regulation 1169/2011 and what changes were introduced by this Regulation.

Rules concerning responsibility of the entities on the market can be found in Article 8, entitled "Responsibilities".

First of all, the provision clearly states which of the entities in the food supply chain are responsible for labelling. According to paragraph 1 of this Article: "The food business operator responsible for the food information shall be the operator under whose name or business name the food is marketed or, if that operator is not established in the Union, the importer into the Union market." In other words, the entity that "undersigns" the product is responsible for it. It would appear therefore, that if the label contains the manufacturer's identification data (i.e. name and address), then in principle the manufacturer should be held responsible for labelling,

---

9 On this subject see more, for example, Michał Trempała, 'Odpowiedzialność administracyjna sprzedawcy detalicznego za wprowadzenie do obrotu artykułu rolno-spożywczego zafałszowanego' (2012) 2 (11) Przegląd Prawa Rolnego 141.

regardless of the stage in which any irregularity would be detected[10]. Correspondingly, if the label contains identification data of the distributor, which is a very common market practice especially with regards to private labels, then it is this entity that should be held responsible for the product's labelling, also in cases where such irregularities were made in the manufacturing stage (product packaging).

However, a question arises whether a lack of data identifying the distributor/vendor on the label really releases him from responsibility under Regulation 1169/2011. Such an interpretation would be too far-reaching and might allow for various abuses. It does not seem that this was the intention of EU legislators. This interpretation is, indeed, unfounded in the light of further paragraphs of Regulation 1169/2011.

Firstly, pursuant to Article 8 (3): "Food business operators which do not affect food information shall not supply food which they know or presume, on the basis of the information in their possession as professionals, to be non-compliant with the applicable food information law and requirements of relevant national provisions". This provision clearly distinguishes a category of entities which "do not affect food information". It can be assumed that the quoted phrase mainly refers to entities that do not participate in the process of labelling food products and whose identification data are not shown on the labels. With regards to such entities, the regulations seem to exclude *a contrario* their responsibility for also selling improperly labelled food if the entities were not aware of and did not suspect any such irregularities based on information and knowledge they should have as professionals acting in the food business sector.

It appears therefore that even if a given entity was not named on the label it does not mean that it is absolutely released from responsibility for the product. The above provision introduces clear criteria based on which the responsibility of a given entity (vendor) should be assessed each time. Considering this provision, the release from responsibility seems to be possible only when these three conditions are jointly met, i.e. the entity under review had no influence on the labelling, did not know about the irregularity and did not suspect that it might occur.

---

10 Here the divergence between the new regulation introduced by the art 8 and the previous approach of the European Court of Justice expressed in the Case C-315/05 *Lidl Italia Srl v Comune di Arcole (VR)* [2006] ECR I-11200 is particularly clear.

Secondly, pursuant to Article 8 (4) (2): "Food business operators are responsible for any changes they make to food information accompanying a food." This provision also confirms that a lack of a "signature" on the labelling does not constitute an absolute release from responsibility. If the vendor changes the label on the product (e.g. by adding or removing some of its components), then he bears full responsibility for such changes.

Finally, Article 8 (5) of Regulation 1169/2011 must be considered. This provision is of the utmost importance in the context under review. According to this provision: "Without prejudice to paragraphs 2 to 4, food business operators, within the businesses under their control, shall ensure compliance with the requirements of food information law and relevant national provisions which are relevant to their activities and shall verify that such requirements are met." In the context of this provision we should direct our attention to the phrase reading "without prejudice to paragraphs 2 to 4", and note what this fragment does not include, namely paragraph 1 of Article 8. This leads to the conclusion that even if the labelling does not contain any identification data of the entity within the business of which an irregularity was identified (e.g. in a shop, in the retail stage), it is possible to apply Article 8 (5), i.e. the rule according to which everyone in the food supply chain has to take responsibility for ensuring that the information is accurate, analogous to the rule specified in Article 17 (1).

This solution should be evaluated positively, as it prevents entities with significant contractual power to force their clients to place their identification data on labels to evade responsibility for the labelling of products that they influenced. It is worth noting that the European Commission also stated the following when responding to questions posed by the European Parliament in respect of Article 8 (5): "Due to the complexity of interactions and contractual obligations, and in particular the potential for future technical developments or logistical synergies in the food supply chain, this general provision operates mainly as a 'safety net' against legal gaps."

There is one more conclusion resulting from Article 8 (5) which is of utmost importance to the entire system of responsibility of entities active on the food market. The fact that the principle expressed by Article 8 (5) does not prevent the application of Article 8 (3) "revolutionises" previously existing rules concerning the responsibility of the distributor for labelling food introduced into the market and in particular, the manner of its interpretation[11]. This rule means that the responsibility of distributors should not be of an objective nature. As stated above, when determining the distributors responsibility, the conditions specified in Article 8 (3) should always be taken into account. These in principle prevent the automatic imposing of penalties on distributors (contrary e.g. to regulatory practices previously applied in Poland).

It seems that the European Commission confirms this interpretation to be correct. When replying to the following question posed by the European Parliament: "Taking account of Article 38 of the regulation, does the Commission believe that para 5 of Article 8 allows a Member State, by way of a national rule or regulatory practice, to consider any food business operator on its territory to be responsible for, and bound by, an obligation to verify the correctness of the mandatory information that must accompany a food product which originates from another Member State?", the Commission answered: "Given that the aim of the article is to prevent a fragmentation of the rules on the responsibility of food business operators, para 5 cannot be used in conjunction with Article 38 to invalidate the legal effect of paras 1 to 4. This is further explained by the use of the wording 'without prejudice to' in that paragraph. Thus, Member States may not, through national law, require that a food business operator who is not involved in the labelling of food information be obliged to check for the presence or accuracy of food information".

---

11 See for example, Fausto Capelli, 'Prodotti agroalimentari di qualità: controlli e responsabilità' (2011) 4 Rivista di Diritto Alimentare 1 <http://www.rivistadirittoalimentare.it/rivista/2011-04/CAPELLI.pdf> accessed 14 September 2015, who stressed out that in the light of the Regulation (EU) 1169/2011 of the European Parliament and of the Council of 25 October 2011 on the provision of food information to consumers, amending Regulations (EC) 1924/2006 and (EC) 1925/2006 of the European Parliament and of the Council, and repealing Commission Directive 87/250/EEC, Council Directive 90/496/EEC, Commission Directive 1999/10/EC, Directive 2000/13/EC of the European Parliament and of the Council, Commission Directives 2002/67/EC and 2008/5/EC and Commission Regulation (EC) 608/2004 [2011] OJ L 304/18, the judgment of the ECJ in Case C-315/05 *Lidl Italia Srl v Comune di Arcole (VR)* [2006] ECR I-11200, can be seen as 'interpretation's error'; see also Luigi Russo, 'La responsabilità del produttore e del distributore' (2014) 1 Rivista di Diritto Alimentare 34 <http://www.rivistadirittoalimentare.it/rivista/2014-01/RUSSO.pdf> accessed 14 September 2015.

C. Summary

Taking into consideration the above analysis, it appears that we can state, including some justification, that Regulation 1169/2011 revolutionised existing rules concerning responsibility of food vendors and distributors for complying with requirements concerning the labelling of food products. While Article 17 (1) of Regulation 178/2002, which – according to judicial practice of the ECJ (as well as e.g. Polish administrative courts) – allowed holding entities objectively responsible regardless of the degree of their fault, had previously been applied before the above regulation entered into force, the continued application of this approach appears no longer possible since the rules have been specified in Article 8 of Regulation 1169/2011 and came into force.

As stated in this article, if an official food control body detects any irregularities in the labelling of food products in the retail stage, before imposing any penalties, such bodies should first consider whether any circumstances exist to preclude the vendor from being held responsible for such irregularities. In the light of Article 8 (3) of Regulation 1169/2011 it appears possible that such responsibility can be precluded if the vendor had no influence on the labelling, did not know about the irregularity and did not suspect any of such irregularity could be present. Only if the above conditions are not met it is possible to hold the vendor responsible for the irregularity.

The legislator thus seems to rationalise previously existing rules for determining responsibility and moves away from the principle of automatically imposing penalties on distributors when any irregularities are identified with regards to the labelling of food they distribute, regardless of whether they had any influence on the labelling, whether they had any knowledge of such irregularities and whether it was possible for them to identify such irregularities.

There is one more important conclusion that needs to be made in this context, namely, that given the new rules concerning responsibility, implemented by Regulation 1169/2011, it is once again worth quoting section 21 of the preamble to this Regulation, which states: "In order to prevent a fragmentation of the rules concerning the responsibility of food business operators with respect to food information it is appropriate to clarify the responsibilities of food business operators in this area. That clarification should be in accordance with the responsibilities regarding the consumer referred to in Article 17 of Regulation (EC) No 178/2002". In this section, the legislator clearly determines that provisions implemented by Regulation 1169/2011 only "clarify" already existing rules concerning responsibility and that Article 17 of Regulation 178/2002 constitutes the main basis for these rules. In other words, according to the EU legislator the departure from the principle of automatism in imposing penalties confirmed in Article 8 (3) of Regulation 1169/2011 only constitutes a "clarification" of the general rule concerning responsibility specified in Article 17 of Regulation 178/2002. It leads to the conclusion that also Article 17 of Regulation 178/2002 itself allows for the possibility of differentiating the rules used to determine the responsibility of individual entities comprising the food supply chain. The clause included in the above article, requiring entities active on the food market to comply with and review their compliance with "requirements of food law which are relevant to their activities" seems to constitute a basis for such differentiation.

§ 8 The New Opt-Out Rule – new challenges in the legal multi-level system of the usage of GMOs

Johanna Monien

A. Introduction

The use of genetically modified organisms (GMOs) remains the subject of controversy. Whereas supporters highlight the advantages of developing, for example, pest or drought resistant plants, and thus allowing more economic production, even in areas with difficult agricultural conditions, sceptics point to the risks of green genetic engineering for the environment, above all, the risk of out crossing with natural varieties which could lead to a loss of biodiversity. Also, the sole cultivation of only a few sorts of genetically modified (GM) crops instead of the variety of traditional types might endanger agricultural biodiversity.[1]

Within the EU Member States, the attitude towards GMOs also differs. The main user and supporter is Spain, where the GM maize MON810 is cultivated on 137.000 hectares.[2] On the other hand, France, Germany and Austria oppose the use of GMOs on their territory and were main drivers for the Opt-Out Rule.

These conflicting points of view of the EU Member States concerning the use of GMOs led to difficulties within the authorisation process for GMOs on an EU level and led to the introduction of the Opt-Out Rule in European law[3]. Under Directive 2001/18/EC (Deliberate Release Direc-

---

1 For a summary of advantages and disadvantages of GMO use see Christian Grimm, *Agrarrecht* (3rd edn, C.H. Beck 2010) 323.
2 European Commission, 'MEMO/15/4778 - Fact Sheet: Questions and Answers on EU's policies on GMOs' (22 April 2015) 2 <http://europa.eu/rapid/press-release_M EMO-15-4778_en.htm> accessed 21 September 2015.
3 Astrid Strack, 'Der lange Weg zum Opt-out von der Gentechnik' (2014) 36 NuR 829; European Commission, 'Communication from the Commission to the European Parliament, the Council, the European Economic and Social Committee and the Committee of the Regions of 22 April 2015 - Reviewing the decision-making process on genetically modified organisms (GMOs)' COM (2015) 176 final, 6.

tive[4]) and Regulation 1829/2003/EC (GM Food and Feed Regulation[5]), the authorisation of GMOs for cultivation and market placement of GMOs has been harmonised. According to the original conception before introducing the Opt-Out Rule, after obtaining an EU-wide valid authorisation for a GMO, Member States only had the possibility to "provisionally restrict or prohibit the use and/or sale of that GMO as or in a product on its territory" (Article 23 Deliberate Release Directive).

However, some Member States tried to restrict the cultivation of GMOs on their territory based on Article 95 (5) TEC – now Article 114 (5) TFEU – which allows Member States to "introduce national provisions based on new scientific evidence relating to the protection of the environment or the working environment on grounds of a problem specific to that Member State arising after the adoption of the harmonisation measure". In the case "Oberösterreich" the European Court of Justice (ECJ) rejected the "Gene Technology Prohibition Act" of the Austrian region Oberösterreich which prohibited the cultivation of GMOs in this region. The court reasoned that the Republic of Austria could not allege new scientific evidence for environmental risks of the use of GMOs in the region of Oberösterreich nor prove that there are specific environmental conditions which would allow the restriction of the cultivation of GMOs in this area.[6]

Because of continued Member States' concerns towards cultivation of GMOs, in 2010 the European Commission forwarded a first proposal to introduce the possibility for Member States to prohibit or restrict the use of GMOs on their territory (Opt-Out Rule) in European GMO legislation[7]. This first proposal did not substantiate on which grounds Member States could rule restrictions on GMOs. Therefore in 2012 it could not find a majority in the Council. After an international seed company brought proceedings against the failure to act before the ECJ because of delays in the

---

4 Directive 2001/18/EC of the European Parliament and of the Council of 12 March 2001 on the deliberate release into the environment of genetically modified organisms and repealing Council Directive 90/220/EEC [2001] OJ L 106/1.
5 Regulation (EC) 1829/2003 of the European Parliament and of the Council of 22 September 2003 on genetically modified food and feed [2003] OJ L 268/1.
6 Case C-439/05 P and C-454/05 P *Land Oberörsterreich v. Comission* [2007] ECR I-7185, para 61.
7 European Commission, 'Communication from the Commission to the European Parliament, the Council, the European Economic and Social Committee and the Committee of the Regions of 22 April 2015 - Reviewing the decision-making process on genetically modified organisms (GMOs)' COM (2015) 176 final, 6.

authorisation process of its GMO, the debate was revitalised[8]. On 12th of June 2014 the Council adopted the Amendment of the Deliberate-Release-Directive by Directive 2015/412 (Amending Directive) to implement the Opt-Out Rule. Parallel to this amendment, the European legislators are discussing the implementation of an Opt-Out Rule in the GM Food and Feed Regulation.

B. The Opt-Out Rule

I. Content of the Amending Directive

With the Amending Directive the authorisation regime for GMOs itself remained unchanged. However, a new Article 26 b has been added to the Deliberate-Release-Directive, which introduces two options on restrictions of GMOs: During the authorisation process and after an obtained authorisation.

1. Restrictions during the authorisation process

During the authorisation process a Member State may demand from the applicant – without having to state reasons – that the geographical scope of the authorisation be adjusted and all or part of the territory of that Member State is to be excluded from cultivation (Article 26 b (1) of the amended Deliberate-Release-Directive). The applicant may voluntarily adjust the geographical scope of its notification and exclude this area. If he rejects this exclusion, the authorisation of the cultivation of GMOs will be valid for the whole territory of the EU.

As the applicant would not have any legal remedies if he agreed to the geographical restriction of his application, it is quite doubtful whether this procedure will have any effects in practise.[9]

---

8 Astrid Strack, 'Der lange Weg zum Opt-out von der Gentechnik' (2014) 36 NuR 829.
9 Ibid.

2. Opt-Out After the Authorisation

Probably more repercussions can be expected from the Opt-Out after the authorisation. Where the applicant has confirmed the geographical scope of its initial application or no demand in this direction was made, a Member State may adopt measures restricting or prohibiting the cultivation in all or part of its territory of a GMO, or of a group of GMOs. The conditions for restrictions or prohibitions are stated in Article 26 b (3) Deliberate-Release-Directive: restrictions or prohibitions have to be "in conformity with Union law, reasoned, proportional and non-discriminatory and, in addition, are based on compelling grounds such as those related to:

(a) environmental policy objectives;
(b) town and country planning;
(c) land use;
(d) socioeconomic impacts;
(e) avoidance of GMO presence in other products without prejudice to Article 26 a;
(f) agricultural policy objectives;
(g) public policy."

Those grounds may be invoked individually or in combination. However, they may not conflict with the environmental risk assessment carried out by EFSA during the authorisation process. This condition mainly limits the possibility to base restrictions or prohibitions on the first ground in Article 26 b (3) (a) Deliberate-Release-Directive "environmental policy objectives".

The environmental risk assessment is the centre piece of the authorisation process for GMOs. It is one element of the precautionary principle, which underlies European law on GMOs.[10] However, one has to distinguish between risk assessment and risk management. While the environmental risk assessment considers the impact of the cultivation of GMOs on the environment and therefore includes scientific assessment of possible adverse effects and the extent of possible risks, the risk management considers which measures can be adopted to cope with those possible

---

10 Johanna Monien, *Prinzipien als Wegbereiter eines globalen Umweltrechts? - Das Nachhaltigkeits-, Vorsorge- und Verursacherprinzip im Mehrebenensystem* (Forum Umwelt-, Agrar- und Klimaschutzrecht, vol 4, Nomos 2014) 282 – 287.

risks.[11] Also the definition of the protection level forms part of the risk management.[12] Member States may therefore not diverge from the risk assessment, but from grounds stated in the risk management decision of EU Commission. According to the Council, permissible environmental policy objectives are, for example, "the maintenance of certain type of natural and landscape features, certain habitats and ecosystems as well as specific ecosystem functions and services."[13]

As other grounds for restrictions or prohibitions of GMOs, Article 26 b Deliberate-Release-Directive names "town and country planning" and "land use". While the former is related to planning law, as in German Law enshrined in the Federal Building Code (Baugesetzbuch) or the Regional Planning Act (Raumordnungsgesetz), as well as in spacial planning laws e.g. planning for natural conservation (naturschutzfachliche Planung)[14], land use means the conditions for the use of soils[15]. However, planning law or land use are no independent goals, but rather instruments to reach environmental or agro-political goals. Thus, the grounds mentioned in lit. b) and c) have to be seen in connection with the other grounds like lit. a) environmental policy objectives or lit. d) socioeconomic impacts.[16]

The notion "socio-economic impacts" does not allow for just base restrictions on environmental effects, which mainly form part of the risk assessment and therefore cannot be evoked for restrictions, but also to consider social and economic effects of the use of GMOs. The Council refers

---

11 Commission of the European Communities, 'Communication from the Commission of 2 February 2000 on the Precautionary Principle' COM (2000) 1 final, 13.
12 Ibid.
13 Council of the European Union, 'document 10271/14 of 28 May 2014 - Proposal for a Regulation of the European Parliament and of the Council amending Directive 2001/18/EC as regards the possibility for the Member States to restrict or prohibit the cultivation of GMOs in their territory' 2010/0208 (COD) 7 recital 11.
14 Matthias Herdegen, 'Die geplante Opt-Out-Regelung zum Anbau gentechnisch veränderter Organismen (Änderung der Richtlinie 2001/18/EG) – Rechtliche Spielräume für die Mitgliedstaaten' (legal opinion commissioned by the German Federal Ministry of Food and Agriculture, 2014) 29 <https://www.bmel.de/Shared Docs/Downloads/Landwirtschaft/Pflanze/GrueneGentechnik/OptOut-Regelungen Geplant.pdf?__blob=publicationFile> accessed 7 December 2015.
15 Ibid 31.
16 Gerd Winter, 'Nationale Anbaubeschränkungen und -verbote für gentechnisch veränderte Pflanzen und ihre Vereinbarkeit mit Verfassungs-, Unions- und Völkerrecht' (legal opinion commissioned by the German Federal Agency for Nature Conservation, 2015) 17.

to these socioeconomic impacts and describes them in reference to the principle of coexistence of GMOs and conventional or organic production:

In cases of "impracticability or the impossibility of implementing coexistence measures due to specific geographical conditions or the need to avoid GMO presence in other products such as specific or particular products or the need to protect the diversity of agricultural production or the need to ensure seed and plant propagating material purity", socio-economic impacts may justify restrictions or prohibitions.[17]

In regards to further socio-economic objectives the conservation of conventional or organic agriculture in a certain scale are mentioned: As industrialisation of agriculture often is an effect of the use of GMOs, restrictions of cultivation of GMOs could preserve small scale farming.[18] This point shows the connection between socio-economic and agricultural policy objectives (lit. f), because the preservation of certain diversity in agricultural structures and ways of production can be assigned with both objectives.

Furthermore, the purity of seeds or avoidance of GMO presence in other products – as explicitly named in lit e) – can be seen as socio-economic objectives.

The last ground of justification – public policy – may not be evoked individually, Article 26 b (3) Deliberate-Release-Directive. Public Policy is already recognised as justification for restrictions of the free movement of goods according to Article 36 TFEU or other market freedoms and serves as catch-all provision.

II. Conformity with EU Law

Irrespective of the ground on which restrictions or prohibitions of GMOs are based, they have to be consistent with EU primary law. Primarily, they have to be in conformity with the free market. Because prohibitions of the

---

17 Council of the European Union, 'document 10271/14 of 28 May 2014 - Proposal for a Regulation of the European Parliament and of the Council amending Directive 2001/18/EC as regards the possibility for the Member States to restrict or prohibit the cultivation of GMOs in their territory' 2010/0208 (COD) 8 recital 12.

18 Gerd Winter, 'Nationale Anbaubeschränkungen und -verbote für gentechnisch veränderte Pflanzen und ihre Vereinbarkeit mit Verfassungs-, Unions- und Völkerrecht' (legal opinion commissioned by the German Federal Agency for Nature Conservation, 2015) 21.

cultivation of GMOs can restrict the free movement of goods a justification according to Article 34 TFEU in connection with the Cassis de Dijon principles is necessary. However, the grounds listed in Article 26 b (3) Deliberate Release Directive are more specific and therefore apply prior to the more general justifications of trade restrictions.[19] Another primary law restriction for Member States' prohibitions of cultivation is the principle of proportionality. Measures may not restrict the internal market or fundamental rights of farmers who want to cultivate GMOs and seed companies more than necessary. Generally, this means a high hurdle – especially taking into account that the risk assessment conducted in the authorisation process had shown no adverse effects of those GMOs. Nonetheless, one has to consider that the Amending-Directive was designed to enable Member States to introduce prohibitions or restrictions of GMOs. To give this Directive the necessary *effet utile*, requirements for justifications of national restrictions may not be set too high so that no scope of application of the Opt-Out Rule remains.[20]

III. Conformity with International Law

However, in a multi-level regulated field, prohibitions and restrictions must not only be in line with EU primary law, they also must be measured against international law, above all, world trade law. Particularly the conformity of national prohibitions of GMO cultivation with the General Agreement on Tariffs and Trade (GATT) and the Agreement on Sanitary and Phytosanitary Measures (SPS-Agreement) is questioned.[21]

---

19 Gerd Winter, 'Nationale Anbaubeschränkungen und -verbote für gentechnisch veränderte Pflanzen und ihre Vereinbarkeit mit Verfassungs-, Unions- und Völkerrecht' (legal opinion commissioned by the German Federal Agency for Nature Conservation, 2015) 28.
20 Achim Willand / Georg Buchholz / Malika Meyer-Schwickerath, 'Rechtsfragen einer nationalen Umsetzung der Opt-out-Änderungsrichtlinie' (legal opinion commissioned by the German Federal Agency for Nature Conservation, 2015) 116 <http://www.bfn.de/fileadmin/BfN/recht/Dokumente/Opt_Out_RGutachten_Buchholz_Willand.pdf> accessed 7 December 2015.
21 Astrid Strack, 'Der lange Weg zum Opt-out von der Gentechnik' (2014) 36 NuR 829, 830 ff.; Achim Willand / Georg Buchholz / Malika Meyer-Schwickerath, 'Rechtsfragen einer nationalen Umsetzung der Opt-out-Änderungsrichtlinie' (legal opinion commissioned by the German Federal Agency for Nature Conservation,

On first glance, prohibitions of cultivation of GMOs just affect the interior use and not international trade, but the scope of application of WTO law, above all the SPS-Agreement, is very extensive. Legal uncertainty of national GMO bans or restrictions will be illustrated exemplarily on compatibility with the SPS-Agreement.

The scope of application of this agreement is opened up for sanitary and phytosanitary measures as defined in annex A (1). Still, in the Panel decision "Biotech Products"[22] this provision was interpreted in an extensive way, justified with the fact, that the notion "other damage" in annex A (1) d) also covered environmental damages.[23] Thus, also provisions on environmental protection were measured against the SPS-Agreement. Furthermore, the SPS-Agreement just applies to measures that can affect international trade and restrictions on cultivation do not affect international trade directly. They just regulate internal use of GMOs. However, a nationwide prohibition of GMO cultivation could have indirect effects on international trade. Because of the tendency of the Panels to interpret the SPS-Agreement in a very wide way, Member States restrictions on GMOs could be covered by the SPS-Agreement.[24]

This extensive interpretation of the Panel has received criticism, because uncountable internal provisions on environmental protection and food safety and security could fall under the SPS-Agreement. Thus, the scope of application of the Agreement would be extended to mere internal provisions without clear connection to international trade.[25]

2015) 134 ff. <http://www.bfn.de/fileadmin/BfN/recht/Dokumente/Opt_Out_RGut achten_Buchholz_Willand.pdf> accessed 7 December 2015.

22　WTO, 'European Communities – Measures affecting the approval and marketing of biotech products' (Report of the Panel 2006) WT/DS291/R, EC.

23　Ibid para 7.208.

24　Astrid Strack, 'Der lange Weg zum Opt-out von der Gentechnik' (2014) 36 NuR 829, 832; Achim Willand / Georg Buchholz / Malika Meyer-Schwickerath, 'Rechtsfragen einer nationalen Umsetzung der Opt-out-Änderungsrichtlinie' (legal opinion commissioned by the German Federal Agency for Nature Conservation, 2015) 145 ff. <http://www.bfn.de/fileadmin/BfN/recht/Dokumente/Opt_Out_RGut achten_Buchholz_Willand.pdf> accessed 7 December 2015.

25　Achim Willand / Georg Buchholz / Malika Meyer-Schwickerath, 'Rechtsfragen einer nationalen Umsetzung der Opt-out-Änderungsrichtlinie' (legal opinion commissioned by the German Federal Agency for Nature Conservation, 2015) 146 <http://www.bfn.de/fileadmin/BfN/recht/Dokumente/Opt_Out_RGutachten_Buch holz_Willand.pdf> accessed 7 December 2015.

However, once the SPS-Agreement is applicable, it requires a strict scientific foundation. SPS-measures are only permitted after a risk assessment has proved risks for legally protected goods like the environment or health.[26] In the case of GMO authorisation such a risk assessment had been run on EU level and shown no adverse effects. Therefore, it is quite doubtful whether restrictions on GMO use could stand its grounds against a Panel revision. Up to now, there is no Appellate Body decision on this matter. Therefore, there is a wide legal uncertainty concerning comparability of GMO restrictions with the SPS-Agreement.[27]

IV. Commissions proposal for amending the GM Food and Feed Regulation

After the amendment of the Deliberate-Release-Directive, also the GM Food and Feed Regulation shall be amended by an Opt-Out Rule. Therefore, according to the Commission's proposal[28], an Article 34 a shall be introduced to this Regulation, which allows Member States to enact measures to restrict or prohibit food, food ingredients or feed which contain, consist of, or are produced from GMOs. These measures must be reasoned and may not conflict with the conducted risk assessment. Furthermore, they have to be proportional and non-discriminatory. Because of the variety of possible measures in this context, the proposal renounces to list grounds of justification like those in Article 26 b of the amended Deliberate-Release-Directive.[29] Therefore, measures based on Article 34 a of the new GM Food and Feed Regulation will have to be measured against the

---

26 WTO, 'Agreement on Sanitary and Phytosanitary Measures' (1995) art 5.1.

27 Achim Willand / Georg Buchholz / Malika Meyer-Schwickerath, 'Rechtsfragen einer nationalen Umsetzung der Opt-out-Änderungsrichtlinie' (legal opinion commissioned by the German Federal Agency for Nature Conservation, 2015) 152 <http://www.bfn.de/fileadmin/BfN/recht/Dokumente/Opt_Out_RGutachten_Buchholz_Willand.pdf> accessed 7 December 2015.

28 European Commission, 'Proposal for a Regulation of the European Parliament and the Council of 22 April 2015 amending Regulation (EC) 1829/2003 as regards the possibility for the Member States to restrict or prohibit the use of genetically modified food and feed on their territory' COM (2015) 177 final.

29 European Commission, 'Proposal for a Regulation of the European Parliament and the Council of 22 April 2015 amending Regulation (EC) 1829/2003 as regards the possibility for the Member States to restrict or prohibit the use of genetically modified food and feed on their territory' COM (2015) 177 final, 7.

general grounds of justification for trade restrictions pursuant to Article 36 TFEU together with the Cassis de Dijon-principles. According to the previous statement, measures have to be necessary for fixed derogations such as "the effectiveness of fiscal supervision, the protection of public health, the fairness of commercial transactions, and the defence of the consumer". As Member States' measures may not conflict with the risk assessment run by EFSA, a justification with the protection of public health or environmental protection will hardly be possible.

According to the wording, and also to recital 9, of the proposal, measures should apply to the "use" of GM food and feed, not to the free trade of them or their importation. However, the accordance with world trade law is also doubtful here if one lays down an extensive interpretation of the SPS-Agreement like the WTO-Panel in the "Biotech products"-decision did, because even internal provisions on the use of GMOs might indirectly affect international trade, as mentioned above.

C. Conclusions and outlook

The new Opt-Out Rule means a realignment in the field of tension of green genetic engineering law. The compromise between the use of new technologies and precaution against their risks no longer remains unified EU-wide. After long discussions, Member States reached a re-nationalisation of the decision of the use of GMOs in their territory. This is an innovation in EU law, because until now, European integration almost only worked in the direction of more harmonisation.

At the same time the Opt-Out Rule implies new challenges for Member States. In a legal multi-level system, prohibitions of GMOs must be compatible not only with national or European but also with international law. Here, major legal uncertainties remain so that some voices suppose that national bans on GMOs will not be consistent with WTO law. Thus, the Opt-Out, which was meant as an opportunity for Member States to renounce the use of GMOs and therefore prevent the blockade of the authorisation process, might be a door opener for European wide use of this technology.

Hence, in the context of GMO law, scientific investigation and public discussion remain in further movement, as well as legal regulation. In Germany, the government plans to take advantage of the Opt-Out Rule. For this purpose in June 2015 the Ministery of Agriculture forwarded a draft to amend the Genetechnology Act (Gentechnikgesetz) to enable the federate states as well as the federal republic, to enact GMO prohibitions or restrictions.[30] Also the federate states presented a legislative draft to introduce the possibility of GMO prohibitions.[31] It remains to be seen how the WTO reacts on the new Opt-Out Rule in European law. Possibly, other WTO Members decide to apply for judicial review by a WTO Dispute Settlement Body. An Appellate Body decision on the question of the application of the SPS-Agreement on national, non trade related provisions for environmental protection or on agricultural or socio-economic grounds would be welcome to answer outstanding issues on food safety and security in a multi-level legal system.

---

30 Arbeitsgemeinschaft bäuerliche Landwirtschaft, 'Bewertung des überarbeiteten Gesetzentwurfs des BMEL vom 04.06.2015 zur Änderung des Gentechnik-Gesetzes (opt-out im Anbau)' (2015) <http://www.abl-ev.de/fileadmin/Dokumente/AbL _ev/Gentechnikfrei/Hintergrund/AbL-Bewertung_BMEL-%C3%84nderungen_Ge nTG_1_07_2015.pdf> accessed 21 September 2015.
31 BR-Drs. 317/15 of 2 July 2015.

§ 9 Food safety and food security in the light of the European Court of Justice judgment concerning the presence of GMO`s pollen in honey and its influence on the Honey Directive and relevant existing legislation

Krzysztof Różański

A. The role of honey in the European Union from the perspective of Food Law

I. The importance in modern economic relations and trade

According to the Food and Agriculture Organization of the United Nations (hereinafter referred to as FAO), humans have practised honey hunting and beekeeping, (i.e. keeping bees inside man-made hives and harvesting honey from them) for at least 4500 years[1]. The reasons for that have been quite clear: human societies from the earliest times have been aware of the worthwhile benefits to be gained from bees. On the one hand the profits are closely related to various services which bees can render, such as the maintenance of biodiversity by the pollination of flowering plants, the pollination of crops as well as medicine using bees' products (the so called "apitherapy")[2]. On the other hand, the benefits derive also from products harvested from bees such as beeswax, pollen, propolis, royal jelly, venom, and the product considered to be the most important effect of beekeeping - honey[3].

Its important role is reflected in the European Union economy. Nowadays more than 16 million hives kept by nearly 700.000 beekeepers producing approximately 200,000 tons of honey every year are installed on its

---

1 Nicola Bradbear, *Bees and their role in forest livelihoods. A guide to the services provided by bees and the sustainable harvesting, processing and marketing of their products* (FAO 2009) 1 f.
2 Ibid 2 f.
3 European Commission, 'Communication from the Commission to the European Parliament and the Council of 6 December 2010 on Honeybee Health' COM (2010) 714 final.

territory[4]. It is estimated that the beekeeping and pollination business provides nearly 22 billion Euro profit per year to the EU agriculture[5]. It should be emphasized that the European Union is the second largest producer of honey in the world (after China), generating more than 200,000 tons of product per annum, representing 13.3% of the world production[6]. It is also essential to mention that the EU accounts for approximately 20-25% of global consumption of honey, amounting to almost 352,000 tons consumed in 2011[7]. However, the demand for honey is still higher than its production. For that reason the EU is still the biggest importer of honey in the world, importing approximately 78% of its demand from Latin America and Asia[8].

The expanding production of honey has raised questions concerning the actual level of its protection from the presence of genetically modified organisms (hereinafter referred to as "GMO's") and other issues related to food safety and food security. In order to protect the quality of honey and - what is even more important – the health of its consumers, the EU has adopted a number of specific acts supplementing the legislation applicable to foodstuffs.

---

4 Ibid.
5 The European Commission, 'Honey Bees' <http://ec.europa.eu/food/animals/live_animals/bees/index_en.htm> accessed 2 March 2015.
6 European Commission, 'Report from the Commission to the European Parliament and the Council of 16 August 2013 on the implementation of the measures concerning the apiculture sector of Council Regulation (EC) 1234/2007' COM (2013) 593 final.
7 Centre for the Promotion of Imports from developing countries, 'CBI Market Survey: The honey and other bee products market in EU' (2009) 2 <http://www.fepat.org.ar/files/eventos/759630.pdf> accessed 14 September 2015; European Commission, 'EU Market Situation for Honey' (Honey reports, statistics and presentations, DG AGRI UNIT C4, 18 April 2013) 20 <http://ec.europa.eu/agriculture/honey/reports/market-situation_en.pdf> accessed 14 September 2015.
8 European Parliament, 'Clarifying the Status of Pollen in Honey: Substitute Impact Assessment of EC Directive Amending Council Honey Directive 2001/110/EC' (September 2013) 21 f. <http://www.europarl.europa.eu/RegData/etudes/etudes/join/2013/514066/IPOL-JOIN_ET%282013%29514066_EN.pdf> accessed 14 September 2015.

II. The European Union legal framework

The most significant of them constitutes Council Directive 2001/110/EC of 20 December 2001 (hereinafter referred to as: "the Honey Directive") which provides the legislative criteria for honey and specifies the definition of honey, sales names, labelling, presentation and information on origin.

It is the only legal act in all of the EU legislation which sets out the composition criteria for honey defining it in its Annex 1.1 as the natural sweet substance, produced by *apis mellifera* bees from the nectar of plants or from secretions of living parts of plants, or excretions of plant-sucking insects on the living parts of plants, which the bees collect, transform by combining with specific substances of their own, deposit, dehydrate, store and leave in honeycombs to ripen and mature[9]. It is vital to add that pursuant to its Annex 2 honey consists essentially of different sugars, predominantly fructose and glucose, as well as other substances such as organic substances, organic acids, enzymes and solid particles derived from honey collection[10]. Apart from defining the term "honey", the Honey Directive does not state whether pollen is or is not an "ingredient" of honey in sense of the Directive No 2000/13/EC [11].

It is vital to add that the Honey Directive also limits human intervention that could alter the composition of honey, and thereby allows for the preservation of the natural character of honey. In particular – pursuant to paragraph 3 of Annex 2 of this Act – it is prohibited to add any kind of food ingredient to honey, including food additives, and any other addition other than honey. Furthermore, it is also not allowed to remove any constituent particular to honey, including pollen, unless such removal is unavoidable in the removal of foreign inorganic or organic matter[12]. It

---

9 Council Directive 2001/110/EC of 20 December 2001 relating to honey [2001] OJ L 10/47, Annex I no 1.

10 Ibid Annex II no 1.

11 Council Directive 2000/13/EC of 20 March 2000 on the approximation of the laws of the Member States relating to the labelling, presentation and advertising of foodstuffs [2000] OJ L 109/29.

12 Ibid Annex II no 2.

should be stressed that all of these requirements are in line with the Codex Alimentarius standard for honey[13].

In terms of GMO presence in honey, the Honey Directive is in compliance with the provisions of Directive (EC) 2001/18 on genetically modified organisms[14] (which provides that such organisms may be released deliberately into the environment or placed on the market only when prior authorization has been given) and with Regulation (EC) 1829/2003 on genetically modified food and feed[15]. In accordance with the provisions of the mentioned Regulation, GMOs for food use, food containing or consisting of GMOs, or food produced from or containing ingredients produced from GMOs must be authorized before being placed on the market[16]. In the absence of such authorization (which is issued after conducting an assessment of the risks to human health and the environment) the products cannot be marketed[17].

Regulation 1829/2003 also sets out labelling requirements, stating that, generally speaking, there is no obligation to indicate the presence of genetically modified substances in honey on labels, on condition that the amount of such substance does not exceed 0.9% of the honey ingredients, considered individually or honey consisting of a single ingredient, provided that its presence in it is adventitious or technically unavoidable[18].

In that context, it is essential to determine the concept of "an ingredient" in terms of food law. Nowadays it is specified in Article 2 (2) (f) of Regulation (EU) 1169/2011 on the provision of food information to consumers, which states that the term "ingredient" shall be understood as any substance or product, including flavourings, food additives and food enzymes, and any constituent of a compound ingredient, used in the manufacture or preparation of a food and still present in the finished product,

---

13 World Health Organization, Food and Agriculture Organization of the United Nations, *Codex Alimentarius* Standard for honey (Codex Stan 12-1981, Adopted in 1981, Revisions 1987 and 2001).

14 Directive 2001/18/EC of the European Parliament and of the Council of 12 March 2001 on the deliberate into the environment of genetically modified organisms and repealing Council Directive 90/220/EEC [2001] OJ L 106/1.

15 Regulation (EC) 1829/2003 of the European Parliament and of the Council of 22 September 2003 on genetically modified food and feed [2003] OJ L 268/1.

16 Regulation (EC) 1829/2003 of the European Parliament and of the Council of 22 September 2003 on genetically modified food and feed [2003] OJ L 268/1, art 3.

17 Ibid art 4 (2).

18 Ibid art 2. (2 f.).

even if in an altered form. Residues shall not be considered as ingredients[19]. That definition implies deliberate use of a substance in the manufacture or preparation of food. Before the entering into the force the Regulation (EU) 1169/2011 an ingredient was defined slightly different in the Directive 2000/13/EC as any substance, including additives, used in the manufacture or preparation of a foodstuff and still present in the finished product, even if in altered form.

The above mentioned legal issues constituted the subject of the European Court of Justice (ECJ) judgment in the case of Karl Heinz Bablok and others against Freistaat Bayern on 6 September 2011[20]. To be more specific, the ruling concerned the legal status of pollen in honey: if it should be recognized as "a natural constituent" particular to honey, or its "ingredient" within the meaning of the Regulation 1829/2003.

According to the Honey Directive pollen constitutes part of the composition criteria for honey. Available evidence, including empiric and scientific data, confirm that bees are the origin of the presence of pollen in honey. Pollen grains fall into nectar which is collected by bees. In the hive, collected nectar containing pollen grains is transformed into honey by bees. In accordance with the available data, additional pollen in honey can come from pollen on bees' hair, from pollen in the air inside the hive and from pollen that was packed in cells by bees and released as a result of the accidental opening of those cells during the extraction of honey by food business operators. Pollen can therefore be said to enter the hive as a result of the activity of bees and is naturally present in honey regardless of whether or not food business operators extract that honey. Furthermore, the deliberate addition of pollen to honey by food business operators is prohibited under the Honey Directive.

All of the abovementioned acts constitute the legal framework relating to honey. They are supported by a number of implementing rules or by recommendations and guidelines.

---

19 Regulation (EU) 1169/2011 of the European Parliament and of the Council of 25 October 2011 on the provision of food information to consumers, amending Regulations (EC) 1924/2006 and (EC) 1925/2006 of the European Parliament and of the Council, and repealing Commission Directive 87/250/EEC, Council Directive 90/496/EEC, Commission Directive 1999/10/CE, Directive 2000/13/EC of the European Parliament and of the Council, Commission Directives 2002/67/EC and 2008/5/EC and Commission Regulation (EC) 608/2004 [2011] OJ L 304/18.

20 Case C-442/09 *Karl Heinz Bablok and others v Freistaat Bayern* [2011] ECR I-07419.

B. The influence of the Judgment concerning the presence of GMO`s pollen in honey on the Honey Directive and Relevant Existing Legislation

I. Overview of the case

All of the acts mentioned in Section had been applied in judgement of the European Court of Justice (hereinafter referred to as "ECJ") n C-442/09 in the case of Karl Heinz Bablok and Others v. Freistaat Bayern in which ECJ had to determine the status of pollen in honey by figuring out whether the pollen should be considered as a natural ingredient of honey or not.

Mr Bablok was an amateur beekeeper in German, who brought legal proceedings against Freistaat Bayern (Germany). He produced honey as well as pollen-based foodstuffs both for sale and for his own personal consumption[21]. His beehives were situated close to the plots of land on which the Freistaat Bayern authorised the cultivation of transgenic maize MON 810 for research purposes. In 2005, the presence of MON 810 maize DNA was detected in the maize pollen harvested by Mr Bablok and, in a smaller quantity, in his honey.

Having taken legal proceedings against Freistaat Bayern, Mr Bablok pointed out that his products have been subjected to a material interference and can no longer be marketed without authorisation and, where appropriate, without labelling mentioning the genetic modification, which, under national law, entitles him to monetary compensation. The Administrative Court of Augsburg concurred, considering that, due to the contamination through pollen from MON 810 maize, Mr Bablok's honey and pollen-based food supplements were foods which required authorisation under Article 4 (2) of Regulation (EC) 1829/2003. In the absence of such authorisation, which is issued, where appropriate, after assessment of the risks to human health and the environment, Mr Bablok's products cannot be marketed.

In questions referred by the Bayerischer Verwaltungsgerichtshof court to which Freistaat Bayern and Monsanto appealed, the Court of Justice confirmed the application of Regulation (EC) 1829/2003 in the present case. In fact, although the pollen at issue, derived from a variety of geneti-

---

21 Case C 442/09 *Karl Heinz Bablok and others v Freistaat Bayern* [2011] ECR I-07419.

cally modified maize, was not a GMO as such, as it had lost its ability to reproduce and was totally incapable of transferring the genetic material, the food supplements and honey containing it must be regarded as 'food for human consumption containing ingredients produced from GMOs within the meaning of the Regulation. On this point, the Court primarily took as a basis an interpretation of the concept of 'ingredient' in the light of the objective of protecting human health pursued by the Regulation (EC) 1829/2003 and the need to avoid products containing significant quantities of genetically modified material escaping any safety checks.

The honey and pollen-based food supplements must therefore be subject to assessment and authorisation. The circumstance that the introduction of the pollen was adventitious and not intentional has no influence on the classification of the products at issue or on the applicability of the authorization scheme. Likewise, the obligation of authorisation exists irrespective of the proportion of genetically modified material contained in the product in question. On the other hand, labelling is compulsory only beyond a tolerance threshold of 0.9% per ingredient[22].

II. The aftermath of the legal implications on issues related to Food Safety and Food Security

Prior to the ECJ ruling, pollen was considered to be a component of honey and as such the pollen did not require any specific labelling[23]. Whilst methods exist to remove pollen from honey (ultra-filtration), the compositional criteria state that pollen should not be intentionally removed and where filtration has been used consumers should be informed. Therefore, where pollen is present, packers have no alternative but to leave it in place unless it is unintentionally removed during filtering to take out foreign inorganic or organic matter and labelled as 'filtered'. The ECJ ruling how-

---

22 European Commission, 'Summary of important judgements', C-442/09 *Karl Heinz Bablok and others v Freistaat Bayern, judgement of 6 September 2011* [2012] <http://ec.europa.eu/dgs/legal_service/arrets/09c442_en.pdf> (accessed 2 February 2015).

23 Ewelina Żmijewska / Dariusz Teper / Anna Linkiewicz / Sławomir Sowa, 'Pollen from Genetically Modified Plants in Honey – Problems with Quantification and Proper Labelling' (2013) 57 Journal of Apicultural Science 5 <http://www.degruyter.com/view/j/jas.2013.57.issue-2/jas-2013-0013/jas-2013-0013.xml> (accessed 5 August 2015).

ever states that pollen is considered to be an ingredient of honey. Regulation 1169/2011 repealed Directive 2000/13 and as it was presented in point A para II of the Article, the concept of an "ingredient" is now defined slightly different. According to its provisions, honey is required to carry an ingredients list in which pollen would need to be included. Article 18 of the Regulation 1169/2013 states: "The list of ingredients shall be headed or preceded by a suitable heading which consists of or includes the word 'ingredients'. It shall include all the ingredients of the food, in descending order of weight, as recorded at the time of their use in the manufacture of the food". On the package, this would appear as 'Ingredients: honey, pollen'. Although comprising more than one ingredient, honey could be exempted from the requirement to carry an ingredients list by an appropriate amendment to the Regulation 1169/2011 perhaps by extending Article 19 (1) (d) which already provides a similar exemption for cheese, butter, fermented milk and cream.

A change in the status of pollen in honey from an ingredient to a natural constituent could be predicted to cause the following impacts: increased honey imports to countries in the European Union (EU) from non-EU countries; less disruption to the international trade regime; less stringent requirements to mention pollen on the honey's label may facilitate the cultivation (pollination) of GM crops insofar that beekeepers will face less restrictions in locating their hives near GM fields; no significant cost change for stakeholders in the honey industry[24].

C. The consequences of entering into force of the ruling

I. The aftermath of the ruling

Under legislative requirements for labelling in the EU, both honey produced in Member States, and honey imported from third countries would be affected by the ECJ ruling. For producers in EU Member States the chief impacts arise due to testing that would be required to determine

---

24 European Parliament, 'Clarifying the Status of Pollen in Honey: Substitute Impact Assessment of EC Directive Amending Council Honey Directive 2001/110/EC' (September 2013) 25 – 30 <http://www.europarl.europa.eu/RegData/etudes/etudes/join/2013/514066/IPOL-JOIN_ET%282013%29514066_EN.pdf> accessed 7 September 2015.

whether honey contains pollen from GMOs or not. Likewise, any honey imported from third countries that grow GM crops would need to be tested to determine whether pollen was produced from GMOs and whether or not those GMOs were authorised in the EU.

Whilst the majority of cotton, soybean, maize and oilseed rape varieties are approved in the EU, herbicide tolerant alfalfa (lucerne) grown in the US is not yet approved. For any honey products adhering to specific GM-free product schemes, the threshold stipulated in these agreements for presence of GM ingredients will need to be adhered to.

The marketing of non-authorised GMOs, and ingredients derived from them, is not permitted in the EU. Honey producers in areas that conduct GM crop testing (where the GM crop is not yet authorised) may need to consider adoption of organic standards in order to establish a case to demonstrate that the pollen in the honey does not originate from GMOs. Honey imported from third countries will have to comply with EU legislation in order to be placed on the EU market, but since there are GM crops which grow in third countries that are not EU authorised, there may be a greater chance of unauthorised GM pollen being present in honey from third countries.

Coexistence measures are decided on at the EU Member State level and are principally there to ensure adequate separation of GMOs from conventional and organic varieties, and are not specifically developed to ensure adequate separation distances for honey producers wishing to keep their honey 'GM-free'. There is a high level of uncertainty in terms of bee foraging behaviour, and various studies suggest this can be anywhere from 5-13.5 km[25]. In addition, volunteer plants from the GM crop may appear up to 10 years after cultivation (for oil seed rape), and thus coexistence requirements may also need to take into account temporal separation. As such, if a honey producer is located in a country widely growing GM crops (such as Spain) then ensuring that bees do not forage on GM crops may be difficult and testing would be required to prove that the honey is free from pollen produced from GMOs.

---

25 Ivelin Rizov / Emilio Rodriguez Cerezo, 'Coexistence of Genetically Modified Maize and Honey Production' (2013) <http://bookshop.europa.eu/en/best-practice-documents-for-coexistence-of-genetically-modified-crops-with-conventional-and-organic-farming-pbLBNA26041/?CatalogCategoryID=8CMKABstrPQAAAE-jO5EY4e5L> accessed 2 August 2015.

Under the Organic Regulations (889/2008), for honey to be classed as 'organic', nectar and pollen sources within a 3 km radius of apiaries must be organically produced (or natural). As such, this requirement suggests that a distance of 3 km is adequate for separation of GM crops and organic honey which may inform the debate on appropriate coexistence distances to assure honey can be classed as 'GM-free', or any GM presence classed as 'adventitious or technically unavoidable' and thus without consequence for labelling.

II. The legal actions taken by the European Commission and the European Parliament

Following the ECJ ruling in 2011, the European Commission was asked to clarify the labelling and legal consequences for the honey industry. The European Commission responded by organising workshops and seminars and by proposing to amend the relevant legislation. Nevertheless, at that point there was still no single point of reference providing clear instructions on honey labelling and analysis to ensure legal compliance.

The European Commission has tabled a proposal for a Directive of the European Parliament and of the Council amending Directive 2001/110/EC relating to honey. Following the ECJ judgment, this proposal is intended explicitly to classify pollen as a special component of honey rather than an ingredient[26].

Monsanto introduced an application to cover MON 810 pollen in the marketing authorisation, on which EFSA gave a favourable scientific opinion in December 2012.

III. The conclusions: amendment of the Honey Directive

Finally, the European Parliament and the Council of the European Union have adopted Directive (EU) 2014/63 amending Council Directive

---

26 Directive 2014/63/EU of the European Parliament and of the Council of 15 May 2014 amending Council Directive 2001/110/EC relating to honey [2014] OJ L 164/1.

2001/110/EC relating to honey[27]. The long legislative process finally has come to an end. As a result, there are three main objectives:

Firstly, to provide clarification that pollen is a natural constituent of honey and should not be considered an ingredient in honey in the sense of Article 6 (4) (a) 1 of the Directive 2000/13/EC relating to the labelling, presentation and advertising of foodstuffs.

Secondly, to align powers conferred on the Commission from Directive 2001/110/EC 'the Honey Directive' with those contained in the Treaty on the Functioning of the European Union (TFUE) as a consequence of the entry into force of the Lisbon Treaty.

Thirdly, the proposal aimed to provide the Commission with the power to introduce harmonised testing methods[28].

This amending Directive is without prejudice to the application of Regulation (EC) 1829/2003 of the European Parliament and of the Council to honey containing genetically modified pollen, since such honey constitutes food produced from genetically modified organisms within the meaning of that Regulation. In Case C-442/09, Karl Heinz Bablok and Others v. Freistaat Bayern, the Court of Justice of the European Union ruled that the determining criterion for the application of Regulation (EC) 1829/2003, as set out in recital 16 of that Regulation, is whether material derived from the genetically modified source material is present in food. Honey containing genetically modified pollen should therefore be regarded as being 'food (partially) produced from a GMO' within the meaning of point (c) of Article 3 (1) of Regulation (EC) 1829/2003. Laying down a provision to the effect that pollen is not an ingredient of honey does not therefore affect the Court's conclusion in Case C-442/09 that honey containing genetically modified pollen is subject to Regulation (EC) 1829/2003, in particular, to the requirements thereof concerning authorisation prior to placing on the market, supervision and, where applicable, labelling.

---

27 Directive 2014/63/EU of the European Parliament and of the Council of 15 May 2014 amending Council Directive 2001/110/EC relating to honey [2014] OJ L 164/1.

28 European Parliament, 'Clarifying the Status of Pollen in Honey: Substitute Impact Assessment of EC Directive Amending Council Honey Directive 2001/110/EC' (September 2013) 25 – 30 <http://www.europarl.europa.eu/RegData/etudes/etudes /join/2013/514066/IPOL-JOIN_ET%282013%29514066_EN.pdf> accessed 7 September 2015.

It is essential to mention that Directive 2001/110/EC applies from 1 February 2002 while Directive 2014/63/EU applies from 23 June 2014. Honey for sale or labelled before 24 June 2015 may continue to be marketed until the exhaustion of stocks[29].

Directive 2014/63/EU allows the European Commission to adopt further laws (delegated acts) laying down two parameters for the criterion of 'mainly' as regards the floral or vegetable origin of honey and the minimal content of pollen in filtered honey following removal of foreign inorganic or organic matter.

---

29 Directive 2014/63/EU of the European Parliament and of the Council of 15 May 2014 amending Council Directive 2001/110/EC relating to honey [2014] OJ L 164/1, art 2 (2).

§ 10 New regulation on Novel Foods

Łukasz Mikołaj Sokołowski

A. Indroduction

The primary purpose of food law, as underpinned by health laws[1], is to ensure a high level of public health. The same applies to the Regulation on novel foods and food ingredients[2]. In recital 2 of the preamble to Regulation 258/97, the legislator provides that in order to protect public health, novel foods and food ingredients must undergo a single safety assessment. Ensuring the safety of novel foods should be understood as meaning, primarily, the protection of the life and health of the consumer, the environment, and biodiversity. However, other purposes of the Regulation, particularly those of an economic nature, should also be taken into account. A common, uniform authorisation procedure for the placing on the EU market of novel foods is designed to ensure the free movement of goods, including foodstuffs. Otherwise, differences between the national laws of different Member States could result in unfair competition which in turn could directly affect the functioning of the internal market[3].

Save for a few amendments[4], the current legislation has remained essentially the same for nearly 20 years. However, Regulation 258/97 has generated controversy for quite some time. Article 14 of Regulation 258/97 stipulates that the Commission, within five years of the entry into force of the Regulation and in the light of experience gained, is to forward to the European Parliament and to the Council a report on the implementation of the Regulation together with any proposal of suitable amendments.

---

1 Maciej Taczanowski, *Prawo żywnościowe w warunkach członkostwa Polski w Unii Europejskiej* (Wolters Kluwer 2009) 46.
2 See in particular, Regulation (EC) 258/97 of the European Parliament and of the Council of 27 January 1997 concerning novel foods and novel food ingredients [1997] OJ L 43/1.
3 Ibid recital 1.
4 They concern, in particular, GMOs.

Yet already in 2000, it was announced in the White Paper on Food Safety[5] that the procedure for authorising the marketing of novel foods should be modified. The main points of criticism concerned the duration and lack of transparency of the authorisation process[6].

An assessment of Regulation 258/97, carried out in 2002, and the subsequent consultation indicated that changes were needed in several areas. They included: regulating non-genetically modified foods; specifying the addressees of the decision authorising the placing on the market of novel foods; the procedure for the marketing of such foods; and identification of novel foods and food ingredients[7]. This review marked the beginning of the reform efforts which are yet to conclude. On 14 January 2008, the Commission adopted a proposal for a Regulation of the European Parliament and of the Council concerning novel foods[8]. The legislative work focused mainly on rules pertaining to traditional foods from non-EU countries, nanomaterials, animal cloning for food production, the criteria used for risk assessment and risk management, as well as aspects relating to simplifying the procedure for placing novel foods on the market within the European Union. These efforts, however, failed to reach agreement, particularly on the proposed Regulation of animal cloning, and concluded with the legislator rejecting the proposal.

On 18 December 2013, the Commission adopted another proposal for a Draft Regulation of the European Parliament and of the Council concerning novel foods[9], as well as animal cloning. This differentiation follows, *inter alia*, from existing experience and the proposals that resulted from the previous attempts at an amendment. During the meeting of the Committee on the Environment, Public Health and Food Safety on 25 June 2015, parliamentarians voted by a majority to support the Draft Regulation on novel foods and food ingredients. In November 2015, the Parliament and the Council also reached an agreement, and 11 December 2015 saw

---

5 European Commission, 'White Paper on Food Safety' of 12 January 2000 COM (1999) 719 final, ch 5 no 76.
6 Markus Kraus / Alfred Hagen Meyer, 'Zu den Reformbestrebungen der Novel Food Verordnung – eine kritische Bestandsaufnahme' (2009) 10 EWS 414.
7 Ina Gerstberger, 'Die Novel Food Verordnung vor der Reform' (2005) 5 WRP 584.
8 European Commission, 'Proposal for a Regulation of the European Parliament and of the Council of 14 January 2008 on novel foods and amending Regulation (EC) xxx/xxxx [common procedure]' COM (2007) 872 final.
9 European Commission, 'Proposal for a Regulation of the European Parliament and of the Council of 18 December 2013 on novel foods' COM (2013) 894 final.

the publication Regulation (EU) 2015/2283 of the European Parliament and of the Council of 25 November 2015 on novel foods, amending Regulation (EU) No 1169/2011 of the European Parliament and of the Council and repealing Regulation (EC) No 258/97 of the European Parliament and of the Council and Commission Regulation (EC) No 1852/2001[10]. The new Regulation enters into force on 1 January 2018. The changes introduced to the novel food legislation are expected to contribute to improving the access of novel foods to the EU market and to maintaining a high level of health protection[11].

B. Definitional problems

The definition of a novel food included in Regulation 2015/2283 is significantly different from that in Regulation 258/97. In its new form, it describes novel foods as any food that was not used for human consumption to a significant degree within the Union before 15 May 1997, irrespective of the dates of accession of Member States to the Union, and that falls under at least one of the ten categories listed in the Regulation[12]. Despite the fact that initially the legislator proposed to create an open catalogue of novel foods[13], ultimately it was decided that the scope of the new Regulation should remain unchanged as compared to Regulation 258/97.

---

10 Regulation (EU) 2015/2283 of the European Parliament and of the Council of 25 November 2015 on novel foods, amending Regulation (EU) 1169/2011 of the European Parliament and of the Council and repealing Regulation (EC) 258/97 of the European Parliament and of the Council and Commission Regulation (EC) 1852/2001 [2015] OJ L 327/1.
11 Cf Dorota Stankiewicz, 'Nowa żywność' (2014) 13 (117) Analizy BAS 6 and references therein <http://orka.sejm.gov.pl/WydBAS.nsf/0/CD9B3145F0447305C1257D6A003B3D6B/$file/Analiza_BAS_2014_117.pdf> accessed 7 February 2016.
12 Cf Regulation (EU) 2015/2283 of the European Parliament and of the Council of 25 November 2015 on novel foods, amending Regulation (EU) 1169/2011 of the European Parliament and of the Council and repealing Regulation (EC) 258/97 of the European Parliament and of the Council and Commission Regulation (EC) 1852/2001 [2015] OJ L 327/1, art 3 (2).
13 Cf European Commission, 'Proposal for a Regulation of the European Parliament and of the Council of 18 December 2013 on novel foods' COM (2013) 894 final, art 2 (2) lit a). The provisions specify what particularly can be considered a novel food.

However, due to the advances in science and technology, it was necessary to review, clarify and update the categories of food which constitute novel foods. As indicated in the preamble to Regulation 2015/2283, these categories should contain whole insects and their parts; food with a new or intentionally modified molecular structure and food from cell culture or tissue culture derived from animals, plants, microorganisms, fungi or algae; food from microorganisms, fungi or algae and food from material of mineral origin; food from plants obtained by non-traditional propagating practices where those practices give rise to significant changes in the composition or structure of the food affecting its nutritional value, metabolism or level of undesirable substances[14]. The definition of novel food may also cover food consisting of certain micelles or liposomes.

This definition is doubtless more precise and gives more consideration to technological development[15]. At present, novel foods are considered to be products which have hitherto not been used for human consumption to a significant degree within the Community and which fall into one of four legally established categories[16].

The legislator proposes that the word "hitherto", understood as "before the date of the entry into force of Regulation 258/97", be replaced with the expression "before 15 May 1997". According to the legislator, this change would ensure continuity with Regulation 258/97. However, such a solution may raise doubts because it effectively introduces a new definition of a *novel food*. The introduction of new categories may result in a situation whereby products that have not been seen as novel foods will be considered as such[17]. The problem would affect foodstuffs introduced between 15 May 1997 and the date of the entry into force of the new Regulation,

---

14 Cf Regulation (EU) 2015/2283 of the European Parliament and of the Council of 25 November 2015 on novel foods, amending Regulation (EU) 1169/2011 of the European Parliament and of the Council and repealing Regulation (EC) 258/97 of the European Parliament and of the Council and Commission Regulation (EC) 1852/2001 [2015] OJ L 327/1, recital 2 and art 3 (2) lit a).

15 Dorota Stankiewicz, 'Nowa żywność' (2014) 13 (117) Analizy BAS 7 <http://orka .sejm.gov.pl/WydBAS.nsf/0/CD9B3145F0447305C1257D6A003B3D6B/$file/An aliza_BAS_2014_117.pdf> accessed 7 February 2016.

16 The categories are provided in Regulation (EC) 258/97 of the European Parliament and of the Council of 27 January 1997 concerning novel foods and novel food ingredients [1997] OJ L 43/1, art 1 (2).

17 Christian Ballke, 'Die neue Novel Food-Verordnung - Reform 2.0' (2014) 4 ZLR 412, 416.

which would not be categorised as novel foods under Regulation 258/97 but which would fall within that category according to Regulation 2015/2283. Consequently, products that were legally placed on the market would be required to undergo an additional procedure[18]. This could have a negative economic impact, such as a possible ban on the sale, or an increase of the cost and time needed to obtain the authorisation. The legislator, however, has established transitional measures. Such foods may continue to be placed on the market until a decision is taken following an application for authorisation of a novel food or a notification of a traditional food from a third country submitted by the date specified in the implementing rules, but no later than 2 January 2020.

It should be noted that the new definition does not address many of the concerns expressed so far. These refer to, in particular, the imprecision of phrases such as "to a significant degree". It should be pointed out that this particular phrase has been criticised for having too many possible interpretations. The European Commission understood it as meaning "wide availability", i.e. the ability to easily purchase the product from shops, but not pharmacies. This interpretation was criticised as being too limiting, without substance, and not being based on existing legislation, while the differentiation was seen as discriminatory[19]. An altogether different interpretation of the phrase was given by Advocate General L.A. Geelhoed[20]. In his opinion, it cannot be assumed that a product was not used for consumption to a significant degree if it had been on the market of one or more Member States at the date of the entry into force of the Regulation, and which was therefore accessible to consumers. Thus, the phrase should be interpreted broadly and includes all delivery and distribution channels[21]. Regrettably,

---

18 Cf Regulation (EU) 2015/2283 of the European Parliament and of the Council of 25 November 2015 on novel foods, amending Regulation (EU) 1169/2011 of the European Parliament and of the Council and repealing Regulation (EC) 258/97 of the European Parliament and of the Council and Commission Regulation (EC) 1852/2001 [2015] OJ L 327/1, art 35 (2).
19 Ina Gerstberger, 'Die Novel Food Verordnung vor der Reform – Aktuelle Probleme und Änderungsvorschläge für ein verbessertes Gesetzeswerk' (2005) 5 WRP 584, 585 f.
20 Case C-211/03, C-299/03 and C-316/03 to C-318/03 *HLH Warenvertrieb and Orthica* [2005] ECR I-5147, Opinion of AG Geelhoed, paras 96 – 97.
21 Ina Gerstberger, 'Die Novel Food Verordnung vor der Reform – Aktuelle Probleme und Änderungsvorschläge für ein verbessertes Gesetzeswerk' (2005) 5 WRP 584, 585 f.

the new regulation does not resolve this matter, which may lead to a delay in the marketing of some foods[22].

Under Regulation 2015/2283, food business operators may verify whether the food they intend to market falls within the scope of this Regulation. In case of doubt, potential applicants may consult a Member State which may request that the food business operators provide the necessary information to determine the extent to which the food in question was used for human consumption within the Union before 15 May 1997[23].

The new Regulation provides a definition of a "traditional food from a third country". The legislator considers it to be novel foods not covered by the categories listed in the Regulation[24], derived from primary production and having a history of safe food use in a third country. The legislator clarifies the enigmatic phrase "history of safe food use in a third country" as meaning that the safety of the food in question has been confirmed with compositional data and from experience of continued use for at least 25 years in the customary diet of a significant number of people in at least one third country, prior to a notification of the intention to market the food within the European Union[25]. This definition consists of two elements: the quantitative – a long period of use by a significant number of people in at least one third country; and the qualitative – ensuring safety of the food based on compositional data and existing experience[26]. However, these expressions also create interpretation problems. While the phrase "customary diet" may be interpreted as 'daily consumption', although even that is not completely clear, the meaning of the phrase "a significant number of people in at least one third country" is ambiguous. Consequently, such

---

22 Cf Dorota Stankiewicz, 'Nowa żywność' (2014) 13 (117) Analizy BAS 7 f. <http://orka.sejm.gov.pl/WydBAS.nsf/0/CD9B3145F0447305C1257D6A003BD6B/$file/Analiza_BAS_2014_117.pdf> accessed 7 February 2016.
23 Cf Regulation (EU) 2015/2283 of the European Parliament and of the Council of 25 November 2015 on novel foods, amending Regulation (EU) 1169/2011 of the European Parliament and of the Council and repealing Regulation (EC) 258/97 of the European Parliament and of the Council and Commission Regulation (EC) 1852/2001 [2015] OJ L 327/1, art 4.
24 Ibid art 3 (2) lit c).
25 Ibid art 3 (2) lit b).
26 Christian Ballke, 'Die neue Novel Food-Verordnung - Reform 2.0' (2014) 4 ZLR 412, 418.

wording of the provisions may result in limiting the access of some third-country food producers to the Union market[27].

Furthermore, it should be pointed out that, paradoxically, instead of opening the market to these kinds of foodstuffs, the new Regulation may in fact exclude them. This is primarily due to high quantitative and qualitative requirements, especially if the suspicion that no evidence of "safe food use" has been collected so far proves true[28]. At this point, however, it is difficult to predict whether the new proposals will be justified by practice, or proved dead, in which case the only way of introducing novel foods onto the market will be through obtaining an authorisation.

By contrast, the proposed definition of an applicant should be viewed in a more positive light. The current legislation defines an applicant as the person responsible for placing the novel food on the Community market[29]. The new Regulation provides for a large group of entities entitled to do so; that is not only the party to the process, but also the Member State or the third country or an interested party who may represent several interested parties[30]. It is noted in the literature that this change should not result in a dramatic increase in the number of applications, while the option whereby a third country may submit a separate application seems very attractive[31].

C. Placing novel foods on the market within the European Union

Regulation 2015/2283 on novel foods determines the requirement of establishing and updating a Union list of novel foods. It is worth noting that

---

27 Dorota Stankiewicz, 'Nowa żywność' (2014) 13 (117) Analizy BAS 8 <http://orka.sejm.gov.pl/WydBAS.nsf/0/CD9B3145F0447305C1257D6A003B3D6B/$file/Analiza_BAS_2014_117.pdf> accessed 7 February 2016.

28 Christian Ballke, 'Die neue Novel Food-Verordnung - Reform 2.0' (2014) 4 ZLR 412, 418.

29 Cf Regulation (EC) 258/97 of the European Parliament and of the Council of 27 January 1997 concerning novel foods and novel food ingredients [1997] OJ L 43/1, art 4 (1).

30 Regulation (EU) 2015/2283 of the European Parliament and of the Council of 25 November 2015 on novel foods, amending Regulation (EU) 1169/2011 of the European Parliament and of the Council and repealing Regulation (EC) 258/97 of the European Parliament and of the Council and Commission Regulation (EC) 1852/2001 [2015] OJ L 327/1, art 3 (2) lit d).

31 Christian Ballke, 'Die neue Novel Food-Verordnung - Reform 2.0' (2014) 4 ZLR 412, 418.

a catalogue of novel foods already exists[32]. However, it is not an exhaustive list and, given its approximate nature, helps to perform an initial assessment to determine whether a food belongs to the novel food category[33]. The new solution is that in order to be introduced onto the Union market, a food product must not only be given an appropriate authorisation but must also be included in the Union list. The inclusion in the Union list is therefore constitutive in character. Accordingly, the catalogue will be updated to include foods which were authorised under present rules, or which were successfully notified. The Regulation will introduce certainty in business transactions and therefore should be viewed positively. This is even more so since the list is to define the conditions of use of novel foods, which will facilitate control and thus will help to ensure the safety of these products.

One of the most significant changes is the replacement of the current system of individual authorisations with generic authorisations. Accordingly, the notification procedure is to be removed. A generic, centralised procedure will be initiated by the Commission, although this is not expected to be a common practice[34], or will require that applications for the authorisation of novel foods be submitted directly to the European Commission. The applications must include, *inter alia,* the name, description and composition of the novel food, as well as a description of the production process and scientific evidence demonstrating that the food does not pose a safety risk. Furthermore, the applications must be accompanied by proposals for the conditions of use and specific labelling requirements which do not mislead the consumer.

The European Commission may request the European Food Safety Authority[35] to issue an opinion if the update of the Union list is likely to have an effect on human health[36]. This implies that the Commission may exer-

---

32 Available at European Commission, Novel Food catalogue, <http://ec.europa.eu/fo od/food/biotechnology/novelfood/nfnetweb/mod_search/index.cfm> accessed 7 February 2016.
33 Cf European Commission, Novel Food catalogue <http://ec.europa.eu/food/food/ biotechnology/novelfood/novel_food_catalogue_en.htm> accessed 7 February 2016.
34 Christian Ballke, 'Die neue Novel Food-Verordnung - Reform 2.0' (2014) 4 ZLR 412, 420.
35 Referred to in this paper as: EFSA.
36 Cf Regulation (EU) 2015/2283 of the European Parliament and of the Council of 25 November 2015 on novel foods, amending Regulation (EU) 1169/2011 of the

cise its discretion in almost every case which will undoubtedly have an impact on the duration of the process, already expected to last a minimum of 16 months. EFSA must adopt its opinion within nine months of receiving a valid application[37]. The Commission, within seven months of the date of publication of EFSA's opinion, submits to the Standing Committee on the Food Chain and Animal Health a draft implementing act taking into account the conditions for inclusion in the Union list, relevant provisions of Union law, EFSA's opinion, and other legitimate factors relevant to the application under consideration[38]. There are doubts, particularly about what should be considered legitimate factors, or even whether there are any other factors that could be the reason for refusing to authorise the marketing of a foodstuff[39].

In assessing the safety of foods, EFSA will take into account whether the composition of the novel food and the conditions of its use pose a safety risk to human health in the Union, and whether the novel food is as safe as foods from a comparable food category already present on the market within the EU[40]. According to the literature, the latter condition is unclear, *inter alia*, because it does not belong to the general criteria for inclusion in the list of novel foods[41]. The Regulation is also criticised for the fact that a general safety requirement for all food categories was defined in Article

---

European Parliament and of the Council and repealing Regulation (EC) 258/97 of the European Parliament and of the Council and Commission Regulation (EC) 1852/2001 [2015] OJ L 327/1, art 10 (3).

37 Cf ibid art 11 (1).

38 Cf ibid art 12 (1).

39 Christian Ballke, 'Die neue Novel Food-Verordnung - Reform 2.0' (2014) 4 ZLR 412, 421 f.

40 Cf Regulation (EU) 2015/2283 of the European Parliament and of the Council of 25 November 2015 on novel foods, amending Regulation (EU) 1169/2011 of the European Parliament and of the Council and repealing Regulation (EC) 258/97 of the European Parliament and of the Council and Commission Regulation (EC) 1852/2001 [2015] OJ L 327/1, art 11 (2).

41 Christian Ballke, 'Die neue Novel Food-Verordnung - Reform 2.0' (2014) 4 ZLR 412, 421.

14 of Regulation 178/2002[42], and Union law does not recognise phrases such as: "equally safe", "less safe", or "safer"[43].

Shortening the authorisation procedure is one of the most significant changes that the new Regulation is to implement. According to the British agricultural economist G. Brookes, an authorisation procedure which takes more than three years to complete is not economically viable and hinders innovation[44]. The Union procedure, lasting on average 35 months, compared to the procedures adopted in Brazil (up to 1 month), the United States (up to 3 months), Australia (up to 14 months), or Japan (up to 18 months)[45], seems too long and limits the access of new production methods to the Union market. However, it is unlikely that the Commission will grant authorisations within the planned period of 16 months[46], which is already longer than in other countries. All the more so since in exceptional circumstances the Commission may extend the deadline, not only at EFSA's request but also on its own initiative[47].

Regulation 2015/2283 provides for a detailed authorisation procedure for the placing on the Union market of traditional foods from third countries. The process is initiated by the applicant notifying the Commission of its intention. The notification contains information regarding the name, description, composition and country of origin of the traditional food; documented data demonstrating the history of safe food use in a third country; and, where applicable, the conditions of use and specific labelling requirements which do not mislead the consumer[48]. This information is immedi-

---

42 Regulation (EC) 178/2002 of the European Parliament and of the Council of 28 January 2002 laying down the general principles and requirements of food law, establishing the European Food Safety Authority and laying down procedures in matters of food safety [2002] OJ L 31/1.

43 Christian Ballke, 'Die neue Novel Food-Verordnung - Reform 2.0' (2014) 4 ZLR 412, 421.

44 Ina Gerstberger, 'Was lange währt, wird endlich gut? – Zum Vorschlag der Kommission zur Revision der Novel Food Verordnung' (2008) 2 ZLR 175, 218.

45 Cf ibid 185.

46 Christian Ballke, 'Die neue Novel Food-Verordnung - Reform 2.0' (2014) 4 ZLR 412, 422.

47 Cf Regulation (EU) 2015/2283 of the European Parliament and of the Council of 25 November 2015 on novel foods, amending Regulation (EU) 1169/2011 of the European Parliament and of the Council and repealing Regulation (EC) 258/97 of the European Parliament and of the Council and Commission Regulation (EC) 1852/2001 [2015] OJ L 327/1, art 22.

48 Cf ibid art 14.

ately forwarded to EFSA and to Member States which may submit reasoned safety objections within four months. In order to be valid, the objections must meet two criteria: they must concern food safety and they must be justified. If there are no safety objections, or the objections made do not meet the specified criteria, the Commission will authorise the placing on the market of the traditional food concerned and immediately update the Union list. Otherwise, the Commission will not grant the authorisation, in which case the applicant may initiate another process, similar to the authorisation procedure for the marketing of novel foods but with shorter deadlines. This can be done by submitting an application to the Commission containing documented data relating to the reasoned safety objections raised before. In such cases, obtaining EFSA's opinion is necessary. The opinion is adopted in accordance with similar rules as in the case of other novel foods, but within the period of six months, although this deadline may also be extended.

The literature approves of the new solution regarding a simplified authorisation procedure for the placing on the Union market of novel foods from third countries, and considers it particularly attractive[49]. This is so even despite concerns that in most cases, reasoned safety objections will be presented and the final decision will be based on the application process[50].

D. Data protection

It is worth noting that the new Regulation provides for the protection of information contained in the application, especially of any scientific evidence or data used to support it.

Applicants may request confidential treatment of certain information if the disclosure of such information might significantly harm their competitive position[51]. Furthermore, at the request of an applicant, supported with

---

49 Christian Ballke, 'Die neue Novel Food-Verordnung - Reform 2.0' (2014) 4 ZLR 412, 422.
50 Cf ibid 422.
51 Regulation (EU) 2015/2283 of the European Parliament and of the Council of 25 November 2015 on novel foods, amending Regulation (EU) 1169/2011 of the European Parliament and of the Council and repealing Regulation (EC) 258/97 of the European Parliament and of the Council and Commission Regulation (EC) 1852/2001 [2015] OJ L 327/1, art 23 (1).

appropriate and verifiable information, the newly developed scientific evidence and scientific data used to support an application cannot be further used without the agreement of the prior applicant. Data protection is granted for the period of five years if the following conditions are met: the newly developed scientific evidence or scientific data was designated as proprietary by the prior applicant at the time the first application was made; the prior applicant had exclusive right of reference to that evidence or data; and, the novel food could not have been authorised without the submission of the scientific evidence or scientific data[52]. In that case, the authorisation granted during the period of data protection applies to the marketing of a novel food within the Union by the applicant only, unless the subsequent applicant obtains an authorisation without reference to the proprietary evidence[53].

This solution is aimed at stimulating research and development, as well as innovation within the agri-food industry, especially through protecting the costly investments made by innovators in gathering information and data in support of an application for a novel food. It is to serve as an incentive for food business operators. However, the Regulation does not specify when the scientific evidence or data may be considered new[54]. Furthermore, it is claimed in the literature that establishing such a monopoly is inconsistent with the objectives of the Regulation, does not serve to ensure food safety and significantly limits the free movement of goods, while the applicant has other means of data protection at their disposal, such as patent protection, or a utility model[55]. Nevertheless, the above solution could have a positive impact on the economy since it would allow other business operators to market 'substantially similar'

---

52 Cf Regulation (EU) 2015/2283 of the European Parliament and of the Council of 25 November 2015 on novel foods, amending Regulation (EU) 1169/2011 of the European Parliament and of the Council and repealing Regulation (EC) 258/97 of the European Parliament and of the Council and Commission Regulation (EC) 1852/2001 [2015] OJ L 327/1, art 26 (1) and (2).
53 Cf ibid art 27 (1).
54 Cf Ina Gerstberger, 'Was lange währt, wird endlich gut? – Zum Vorschlag der Kommission zur Revision der Novel Food Verordnung' (2008) 2 ZLR 175, 217.
55 Cf Ina Gerstberger, 'Die Novel Food Verordnung vor der Reform – Aktuelle Probleme und Änderungsvorschläge für ein verbessertes Gesetzeswerk' (2005) 5 WRP 584, 590.

products, provided that they participate in the cost of implementing the innovation on the basis of obtained licenses, or grant compulsory licences[56].

E. Conclusion

There have long been unsuccessful attempts to amend the current Regulation on novel foods. The new Regulation, similarly to its predecessors, has its strengths, but it is not without weaknesses.

By far the greatest advantage of the new solutions is the simplified, shortened and centralised procedure for obtaining general authorisations for the marketing of novel foods. The solutions regarding traditional foods from third countries also deserve a positive assessment, as does the fact that the new Regulation addresses the needs and opportunities of the food industry. The changes clearly aim to reduce the cost of implementing innovations and encourage food business operators to use new, never-before-used production methods and previously unknown foods, while ensuring a high level of public health. The fact that the general authorisation system attempts to consider the stimulation of research and development within the agri-food industry should be viewed as positive, even though these attempts form the basis for disputes regarding the protection of data and scientific evidence. Indeed, these ends could be achieved using existing legal measures.

Nevertheless, despite being based on previous reform efforts and experiences gained from unsuccessful amendment attempts, Regulation 2015/2283 is affected by numerous weaknesses. According to the Committee on the Environment, Public Health and Food Safety, there remains the issue of specifying the scope of the new Regulation in such a way as to ensure precision and relevance of its provisions, on the one hand, taking into account the food industry characterised by a high level of innovation and, on the other, ensuring a high level of protection of human health, consumer interests and the environment as well as the effective functioning of the internal market[57]. Further doubts are raised by the wording of

---

56 Cf ibid.
57 IGI Food Consulting, 'Aktualności: Nowa żywność – prace nad projektem rozporządzenia nabierają tempa' (17 October 2014) <http://www.igifc.pl/aktualnosci/nowa-zywnosc-prace-nad-projektem-rozporzadzenia-nabieraja-tempa,news,24,27.php> accessed 7 February 2016.

the new Regulation which is in many places unclear, thus creating problems of both a theoretical and a practical nature, notably by lengthening the authorisation process. While the objective of the changes is certainly very positive, it should be concluded that not all the means of achieving it are appropriate. Certainly, in order to clarify the numerous significant matters that still raise doubts, it will be necessary to carry out further legislative work and the law doctrine to continue its research on the regulations on novel foods.

§ 11 Health Claims – challenges and chances for management decisions in food industry

Mathias Olbrisch

A. Introduction

The labelling of food with health claims, according to Regulation (EC) 1924/2006 of the European Parliament and of the Council on Nutrition and Health Claims made on foods [2006] OJ L 404/9 (Health Claims Regulation – abbreviated as HCR), is part of the facultative food labelling law, which stands optionally next to the obligational labelling system.[1] In the first instance, it serves consumer protection because it regulates the use of Health and Nutrition Claims. In this way, it also protects the integrity of advertising statements for foods and supports safeguarding qualitative properties of the corresponding foods.

Keeping compliance with the complex legal provisions of the HCR is, on the one hand a challenge for business operators in nutrition economy and, on the other hand, a chance to improve the amount of product sales, if a product is allowed to be promoted with Health or Nutrition Claims. And, the consumer can rely on the product which has to keep the advertised properties.

For this reason, the following article gives an overview about the basic legal structures for the use of Health and Nutrition Claims. In addition to that, it deals with current developments in this field of nutrition economy law, such as botanicals and recent case decisions.

B. Legal framework and current developments

The structure of the legal framework for Health and Nutrition Claims is comparable to many other regulations of EU food law. In this way, the op-

---

1 Ines Härtel, 'Geographische Herkunftsangaben als Rechtsgut – das Schutzsystem der EU für Agrarerzeugnisse und Lebensmittel' (2014) 2 (15) Przegląd Prawa Rolnego 175.

erative part of the HCR firstly regulates the scope. It follows general principles and conditions that are applicable for all kinds of claims. Finally, there are specific conditions for Health and Nutrition Claims before the regulation ends with general and final provisions. Aside from that, the HCR empowers the EU-Commission to establish nutrient profiles.

I. Scope

The HCR distinguishes between three, respectively four, categories of claims with different legal prerequisites that are legally defined in the regulation. These are Health Claims, Nutrition Claims, Risk Reduction Claims and Child Claims.

1. Health Claims

A Health Claim is, in accordance with HCR, Article 2 no. 5 "any claim that states and suggests or implies that a relationship exists between a food category, a food or one of constituents and health". Decisive is, in so far, the mere suggestion of a causal relationship between the food (respectively its ingredients) and the advertising claim[2], as for example "The juice contains a high amount of vitamin C. Vitamin C contributes to the normal function of the immune system". The benchmark is in accordance with HCR recital 15 the consumer's perspective. In so far, the jurisprudence takes as a basis the model of a normally informed and reasonably attentive and circumspect consumer.[3] The subject of the claim must be an advertising of "particular characteristics", as HCR, Article 2 (2) no. 1 states and which is, for instance, not the case for "energy drink".[4]

---

2 Markus Grube / Nicola Conte-Salinas, *Health Claims Verordnung* (2nd edn, Books on Demand 2013) art 5 recital 2.
3 Decision of the Federal Court of Justice of 26 February 2014 - I ZR 178/12, recital 17.
4 Thomas Bruggmann, 'Neun Jahre Health-Claims-Verordnung – kein Ende der Kinderkrankheiten in Sicht' (2015) LMuR 73, 74.

2. Nutrition Claims

Nutrition Claims are legally defined in HCR, Article 2 (2) no. 4 as a claim "which states, suggests or implies that a food has particular beneficial nutritional properties". One of the most classical examples might be the numerous light-foods. In so far, mere content indications appear problematic.[5] They do not fall under the HCR only, if they are free from assessment, i.e. if their content indication does not suggest that the food has got a prominent position due to its nutritional properties. In this way, the labelling "only 1 gramme fat" would be a Nutrition Claim; the labelling "1 gramme fat" would be neutral.[6] "Other substances" in the sense of HCR, Article 2 (2) no. 4 are, for example, "antioxidants" or "probiotic yoghurt cultures".[7]

3. Risk Reduction Claims

HCR, Article 2 (2) no. 6 defines reduction of disease risk claims (here abbreviated as Risk Reduction Claims) as a claim "that states, suggests or implies that the consumption of a food category, a food or one of its constituents significantly reduces a risk factor in the development of a human disease". An example would be "Plant sterols have been shown to lower/ reduce blood cholesterol. High cholesterol is a risk factor in the development of coronary heart disease".[8]

4. Legal remedies

Due to the fact that the mere suggestion of health or nutritional benefit is included under the HCR, the provisions capture a wide range of factual phenomena. But the far reaching provisions are limited in two ways:

---

5 Markus Weck, *Lebensmittelrecht* (2nd edn, Kohlhammer 2013) recital 431 f.
6 Example similar to Markus Weck, *Lebensmittelrecht* (2nd edn, Kohlhammer 2013) recital 432.
7 Markus Grube / Nicola Conte-Salinas, *Health Claims Verordnung* (2nd edn, Books on Demand 2013) art 2 recital 17.
8 Example taken from Kurt-Dietrich Rathke / Andreas Hahn in Walter Zipfel / Kurt-Dietrich Rathke (eds), *Kommentar zum Lebensmittelrecht* (C.H. Beck 2015) Regulation (EC) 1924/2006, 160 a.d. 2015, art 2 recital 49.

The first limitation can be found in HCR, Article 1 (3) where it states that trademarks, which can be understood as a health or Nutrition Claim, "may be used without undergoing the authorisation procedures provided for in this Regulation". But, as the norm further states, this is only possible if the advertising is combined with a permissible admitted health or Nutrition Claim.

In addition to that HCR, Article 1 (4) contains a privilege rule for generic denominations like "cough drop" which are traditionally used and which imply a benefit for the health.[9] Those denominations do not have to be combined with a permissible claim.[10]

II. General principles and conditions

If the advertising claim can be included under the HCR, then the claims concerned have to fulfil certain general principles and conditions that apply equally to Health and Nutrition Claims.

The general principles are largely self-descriptive and can be found in HCR, Article 3. They ensure essential aspects for the integrity of the use of Health and Nutrition Claims.

1. Scientific proof

Amongst the general conditions HCR, Article 5 (1) (a) plays a central role. This norm says that the causal relationship between the presence or absence of a substance, on the one hand, and the positive effect, on the other hand, has to be proven scientifically.[11] In so far, the one who uses the claims bears the burden of proof, as HCR, Article 6 (2) expresses. According to HCR, recital 23, a scientific assessment has to be based on the highest possible standard. This provision indeed gives a tendency, but it does not concretise, exactly how far the scientific proof has to be performed.

---

9 The example 'cough drop' can be found in recital 5 of the HCR.

10 Andreas Meisterernst / Bernd Haber (eds), *Commentary on the EU Health Claims Regulation* (lexxion 2010) art 1 recital 76.

11 Markus Grube / Nicola Conte-Salinas, *Health Claims Verordnung* (2nd edn, Books on Demand 2013) art 5 recital 2 ff.

Wikipedia-articles[12], studies form non-independent institutes[13] or studies with only 95 samples are not sufficient according to opinions of the German courts.[14] The German Federal Court decided in the Priorin-case in 2008, that for dietary foods a randomised, placebo-controlled double blind study is necessary, and transferred, in this way, the gold standard for medicinal products to dietary foods.[15] In the Vitalpilze-case, the German Federal Court decided that in cases of normal foods it is not necessary to keep the same requirements as for dietary products.[16] This means, that for normal foods a randomized, placebo-controlled double blind study is not obligatory. Exact requirements for scientific proof are thus not given.[17]

In the literature, a schematic perspective for the solution of this problem is refused, and only certain convergences and basic structures can be identified concerning a possible system of requirements for the scientific proof.[18]

---

12 Decision of the District Court Berlin of 23 March 2015 - 101 O 106/14, recital 48 and 50.

13 Ibid recital 46.

14 Decision of the District Court Frankfurt am Main of 17 February 2015 - 3-6 O 69/14.

15 The term 'gold standard' is a description for the best possible method of scientific proving in the medicine; see Irina Grgic, *Gesundheitsbezogene Angaben nach der Health Claims Verordnung* (Verlag Peter Lang 2012) 165.

16 Decision of the Federal Court of Justice of 17 January 2013 - I ZR 5/12.

17 A very differentiated jurisprudential analysis concerning the requirements for the scientific proof can be found in the dissertation of Irina Grgic, *Gesundheitsbezogene Angaben nach der Health Claims Verordnung* (Verlag Peter Lang 2012); see also Andreas Meisterernst / Bernd Haber (eds), *Commentary on the EU Health Claims Regulation* (lexxion 2010) art 6.

18 Kurt-Dietrich Rathke / Andreas Hahn in Walter Zipfel / Kurt-Dietrich Rathke (eds), *Kommentar zum Lebensmittelrecht* (C.H. Beck 2015) Regulation (EC) 1924/2006, 160 a.d. 2015, art 5 recital 8 a; Andreas Meisterernst / Bernd Haber, *Commentary on the EU Health Claims Regulation* (lexxion 2010) art 6 recital 1 ff. suggest system of evidence requirements, which are orientated on art 5 of the Commission Regulation (EC) 353/2008 of 18 April 2008 establishing implementing rules for applications for authorization of health claims as provided for in art 15 of Regulation (EC) 1924/2006 of the European Parliament and of the Council [2008] OJ L 109/11.

Concerning traditional foods, *Grgic* suggests that a long-term traditional use could be sufficient for the scientific proof of the causal relationship.[19] This proposal is based on an *argumentum a majore ad minus*, because for traditional medicaments, such traditional evidence is accepted.[20] Thus, if such relaxed requirements are applied even for medicaments, then *a fortiori* this must be enough evidence for foods, that are traditionally associated with nutritional or health related benefits.[21]

2. Botanicals

The recognition of traditional evidence would be very relevant for the judicial treatment of foods with ingredients taken from plants, so-called botanicals. If the proof of the causal relationship between a botanical ingredient and a nutritional or health related effect is evaluated by the previous (diffuse) standards, then most of the desired Health and Nutrition Claims cannot be allowed.[22] For this reason, the Commission has disconnected the admission procedure for botanicals from the other claim-recognition requests and raised the question whether it might be appropriate to apply another proof method especially for botanicals.[23] In this context, the approach from *Grgic* could eventually be useful, particularly because the effect of botanical ingredients can, in many cases, only be proven by traditional experiences.[24]

Until now, the Commission has not taken a decision about the applicable standards for the scientific evidence. This is why many botanical

---

19 Irina Grgic, *Gesundheitsbezogene Angaben nach der Health Claims Verordnung* (Verlag Peter Lang 2012) 151 ff.; in the same way also Andreas Meisterernst / Bernd Haber (eds), *Commentary on the EU Health Claims Regulation* (lexxion 2010) art 6 recital 28, who suggest traditional knowledge as a supporting source of data; Markus Weck, *Lebensmittelrecht* (2nd edn, Kohlhammer 2013) recital 453.

20 Irina Grgic, *Gesundheitsbezogene Angaben nach der Health Claims Verordnung* (Verlag Peter Lang 2012) 165.

21 Ibid; opposite view, Decision of the District Court Frankfurt am Main of 17 February 2015 - 3-6 O 69/14, recital 49.

22 Markus Weck, *Lebensmittelrecht* (2nd edn, Kohlhammer 2013) recital 453.

23 BT-Drs. 18/1273, 2; Markus Weck, *Lebensmittelrecht* (2nd edn, Kohlhammer 2013) recital 453.

24 In this way also Markus Weck, *Lebensmittelrecht* (2nd edn, Kohlhammer 2013) recital 453.

claims are on-hold.[25] A suit was filed in 2012 at the General Court of the European Union (GC) against the disconnection of the evaluation procedure. The applicants complained, in particular, that a legal basis would be missing for this measure of the Commission.[26] In accordance with HCR, Article 13, there could be only one single list; consequently the establishment of various lists and of a staged admission-process would not be covered by the HCR.[27] In so far, the GC replied that HCR, Article 13, does contain a legal basis for the creation of the lists.[28] Although this provision does not contain any indications concerning the possibility of disconnecting the admission procedure, it would grant the Commission a wide scope of discretion concerning the arrangement of the admission procedure in order to realise the legislative goals apparent in recitals 1, 2 and 14 of the HCR.[29] Furthermore, the procedure to change the lists for admitted claims show, that a staged procedure must be possible.[30] In addition to that, the splitting would be justified by the high degree of complexity of the subject-matter.[31]

That the deadline for the adoption of the admission list was exceeded, was also recognised by the GC.[32] But the GC argued, that exceeding the deadline was of no importance, if, within the time window, nothing else would have been regulated, either.[33]

Moreover, the applicants argued that the requirements for the scientific proof would be too strict.[34] But the GC also rejected this argument and referred, in so far, to recitals 17 and 23 of the HCR, which would express

---

25 Markus Grube / Nicola Conte-Salinas, *Health Claims Verordnung* (2nd edn, Books on Demand 2013) recital 6.
26 Case T-296/12 *The Health Food Manufacturers' Association et al v European Commission* [2015] para 53 ff. (not yet published in ECR II) <http://curia.europa.eu/juris/document/document.jsf?docid=165021&mode=req&pageIndex=1&dir=&occ=first&part=1&text=&doclang=EN&cid=263110> accessed 25 January 2016.
27 Ibid para 55.
28 Ibid para 64 f.
29 Ibid.
30 Ibid para 66.
31 Ibid para 73.
32 Ibid para 71.
33 Ibid. According to art 13 (3) HCR the deadline was on 31 January 2010.
34 Ibid para 123.

the legislative intention of highest possible standards.[35] Also, the applicants' assertion that the criteria of the EFSA would be unclear, were rejected by the GC with regard to chapter III of Regulation (EC) 178/2002 of the European Parliament and of the Council laying down the general principles and requirements of food law, establishing European Food Safety Authority and laying down procedures in matters of food safety [2002] OJ L 031/1, which would regulate the work of the EFSA in detail.[36] Specific guidelines in advance of the admission procedure itself would not be necessary.[37]

In summary, with its decision of June 12, 2015, the GC took a stand on many controversial legal questions, but the statements concerning the scientific evidence remained at the abstract level only.

3. Further judgments and general conditions

Currently, actions for failure in cases no. T-619/14 and no. T-578/14 are pending at the GC, which are challenging the long-lasting inactivity of the Commission with regard to the admission of botanical-claims. Further general conditions can be derived from the wording of HCR, Article 5, which is largely comprehensible in itself.

III. Specific conditions

In addition to the general principles and conditions, the HCR contains specific rules that are only applicable for either Health Claims or for Nutrition Claims.

---

35 Case T-296/12 *The Health Food Manufacturers' Association et al v European Commission* [2015] paras 126, 129 (not yet published in ECR II) <http://curia.europa.eu/juris/document/document.jsf?docid=165021&mode=req&pageIndex=1&dir=&occ=first&part=1&text=&doclang=EN&cid=26311> accessed 25 January 2016.
36 Ibid para 148.
37 Ibid para 149.

1. Specific conditions for Health Claims

Essential for the field of Health Claims – in accordance with HCR, Article 10 - is the general ban on the use of health claims, if the corresponding claim does not appear on a certain list for allowable claims. This means that the claim can only be used if it was allowed by the Commission and put on the list according to HCR, Article 13 and HCR, Article 14 respectively.[38]

a) List of allowable claims

HCR, Article 14, in so far, refers to specific procedure rules for Risk Reduction and Child Claims that are located in HCR, Article 15-19, and that are more strict; so the legislator must consider those claims as being particularly problematic. In contrast, HCR Article 13 contains rules concerning the admission of all other health claims. The corresponding lists can be found in their own regulations and are available in their entirety via the EU Register on Nutrition and Health Claims which can be accessed online.[39]

b) Particular requirements for non-specific Health Claims

According to the fundamental legislative intent, it is necessary to concretise the claims by describing exactly which substance influences human health in what way. If the claims refer just to general, non-specific benefits, then HCR, Article 10 (3) stipulates that such a non-specific claim has to be combined with a specific claim. This legal requirement has a content-related dimension and a spatial or optical dimension. From the content-related point of view, a claim like "the healthy snack"[40], would have

---

38 Markus Weck, *Lebensmittelrecht* (2nd edn, Kohlhammer 2013) recital 427, 445, 450.

39 <http://ec.europa.eu/nuhclaims/> accessed 11 November 2015; Markus Grube / Nicola Conte-Salinas, *Health Claims Verordnung* (2nd edn, Books on Demand 2013) art 13 recital 9.

40 Example similar to Markus Grube / Nicola Conte-Salinas, *Health Claims Verordnung* (2nd edn, Books on Demand) art 10 recital 12.

to be connected with an allowed claim like "calcium contributes to normal muscle function". If, in addition to that, a spatial or optical connection between both claims has to be given, is considered controversial.[41] Non-specific claims have to be differentiated from general wellness-claims without any reference to human health.[42] Those do not fall under the scope of the HCR and can be used without any list admission. In practice, such wellness claims cause legal problems, as two recent court decisions in Germany show.[43]

c) Specific labelling rules and per se unlawful claims

HCR, Article 10 (2), stipulates specific labelling requirements for Health Claims that extend the obligational labelling of Regulation (EU) 1169/2011 of the European Parliament and of the Council on the provision of food information to consumers [2011] OJ L 304, 18[44]. *Per se* unlawful claims are regulated in HCR, Article 12, which contains, for example, claims that make reference to the rate or amount of weight loss such as claims which make reference to recommendations of individual doctors. According to HCR, Article 11, recommendations of national medical associations and health-related are allowed.[45]

2. Specific conditions for Nutrition Claims

HCR Article 8 also regulates a general prohibition with reservation of admittance, so that Nutrition Claims that are not on the list of allowable

---

41 Pro: Kurt-Dietrich Rathke / Andreas Hahn in Walter Zipfel / Kurt-Dietrich Rathke, *Kommentar zum Lebensmittelrecht* (C.H. Beck 2015) Regulation (EC) 1924/2006, 160 a.d. 2015, art 10 recital 41; contra: Markus Grube / Nicola Conte-Salinas, *Health Claims Verordnung* (2nd edn, Books on Demand 2013) art 10 recital 11.
42 Markus Weck, *Lebensmittelrecht* (2nd edn, Kohlhammer 2013) recital 451.
43 Decision of the District Court Ravensburg of 25 August 2015 - 8 O 43/15; Decision of the Higher Regional Court Hamm of 20 May 2014 - 4 U 19/14.
44 Abbreviated as 'Regulation (EU) 1169/2011'.
45 Markus Grube / Nicola Conte-Salinas, *Health Claims Verordnung* (2nd edn, Books on Demand 2013) art 12 recital 6 f.; Markus Weck, *Lebensmittelrecht* (2nd edn, Kohlhammer 2013) recital 452 in so far criticizes, that consequently recommendations of the WHO would be excluded from the reverse exception.

claims, are forbidden.[46] Differently to the Health Claims, the Nutrition Claims can be found in the Annex of the HCR itself. It is possible to find there, for example, the classical Nutrition Claim "low fat" which means that the claim may only be used, if the food contains less than 3 g fat per 100 g. For comparative claims, HCR Article 9, contains specific rules, according to which, the comparison has to be referred to the range of foods from the same category.[47]

IV. Nutrient profiles

HCR, Article 10, empowers the Commission to determine nutrient profiles in order to regulate the characteristic nutrient composition of food advertised by Health or Nutrition Claims.[48] The idea behind this, is to "avoid a situation where Nutrition or Health Claims mask the overall nutritional status of a food product", as recital 11 expresses.

This approach seems to be reasonable and plausible at first sight. Nevertheless, it is heavily criticized, because it would be too bureaucratic[49] and block potential innovations within the nutrition economy.[50] At the moment, a determination of nutrient profiles by the competent Commission is neither planned nor forseeable.

C. Summary and conclusion

With regard to the continuing problem concerning claims on hold for botanicals, and the legal uncertainties connected therewith, health claims, on the one hand, contain a certain potential of risk.

On the other hand, the HCR establishes a standardized procedure for the admittance of Health and Nutrition Claims which counteracts legal un-

---

46 Markus Weck, *Lebensmittelrecht* (2nd edn, Kohlhammer 2013) recital 445.
47 For detailed information see Markus Weck, *Lebensmittelrecht* (2nd edn, Kohlhammer 2013) recital 449 ff.
48 Stefan Leible, 'Nährwert- und gesundheitsbezogene Werbung' in Rudolf Streinz (ed), *Lebensmittelrechts-Handbuch* (C. H. Beck 2015) 36 a.d. 2015, recital 489 b.
49 Markus Weck, *Lebensmittelrecht* (2nd edn, Kohlhammer 2013) recital 427.
50 Irina Grgic, *Gesundheitsbezogene Angaben nach der Health Claims Verordnung* (Verlag Peter Lang 2012) 67 f.

certainty in a structural manner.[51] Moreover, the legal provisions also protect food business operators from unfair competition. In so doing, the consumer´s trust in Health and Nutrition claims is strengthened.

At the political level, an evaluation of the HCR is envisaged in the context of the EU Regulatory Fitness and Performance Programme (REFIT-Programme).[52] In so far, not only an abolishment of nutrient profiles is discussed, but also an abolishment of the HCR itself, because the consumer protective elements would also result from Regulation (EU) 1169/2011.[53] As long as the *status quo* is kept, Health Claims contain certain challenges and chances for management decisions in the nutrition economy.

---

51 Markus Grube / Nicola Conte-Salinas, *Health Claims Verordnung* (2nd edn, Books on Demand 2013) introduction recital 2.
52 'Health-Claims-VO auf dem Prüfstand' *Lebensmittelzeitung* (Frankfurt am Main, 2 April 2015) 22; for further information see the Euorpean Commission´s road map, available online under <http://ec.europa.eu/smart-regulation/roadmaps/docs/2015_sante_595_evaluation_health_claims_en.pdf> accessed 12 November 2015.
53 See Renate Sommer, 'PM Sommer zu EU-Kommission und Nährwertprofile' (evp-Fraktion im Europäischen Parlament, 13 October 2015) <http://www.cdu-csu-ep.de/presse/pressemitteilungen/10279-pm-sommer-zu-eu-kommission-und-naehrwertprofile-13-10 2015.html> accessed 10 November 2015.

§ 12 Food quality in history – the genesis of the Bavarian Purity Law (beer) from 1516 until today

Daniel Brandauer

A. Introduction

The "Bayerisches Reinheitsgebot" or the Bavarian Purity Law for Beer (PLB) from April the 23rd 1516 is considered to be the oldest food law still in effect in the world[1]. Observing the historical development of this norm, the intent and purpose, of what came to be, the modern system of food laws, can be perfectly outlined and tracked down to its roots. Taking this aspect into consideration the Bavarian PLB from 1516 and all it's properly documented predecessors in Germany, are perfect examples for the birth of food law and it's long lasting development.

Also taking into consideration the problems and litigation that arose on a European level in the early 1980's[2] the discussion and importance of the topic has not ceased to exist in any way. The unanswered questions and doubts about the right to existence of this regulation, and future action in relation to this, remain.

How did the purity law come into existence? How did it find its way into the modern legal culture? Is this norm that has found its modern place in the "VorlBierG" (Temporary Beer Law) and the "BierV" (Beer Ordinance), a regulatory anachronism?

The regulation of the production of food, or to be more precise, the food law inside of Germany, can be traced back into the 12th century and goes hand in hand with the development of city organization[3]. Before the

---

1 <http://www.brauer-bund.de/bier-ist-rein/reinheitsgebot/rechtsentwicklung.html> accessed 1 July 2015.
2 Case 178/84 *Kommission v Deutschland* [1987] ECR 1227; Julia Schmidt, 'Ist das Reinheitsgebot für Bier noch zu retten?' (2005) NJW 3617; K. J. Mayer, 'Germany's Reinheitsgebot and brewing in the 20th century' (1983) 20 (4) Technical Quarterly Master Brewers Association of the Americas 138, 139.
3 Axel Meyer-Wölden, *Die Reinheitsgebote im Lebensmittelrecht* (1968) 11.

Bavarian PLB was enacted, there was ample development regarding the handling of this beverage.

B. Development and enactment of the PLB

I. Documented predecessors

1. Arbitration award of emperor Barbarossa-1156

The oldest known and documented regulation was the arbitration award of Emperor Friedrich Barbarossa for the city of Augsburg in the year 1156[4]. In this regulatory paper, the "Schankwirte" (Barkeepers) who sell "bad beer" or sell beer with "a wrong measurement" are addressed[5]. These two crimes were punishable. Also, the question of what should happen to the beer of the barkeeper in case of an infringement was answered. The arbitration only addressed the matter of the accepted ingredients of beer in a rough way. In this way, the question of what should be considered as "bad beer" was probably left open to the judgment of the authorities at the time.

2. The edict of Nürnberg - between 1303 and 1305

An additional documented development took place between 1303 and 1305[6] in the city of Nürnberg. In the book of statutes of this city under nos. 48 and 60 et. Seq., the word "beer" is first mentioned[7]. Under no. 61 a, the brewing of beer is permitted only through the usage of barley. All other types of grain are forbidden[8]. One can assume that the objective of

---

4 Stadtarchiv Augsburg, *700 Jahre Augsburger Stadtrecht* (1976) 27.
5 '[…] Et quando tabernarius vilem facit cervisiam vel etiam dat iniustam mensuram, supradicto ordnine punietur, et insuper eadem cervisia destitietur vel pauperibus gratis erogetur. […]'.
6 Otto Puchner / Rudolf Muck, 'Die frühesten Verordnungen über das Brauwesen in der Freien Reichsstadt Nürnberg' (1950) 59 Deutsche Brauwirtschaft 367.
7 Werner Schultheiß, *Brauwesen und Braurechte in Nürnberg bis zum Beginn des 19. Jahrhunderts* (Nürnberger Werkstücke zur Stadt- und Landesgeschichte 1978) 3.
8 Otto Puchner / Rudolf Muck, 'Die frühesten Verordnungen über das Brauwesen in der Freien Reichsstadt Nürnberg' (1950) 59 Deutsche Brauwirtschaft 367, 368 (Image 1, SB I/A no 61 a).

this restrictive regulation was to secure the continuity and productivity of bread-production. Between the years 750 and 1315 at least 29 famines hit the European continent[9]. Taking into account that a demand of 25-45% came exclusively from the beer industry, a shortage of grain could be devastating for some cities, making a grain shortage even worse[10]. Without any doubt, there was a need to act to secure the most important source of calories, bread. Possibly because of this, the usage of other grain types was forbidden for brewers.

3. The brewing order of Regensburg- 1453 – 1460

In the year 1450, the city medic, Hans von Bayreut, was appointed by the city council of Regensburg to make an extensive analysis of the beer and its – at that time – usual ingredients. Beer was brewed with different kinds of ingredients, ranging from parsley through henbane seeds, tree ashes and others[11]. Von Bayreut catalogued all beers that where brewed with these ingredients as "medicinal beers" and decided that beers which where drunk by an entire community, should be brewed only with "barley, good hops and water"[12]. In this way, the beer wouldn't harm anyone. Possibly because of this recommendation, the brewing order of Regensburg was enacted around the year of 1453 (in 1457 and 1460 new parts were added). The order forbids brewing in connection with the aforementioned ingredients. Also, a measurement for commerce with beer was set. A clear restriction to only using the ingredients barley, hops and water, did not take place.

9 Hans Michael Esslinger, *Handbook of Brewing: Processes, Technology, Markets* (WILEY-VCH 2009) 14 f.
10 Ibid.
11 Karin Hackel-Stehr, *Das Brauwesen in Bayern vom 14. bis 16. Jahrhundert, insbesondere die Entstehung und Entwicklung des Reinheitsgebotes (1516)* (Gesellschaft für Öffentlichkeitsarbeit der Deutschen Brauwirtschaft e.V. 1987) 163.
12 Ibid 163 f.

4. Edicts of the duchy of Bayern-Landshut –from 1409-1493

The edicts of the duchy of Bayern-Landshut are probably the last step before of the Bavarian PLB. The relevant edicts are within the time frame 1409-1493.

The reasons for this brewing order where: the bad beer quality, and the high prices. Also the "gemeine Nutzen" (common use) was given a higher priority[13]. Through this formulation, the tendency of a new consideration towards consumer protection is recognizable. This first brewing order regulated the use of a specific amount of malt, exact brewing times and enacted a prohibition to mix old and new beer[14]. A fairly new instrument of control was added to the brewing order, the "Bierbeschau", here the production of beer was controlled repeatedly every year[15]. To ensure the implementation of the aforementioned regulations, the brewers had to give an oath. There was no strict regulation of ingredients for beer production. In the year 1486, the prohibition of certain ingredients was enacted, and as a result of this prohibition's failure to succeed, a restriction to the sole use of "malt, hops and water" was introduced in 1493[16].

5. Interim findings

On the basis of the documented initial stages of the PLB and the regulation of the beer industry, one can notice the creation of an early consumer protection system. These instruments had the purpose of avoiding dangers that would come from the beer itself and the dangers connected to beer production.

Firstly, the aim was the protection of the population from impure beer, bad beer, fraud and ingredients that could be harmful to human beings[17].

---

13 Karin Hackel-Stehr, Das Brauwesen in Bayern vom 14. bis 16. Jahrhundert, insbesondere die Entstehung und Entwicklung des Reinheitsgebotes (1516) (Gesellschaft für Öffentlichkeitsarbeit der Deutschen Brauwirtschaft e.V. 1987) 33.
14 Ibid 78.
15 Ibid.
16 Ibid 94 ff.: 'Welcher Bierschenk [...] Bier [...] gefährlich mischt, anders als Malz, Hopfen und Wasser dazu nehme oder sonst Gefährliches tue, wird bestraft'.
17 Also one opinion calls the purity law "the first drug law in Germany", and specifically talks about the prohibition of henbane. Henbane was used as word for the

These regulations were also a device to protect the population from economic and existential dangers. The goal of the limitation to only one kind of grain in beer production was also to keep the prices of grains inside of an acceptable range. The guaranty of a certain amount of grain for the production of bread was also definitely one of the main motivations[18].

II. The Bavarian Purity Law from the 23rd of April 1516 ·

On the 23rd of April 1516, during the State parliament of the city of Ingolstadt, the first nationwide land order was enacted,[19] and in this order the PLB or Reinheitsgebot was included which also had force of law in the whole Bavarian territory.

The most important factor that led to the enactment of the purity law was the reunification of the Bavarian duchy. Being divided since 1392 into four different dukedoms[20]; Bayern-München, Bayern-Ingolstadt, Bayern-Landshut and Bayern-Staubingen; there was no way to enact a PLB or a beer ordinance with the magnitude of the later enacted purity law for beer, without these dukedoms working as one single unit.

After a succession war between upper and lower Bavaria[21] the dukedom was reunited under the rule of Duke Wilhelm IV and his brother Ludwig. This was one of the key moments for the countrywide enactment of the Bavarian PLB from 1516.

---

beer, because it had an intoxicating and hallucinogenic effect on the user. In this way it is assumable that the purity laws were also predecessors of drug laws in Germany. See Christian Rätsch, *Enzyklopädie der psychoaktiven Pflanzen* (AT Verlag 1998) 277 ff.

18 Hans Michael Esslinger, *Handbook of Brewing: Processes, Technology, Markets* (WILEY-VCH 2009) 14 f.

19 Karin Hackel-Stehr, *Das Brauwesen in Bayern vom 14. bis 16. Jahrhundert, insbesondere die Entstehung und Entwicklung des Reinheitsgebotes (1516)* (Gesellschaft für Öffentlichkeitsarbeit der Deutschen Brauwirtschaft e.V. 1987) 224.

20 Ibid 162 ff.

21 Max Spindler / Andreas Kraus (eds), *Handbuch der bayerischen Geschichte* (C.H. Beck 1981) 318.

1. First assembly of the united State parliament

In the year 1508 the first assembly of the united state parliament was held[22]. During this assembly, one of the main aspects being discussed and decided was the united procedures between the different parliaments of the once divided dukedom[23]. The united procedures of the parliaments were also one of the key-points to achieve a countrywide ordering for the state and, in this way, an important antecedent for the creation of the PLB. Without a united state organ this would not have been accomplished.

2. Enactment at the State Parliament of Ingolstadt -1516

The first order for the dukedom of Bavaria since the reunification was enacted on the 23rd of April 1516[24]. The purpose of the order was to create harmonization of the different law systems in the dukedom. This harmonization affected nearly every aspect of legislation, and in this way the first PLB for the entire Bavarian territory was enacted[25]. It appeared inside of the new Beer Order[26] for the entire Bavarian territory.

The most important points of the Beer Order were: the PLB and the maximum price fixing for beer[27]. The PLB specifically restricted the ingredients for the production of beer in all cities and markets to "barley, hops and water"[28].

Nevertheless, the legislator failed to recognize that the attempt to lay down a set of generalized rules for the regions inside of Bavaria was going to run into problems due to the regional differences that the various parts

---

22 Andreas Kraus, *Geschichte Bayerns* (C.H. Beck 1988) 195.
23 Karin Hackel-Stehr, *Das Brauwesen in Bayern vom 14. bis 16. Jahrhundert, insbesondere die Entstehung und Entwicklung des Reinheitsgebotes (1516)* (Gesellschaft für Öffentlichkeitsarbeit der Deutschen Brauwirtschaft e.V. 1987) 221.
24 Ibid 224.
25 Ibid.
26 Title: 'How beer should be served and brewed during the summer and winter'.
27 Karin Hackel-Stehr, *Das Brauwesen in Bayern vom 14. bis 16. Jahrhundert, insbesondere die Entstehung und Entwicklung des Reinheitsgebotes (1516)* (Gesellschaft für Öffentlichkeitsarbeit der Deutschen Brauwirtschaft e.V. 1987) 229 ff.
28 'In allen Stetten, Märckthen, unn auf dem Lannde, zu keinem Pier merer, dann allain Gersten, Hopfen unn Wasser' (Bayerische Landesordnung 1516).

of the dukedom had. For example, the decision of making barley the only grain allowed, had an impact on the maximum price fixing. The grain was not easy to find on the market and therefore it was expensive[29]. Because of this, the brewers had to import the grain[30] and couldn't compete with the cheaper beer being imported. In reaction to this, the brewers sometimes did not follow the regulation and the purpose was undermined. This problem can be verified through complaint letters of the brewers and a survey made by the dukes[31].

3. Interim findings

The main objectives where: the stabilization of prices, higher quality of beer and a secure food supply for the population. One critical problem of this generalized regulation was the neglect of the regional differences, which ultimately led to the undermining of the regulations in some parts of the dukedom. Brewers couldn't keep the same quality of beer and maintain the fixed prices; they had to lower the quality to be able to survive in the market.

III. Development from 1516 until 1949

Contrary to common belief, the PLB had no continuous development from the year 1516 on. In the year 1616, the law was limbered in Bavaria and other ingredients such as salt and cumin were accepted[32]. It also has to be mentioned that between 1516 and 1871 no clear path of development can be traced. Germany became a united state territory in the year 1871 with the foundation of the "Reich". At this point, Article 35 of the "Reichverfassung" gave the Empire all legislative and revenue powers for the new

---

29 Peter Lietz, 'Überlegungen zum deutschen Reinheitsgebot' (2007) 3 Brauerei Forum 12, 13.
30 Ibid.
31 Karin Hackel-Stehr, *Das Brauwesen in Bayern vom 14. bis 16. Jahrhundert, insbesondere die Entstehung und Entwicklung des Reinheitsgebotes (1516)* (Gesellschaft für Öffentlichkeitsarbeit der Deutschen Brauwirtschaft e.V. 1987) 264.
32 Ibid 291; Walter Schemmel, *Das Reinheitsgebot für Herstellung und Vertrieb von Bier in Bayern* (1968) 5.

brew taxation territory[33]. Baden, Württemberg and Bavaria were exempt from this[34]. The Purity Law was not included in the new BrauStG (Brewing Taxation Law) of 1872. The PLB was first included in the legislation of the Empire in 1906 through the Law to Modify the Law of Beer Taxation on the 3rd of June[35]. The ingredient restriction applied to bottom-fermented beer and the only ingredients allowed were malted barley, hops, yeast[36] and water. In 1909, the term "Bier" was secured and only those fermented beverages that followed the norms of beer production could be sold under the name "Bier"[37].

IV. Purity Law on an European level

After World War II ended in 1945, the "Grundgesetz" was enacted in 1949 and the FRG took administration into its own hands again. On 18th April 1951, the ECSC was founded in Paris through the initiative of France[38]. Through this new treaty the ECJ also was founded.

On 14th March 1952, a new beer taxation law was passed in Germany. Under Article 9 of the BierStG, the production of beer was described, and under Article 10 BierStG the term "Bier" was secured and only to be used for fermented beverages that were in compliance with Article 9 paragraph 1 and 2 of the BierStG. Five years later on 25th March 1957, Germany joined the EEC[39]. This step would proove to be crucial for the development of the PLB, from this time on, Germany was bound to the realization of the Common European Market.

---

33 Michael Heil in Jürgen Paul Birle / Achim Fey et al (eds), *Beck'sches Steuer und Bilanzrechtslexikon* (C.H. Beck 2015) lit B - Biersteuer.
34 Ibid.
35 Holger Gerstenberg in Walter Zipfel / Kurt-Dietrich Rathke, *Kommentar zum Lebensmittelrecht* (2014) VorlBierG § 9 recital 1.
36 Yeast was a new ingredient in the Purity Law, after the discoveries made by Louis Pasteur in his work 'Etudes sur la biere', which was published in the year 1876 in Paris.
37 Walter Schemmel, *Das Reinheitsgebot für Herstellung und Vertrieb von Bier in Bayern* (1968) 16.
38 Andreas Haratsch / Christian König / Matthias Pechstein, *Europarecht* (8th edn, Mohr Siebeck 2012) 4 recital 8.
39 Andreas Haratsch / Christian König / Matthias Pechstein, Europarecht (8th edn, Mohr Siebeck 2012) 5 recital 10.

The Article 3 lit. h) and Article 30 of the EEC treaty were decisive for the future development of the Purity Law. Under Article 3 lit. h) EEC-T the adjustment of national laws was concretized, as long as these laws were crucial for the proper functioning of the common market, and in Article 30 of the EEC-T all import restrictions and all measures with equivalent effect where forbidden.

The conflict arose mainly because foreign beer importers had to follow the PLB to be able to sell their product as "Bier" in Germany. More pressure was laid upon the existence of the PLB through the decision of the ECJ in the famous "Cassis de Dijon" case[40] in the year 1979.

The EEC addressed the PLB on 12th February 1982 opening an infringement procedure against Germany, because of the aforementioned Article 9 and 10 of the BierStG and the factual import restrictions for foreign brewers[41]. The EEC-Commission saw an infringement of Article 30 EEC-T by Germany. The reactions to the infringement procedure in Germany where very emotional. The Foreign Minister, Genscher at that time, said "Courts of justice come and go but the PLB will remain.[42]". The Federal Government responded to this using Article 36 I EEC-T as an argument[43]. Stating that import restrictions in furtherance of the protection of health and the life of human beings and animals were not part of those forbidden restrictions in Article 30 EEC-T.

Following these statements the EC-Commission filed a declaratory action against Germany in concordance with Article 169 of the EEC-T[44] this ended with the decision of the ECJ on 12th March 1987. The ECJ declared, that Article 9 and 10 of the BierStG where infringing against Article 30 of the EEC-T[45]. The argumentation of the Federal Government was discarded by the ECJ[46]. Because of the general prohibition of ingredients the PLB

40 Case 120/78 *Rewe-Zentral AG v Federal Monopoly Administration for Spirits– Cassis de Dijon* [1979] ECR 649.
41 K. J. Mayer, 'Germany's Reinheitsgebot and brewing in the 20th century' (1983) 20 (4) Technical Quarterly Master Brewers Association of the Americas 138.
42 Anonymous (abbrv.: Bw.), *Aktivitäten für das Reinheitsgebot* (1982) 15 Brauwelt 614.
43 K. J. Mayer, 'Germany's Reinheitsgebot and brewing in the 20th century' (1983) 20 (4) Technical Quarterly Master Brewers Association of the Americas 138, 140 (Fig. 1).
44 Case 178/84 *Kommission v Deutschland* [1987] ECR 1227.
45 Case 178/84 *Kommission v Deutschland* [1987] ECR 1274 f.
46 Ibid.

was infringing against the proportionality principle[47]. The consequences
for the PLB were transcendent. After the decision of the ECJ, Germany
had to open its market to foreign beer and let these products enter the market with the denomination "Bier". This didn't apply to German brewers,
who still had to follow the regulation of the PLB. The regulations found
their new places under the Article 9 VorlBierG and Article 1 BierV. An
exception was added for foreign beers under Article 1 paragraph 2
BierV[48]. For German brewers, a violation against Article 9 VorlBierG in
connection with Article 18 VorlBierG, can be punished with up to
10,000 € in penalties in the cases of willful intent and up to 5,000 € in the
case of negligence, Article 17 paragraph 2 OWiG (Law on Misde-
meanors)[49].

C. Resume and future perspectives

Nowadays, the importation of foreign beers that are not in concordance
with the PLB has had no damaging impact on the German beer industry
nor has it caused any health issues. In fact, the PLB has become a respected and renowned quality asset for the majority of German brewers. A bigger threat to the German beer industry is the steady decline of beer consumption[50].

One can realize that there was, in no way, a continuous development of
the PLB. Only until the early 1860's was the PLB re-inacted in Bavaria[51],
afterwards it was taken into the legislation of the German Empire, and
then into the FRG. Questions still arise in connection with the distinction
between bottom and top fermented beers (Article 9 paragraph 1 and 2
VorlBierG). It is clear that the decision of the ECJ made the contradictions
to an enforcement of the PLB clearer for the public and the consumers.

---

47 Ibid.
48 Holger Gerstenberg in Walter Zipfel / Kurt-Dietrich Rathke (eds), *Kommentar zum Lebensmittelrecht* (2014) BierV § 1 recital 3 f.
49 Ibid VorlBierG § 9 recital 55.
50 'Bierkonsum: Deutsche haben weniger Durst' *Wirtschaft.com* (24 September 2013) <http://www.wirtschaft.com/bierkonsum-deutsche-haben-weniger-durst/> accessed 20 July 2015.
51 Walter Schemmel, *Das Reinheitsgebot für Herstellung und Vertrieb von Bier in Bayern* (1968) 6.

This should have opened up a chance for German brewers to compete on a different level and in this way evolve.

At this point, the PLB feels like an anachronistic and outdated regulation, which should be looked at more precisely. Especially when looking at the use of Polyvinylpolypyrrolidone in the production[52]. Taking this into perspective, a bad aftertaste remains. How pure is the PLB in Germany, what else is used during the production?

An initiative of the Brewing Association of Germany has taken care to name the PLB a cultural heritage of Germany[53]. Once again this demonstrates that the PLB is a law of a past time and should be treated as a relict. The PLB should not sit in the way of the development of the German beer industry. It should, contrary to this, become a quality seal, optional to any German brewer. A role that could strengthen the future perspectives of the PLB, could be the fight against modern problems such as side effect of uncontrolled brewing barley or the addition of chemical additives such as stimulating codeine[54]. In this way a purposeful existence of the PLB could be created. Otherwise there is no proper sense to this regulation as has been shown through the development analysis. The problems and main areas that where meant to be regulated ceased to exist hundreds of years ago.

---

52 European Patent Office, Decision of the Technical Board of Appeal of 24 June 1997, Case Number T 0385/94 - 3.3.4, Application Number 86901809.3, Publication Number 0246241 *Bier/HUMS et al.*
53 <http://www.brauer-bund.de/index.php?id=680&ageverify=16> accessed 20 July 2015.
54 Peter Lietz, 'Überlegungen zum deutschen Reinheitsgebot' (2007) 3 Brauerei Forum 12, 15.

Third Chapter:
Agricultural Production, Structure and Reform of Common
Agricultural Policy in the EU

§ 13 Greening the new goal of the Common Agricultural Policy of the European Union for 2020

Johan F. Stoepker

A. Common Agricultural Policy for 2020

Ever since the Common Agricultural Policy (CAP) of the European Union has existed, it has continuously been changing in order to meet new challenges.

Important reforms have been made during the last few years. In 2003 and during the CAP Health-check in 2008, the policy became more market-oriented.[1] The payments were detached from the farmer's income and made equal for all farmers.[2]

Before starting the political debate on the latest reform of the CAP, the European Commission launched a public debate on April 12, 2010 on the future of the CAP[3].

The CAP changed from guaranteeing only the farmer's income and food security, to a policy which is more focused on public goods and ecological interests. As the CAP was already more market oriented, a new challenge appeared to make agriculture more environmentally friendly. Therefore, the EU-legislature created a new component of the direct payment system, the so-called "Greening". Greening is a mandatory policy to support agricultural practices benefiting climate and the environment.

The European Union has the power to define Common Agricultural Policy. This power is granted in Article 43 (2) TFEU. This power has to be interpreted as a broad power: the power to regulate not only specific

---

1 Ines Härtel, 'Agrarrecht' in Matthias Ruffert (ed), *Enzyklopädie des Europarechts*, vol 5 (Nomos 2013) § 7, 395.

2 John Booth, 'Europäisches Marktordnungs- und Beihilfenrecht' in Matthias Dombert / Karsten Witt (eds), *Münchener Anwaltshandbuch Agrarrecht* (C.H. Beck 2011) § 79.

3 Ines Härtel, 'Die Gemeinsame Agrarpolitik der Europäischen Union im föderalrechtlichen Mehrebenenverbund' in Vorstand des Europäischen Zentrums für Föderalismus-Forschung Tübingen (ed), *Jahrbuch des Föderalismus 2014* (Nomos 2014) 269.

agricultural topics, but also related areas, as long as their main rules are related to one or more goals of the CAP as defined in Article 39 TFEU.[4] Support for sustainable agriculture throughout the European Union has been added to the traditional political goals as defined in Article 39 TFEU, like the guaranteed availability of food supplies.

These goals have not changed and sustainability is not something entirely new. For a long time we know that the unbridled use of agricultural practices is unsustainable.

The CAP is composed of two pillars with specific goals. The first pillar regulates the direct payment system: the farmers are paid per hectare of farmland. The second pillar includes specific payments and programmes for the development of rural areas in order to promote a sustainable and environmentally friendly agriculture.

B. Greening as an instrument and the German transition

Greening is a completely new instrument of the CAP for 2020, which is regulated in Article 43 (f) Regulation (EU) 1307/2013. Similar to other regulations and regulatory instruments of the CAP, Greening has to be enacted as national law. The focus of this article will be the implementation into German law.

I. The instrument Greening

Greening is similar to Cross-Compliance; it is not an additional payment for farmers. Greening is a prerequisite for receipt of the full direct payment per hectare from the first pillar.

It became a mandatory part of direct payments to farmers. In Article 1 of Regulation (EU) 1307/2013, Greening is described as "a payment for farmers observing agricultural practices beneficial for the climate and the environment". The greening premium is 30 per cent of the total of direct payments.

Since Greening is mandatory, the direct payments should encourage a more ecologically friendly agriculture. Article 11 TFEU stipulates that en-

---

4 Ines Härtel, 'Agrarrecht' in Matthias Ruffert (ed), *Enzyklopädie des Europarechts*, vol 5 (Nomos 2013) § 7, 395.

vironmental protection has to be considered in the policies of the European Union; this should also apply to the agricultural policy. This policy has been implemented not only through existing practices and regulations, but also through the introduction of a new measure "Greening". "Greening" was introduced in 2013 as part of the latest reform of this policy.

If Greening is described as mandatory, it does not mean that greening measures have to be used by every single farmer. It only means that Greening is mandatory for farmers who apply for direct payments from the Common Agricultural Policy. However Greening is required in order to receive these payments.

As nearly every farmer in the European Union is already receiving direct payments, this measure has nearly the same effect as a general rule.

What is "Greening" in legal terms and what are the implications?

Regulation (EU) 1307/2013 says greening measures are practices which should take the form of simple, generalized, non-contractual and annual actions that go beyond cross-compliance and are linked to agriculture.[5]

If the regulation says that greening measures have to go beyond Cross-Compliance, then we have to take a quick look at Cross-Compliance. Cross-Compliance rules were developed from already existing specific European Union law and the standards for good agricultural and environmental practices established at the national level. A good example without any direct connection to agriculture can be found in environmental law. These rules have to be followed by everyone and they are not prerequisite for direct payments, but they can lead to extra penalties in connection with direct payments in addition to penalties following from specific laws.[6] Besides the introduction of Greening, the Cross-Compliance rules became stricter during the last reform of the CAP.

So Greening has to be more than just a regulation. Therefore legislation was developed on the content of greening measures. The most important fact is that agricultural practices should benefit the climate and the environment. Article 43 (2) Regulation (EU) 1307/2013 indicates three types

---

5 Regulation (EU) 1307/2013 of the European Parliament and of the Council of 17 December 2013 establishing rules for direct payments to farmers under support schemes within the framework of the common agricultural policy and repealing Council Regulation (EC) 637/2008 and Council Regulation (EC) 73/2009 [2013] OJ L 347/608, recital 37.
6 Christian Busse, 'Das Instrument des Greening im Rahmen der GAP-Reform 2014/15' (2015) DVBl 337, 338.

of practices fulfilling these requirements: 1. crop diversification, 2. maintaining existing permanent grassland and 3. maintaining an ecological focus area within the agricultural area.

In addition to these three greening practices, there are also equivalent practices possible in accordance with Article 43 (3) Regulation (EU) 1307/2013. These equivalent practices shall be those which include similar practices yielding an equivalent or higher level of benefit for the climate and the environment when compared to one or several of the practices named in Article 43 (2) Regulation (EU) 1307/2013. Farmers can only decide to use equivalent practices, if these are allowed by their Member State. Therefore Member States first have to establish equivalent practices. The second step is that the European Commission has to review these planned practices and determine whether they are equivalent, and afterwards farmers could use these equivalent practices.[7] The German implementation will be described below:

In accordance with Article 43 (4) Regulation (EU) 1307/2013, the equivalent practices cannot be subject to double funding, for example, through payments from the second pillar of the CAP.

In general, all farmers have to implement greening measures, but there are some exceptions in the Regulation. Article 43 (11) Regulation (EU) 1307/2013 specifies that organic farms are automatically entitled to receive the greening premium without any further action. These farms already benefit the climate or the environment because they have to follow stricter rules for organic farming.[8]

A second group are farmers working fully or partly in areas covered by Directives 92/43/EEC, 2000/60/EC or 2009/147/EC. These farmers are exempt because some greening action may not be in accordance with these directives and farmers should not be disadvantaged as compared to farmers in other areas.[9]

---

7 Regulation (EU) 1307/2013 of the European Parliament and of the Council of 17 December 2013 establishing rules for direct payments to farmers under support schemes within the framework of the common agricultural policy and repealing Council Regulation (EC) 637/2008 and Council Regulation (EC) 73/2009 [2013] OJ L 347/608, art 43 (8).

8 Christian Busse, 'Das Instrument des Greening im Rahmen der GAP-Reform 2014/15' (2015) DVBl 337, 340.

9 Ibid.

The last exception is for farms falling under the small farmers' scheme. This exception is made in Article 61 (3) Regulation (EU) 1307/2013 regarding rules for small farms. These farms only receive a low direct payment, and Member States should reduce the administrative costs linked to management and control of direct support.[10]

Beyond these exceptions, there are also specific rules for farms holding a high proportion of permanent grassland as specified in Article 44 (3) Regulation (EU) 1307/2013.

In cases of serious infringements against greening requirements, the entire premium can even be reduced by more than 30 per cent, which amounts to the total of the greening premium.

Besides the intention to promote a more ecological agriculture, Greening is also a way to make agricultural policy conform to European competition law.[11] This can be obtained by paying farmers for additional environmental services. The idea of greening measures is that farmers take environmentally-friendly actions which exceed the regular farming standards. They receive payments for these ecological and public services, and in this way these payments are neither special favours, nor subsidies.[12]

II. German implementation

The CAP is formulated in the form of a regulation (EU). In accordance with Article 288 TFEU, regulations are binding in their entirety and directly applicable in all Member States. This would lead to the conclusion that, at the national level, no special implementation is needed. However, an exception to the binding character and application of this Regulation is possible, if a Member State can choose between different possibilities

---

10 Regulation (EU) 1307/2013 of the European Parliament and of the Council of 17 December 2013 establishing rules for direct payments to farmers under support schemes within the framework of the common agricultural policy and repealing Council Regulation (EC) 637/2008 and Council Regulation (EC) 73/2009 [2013] OJ L 347/608, recital 54.

11 José Martinez, 'Das Greening der Gemeinsamen Agrarpolitik' (2013) NuR 690, 692.

12 Ibid.

named in the Regulation.[13] If we consider the character of the legislation made for the CAP, it has the character of a Regulation. On the other hand, this Regulation includes a few rules allowing Member States to decide between different options named in the Regulation.

Not only within the European Union a legal multi-level system exists, but also in Germany such a multi-level system exists in form of a national level and a level of the individual federal states. This influences the German implementation due to different legislative authorities at the national level and at the federal state level.

The German national legislature has implemented the Regulation (EU) 1307/2013 of the CAP in the so-called "Direktzahlungen-Durchführungsgesetz (DirektZahlDurchfG)" (Implementing Law concerning direct payments to farmers within the support system of the Common Agricultural Policy). This EU legislation also provided some specifications which are delegated to the Member States. In the implementation of the second pillar of the CAP, the various federal states are more integrated and are also responsible for creating plans to support rural development.[14]

The implementation of Greening into German law is specified in § 13 f. DirektZahlDurchfG. Germany has chosen the regional model for direct payments. The regions coincide with the territories of the federal states. The amount of direct payments per hectare is different in each region. This regional model is not used to determine greening premiums. In accordance with § 13 paragraph 1 DirektZahlDurchfG, the amount of the greening premium is the same within the entire German territory.

The German implementation also includes regulations on greening practices. One interesting Regulation is § 14 DirektzahlDurchfG, which prohibits the use of equivalent practices in Germany. Regulation (EU) 1307/2013 names three greening practices: 1. crop diversification, 2. maintaining existing permanent grassland and 3. having an ecological focus area within the agricultural area. These practices have to be allowed and used in every Member State. Besides the standard practices, the EU

---

13 Christian König, 'Gesetzgebung' in Reiner Schulze / Manfred Zuleeg / Stefan Kadelbach (eds), *Europarecht - Handbuch für die deutsche Rechtspraxis* (2nd edn, Nomos 2010) § 43.

14 Ines Härtel, 'Die Gemeinsame Agrarpolitik der Europäischen Union im föderalrechtlichen Mehrebenenverbund' in Vorstand des Europäischen Zentrums für Föderalismus-Forschung Tübingen (ed), *Jahrbuch des Föderalismus 2014* (Nomos 2014) 269, 277 ff.

Regulation allows equivalent practices instead of the three standard practices as long as these practices are similar and yield an equivalent or higher benefit for the climate and the environment compared to one or more of the standard practices.

The German legislature decided not to allow equivalent practices. These practices have to have an equivalent, or higher level of benefit for the environment, compared to one or several of the standard practices. This means that these practices are limited in number.[15] A second reason is that equivalent practices cannot receive funding from two sources. This could happen when receiving funding through the second pillar of the CAP for environmentally-friendly measures by the farmers. The conclusion of the legislature was that equivalent practices would not have any positive effect for the farmers.[16]

An argument against this view is Article 43 (5) Regulation (EU) 1307/2013; this Article stipulates that Member States may "restrict" the farmers in their use of equivalent practices. The word "restrict" does not have the same meaning as the word "prohibit".[17] Restrict means that some of the equivalent practices may not be allowed, but other practices are allowed. Otherwise, the Regulation should stipulate that Member States can disallow equivalent practices in their entirety.

Other rules specify that it is not mandatory to implement or apply these instruments as stated in Article 11 (3) Regulation (EU) 1307/2013. Also, Article 43 (8) Regulation (EU) 1307/2013 states that Member States shall notify the Commission which equivalent practices they will allow.

This part of the Greening Regulation is not as clear as it should be. If some Member States allow equivalent practices, and others do not, then this Regulation cannot reach its goal and the word "restrict" can be misunderstood.

In this area, the German implementation is characterized by avoiding administrative expenses. This tendency to avoid administrative expenses

---

15 BR-Drs. 82/14 of 28 February 2014, 34.

16 Ibid.

17 'restrict, v.' (OED Online, Oxford University Press June 2015) <http://www.oed.com/view/Entry/164018?isAdvanced=false&result=2&rskey=A4xrVX&> accessed 27 July 2015.

can also be noticed in other parts of the German implementation; in this way, some options allowed by the EU Regulations are not used.[18]

C. Summary

Greening is one of the biggest, and therefore, most discussed reforms in the CAP. Infringements on greening rules can be punished by reducing the direct premium by the total of the greening premium which amounts to 30%. This is considerably more than already existing penalties which can be applied in case of infringement of Cross-Compliance rules. These penalties enhance the power of this new instrument in its efforts to ensure ecological standards.

The German model of disallowing equivalent greening practices limits farmers in their choice of greening practices. Another point is that in its efforts to reach the main goal of the CAP, a more ecological use of agricultural land, Germany did not use all greening practices and created more restrictions for the farmers in the use of their land. Equivalent practices could be a way to choose the most efficient practices for different farming areas, however, the introduction of equivalent practices can increase administrative expenses without proper benefits for farmers and or the environment.[19]

The CAP provided incentives for a market-oriented agriculture, while Greening is a step towards a more ecologically focused agriculture. Through public approval for direct payments to farmers, the CAP will become a matter of public and political discussion. This will not be the last reform, and we can only guess how the actual CAP and Greening will work in practice.

---

18 Christian Busse, 'Das Instrument des Greening im Rahmen der GAP-Reform 2014/15' (2015) DVBl 337, 344.
19 BR-Drs. 82/14 of 28 February 2014, 34.

§ 14 The abuse clause in context of the redistribution premium – a failure in its construction

Jan Hindahl

A. Introduction

The aim of the Common Agricultural Policy (CAP) is, according to Article 39 (1) TFEU, increasing agricultural productivity and agricultural income, stabilization of markets, ensuring food supply and reasonable prices for consumers.[1] In 2013, the Common Agricultural Policy was reformed by the European Union.[2] This reform lays down new rules for agricultural economic law from the time 2014-2020. For this reform, it was originally planned on EU level that direct payment to the farmers should be reduced by at least 5% for that part of the amount exceeding 150,000 €. Even if this plan found its way into EU-Regulation 1307/2013, Member States would get the option not to cut the direct payments, but instead to introduce a redistribution payment.[3] Due to much pressure on the German Government from the German farmers association, Germany stood up for the option of a redistribution payment and made use of it in Germany.[4] Germany does this by paying a nationwide premium of 50 € for the first 30 hectares and another 30 € for an additional 16 hectares. It does not distinguish between small and large farmers, and it will be paid to every

---

1 Christian Busse / Jens Haarstrich, *Agrarförderrecht, einschließlich EU-Primärrecht, EU-Kartellrecht und EU-Gerichtsbarkeit* (Berliner Wissenschafts-Verlag 2012) 25; Mechtild Düsing in Matthias Dombert / Karsten Witt et al (eds), *Münchener Anwaltshandbuch Agrarrecht* (C.H. Beck 2011) § 26 recital 119.
2 Ines Härtel, 'Die Gemeinsame Agrarpolitik (GAP) der Europäischen Union nach 2013 in juristischer Perspektive' in Landwirtschaftliche Rentenbank (ed), *Die Gemeinsame Agrarpolitik der Europäischen Union nach 2013* (Schriftenreihe der Rentenbank, vol 27, 2011) 42.
3 Ines Härtel, 'Die Gemeinsame Agrarpolitik der Europäischen Union im föderalrechtlichen Mehrebenenverbund' in Europäisches Zentrum für Föderalismus-Forschung Tübingen (ed), *Jahrbuch des Föderalismus 2014* (Nomos 2014) 269, 277 ff.
4 Ibid.

farmer for the first 46 hectares. However, in regard to this rule, the prob-lem arose that the farmers might possibly split their companies to be able to get more out of the redistribution premium programme, than they would get if they operated their farm as a single company. Because of this abuse risk, an abuse clause was added to the redistributive payment programme. However, the abuse clause was put in a legal framework that can be sub-ject to many legal problems, as is outlined below.

B. The anti-abuse clause against the abuse of the redistributive payment

Germany has used the leeway, which was given to the Member States in Article 11 (3) of Regulation 1307/2013 to introduce a redistributive pay-ment (see above) (§ 21 Direktzahlungen-Durchführungsgesetz– Direkt-ZahlDurchfG (Implementing Law concerning direct payments to farmers within the support system of the Common Agricultural Policy)). To avoid abuse in the form of splitting one farm/company into several with the aim to gain more of the redistribution premium, Germany introduced in § 24 DirektZahlDurchfG, an abuse clause that is based on Article 41 (7) Regu-lation (EU) 1307/2013[5]. This clause states "Member States shall ensure that no advantage (…) is granted to farmers in respect of whom it is estab-lished that, after 18 October 2011, they divided their holding for the sole purpose of benefiting from the redistributive payment"[6].

I. Interpretation of the anti-abuse clause of § 24 DirektZahlDurchfG

The abuse clause states that the granting of a redistribution premium is ex-cluded if a farmer has split his company after 18/10/2011 proven to be for the sole purpose to enjoy a redistribution premium.

---

5 Regulation (EU) 1307/2013 of the European Parliament and of the Council of 17 December 2013 establishing rules for direct payments to farmers under support schemes within the framework of the common agricultural policy and repealing Council Regulation (EC) 637/2008 and Council Regulation (EC) 73/2009 [2013] OJ L 347/608.
6 Ibid art 41 (7).

1. Granting a redistribution premium

The abuse facts have not been well formulated linguistically. § 21 Direkt-ZahlDurchfG states that upon request, each farmer will get a redistribution premium per activated pecuniary claim of not more than 46 hectares The redistribution premium is laid down in § 21 DirektZahlDurchfG, which bears the heading "redistribution premium". So there is no need for splitting farms to benefit from the redistribution premium for the first 46 hectares in this respect, an abuse is not possible. So an abuse can only occur in that a farmer uses a company split to get more payment entitlements of the redemption premium than without splitting a company.

The wording is based on Article 41 (7) Regulation (EU) 1307/2013 which contains provisions concerning the abuse clause as well as other provisions on the design of the redistribution premium.

In the explanatory memorandum to § 24 DirektZahlDurchfG only the obligation laid down in Regulation (EU) 1307/2013 to implement such a clause is referenced.

To give the Union law maximum effectiveness (*effet utile*), the abuse clause can only be interpreted teleologically in a way that cases should be included, where a company split takes place, to be eligible for a redistribution premium for additional pecuniary claims.

This interpretation, however, raises the question of the sanction: "granting a premium redistribution is excluded". It seeks to combat the misuse of company split to increase the distributing premium. Shall only the abuse brought by trying to gain further distribution premium be excluded, or is the abuse perpetrator excluded from the redistribution premium that he would have received without company split? The text seems to favor the latter. That interpretation is also the aim of more effective sanctions.

2. Company split

The abuse fact is linked to company splitting without defining this. In the legal acts passed, no binding definition is given. Therefore, the question arises whether this concept is perhaps already defined for other areas of law, or how this concept could be defined.

a. Definition of the Federal Fiscal Court

The Federal Fiscal court has defined the concept of company splitting for tax structures as follows: A company splitting is an institute in which a company is divided into two or more separate legal entities, where the units involved remain personally and economically bound together.[7] A company split exists when a company leaves a substantial operating basis to a commercially active denominator or corporation for use, and the original company dominates the new company, which is the case when both a transfer of essential operating base as well as a majority of the voting rights of the partnership or corporation takes place.[8] This would limit the term "company split" to a very limited scope, and does not take into account the fact that the company split is not used to limit the scope since this is done for the fact that the company split is used "solely" for the purpose of obtaining the redistribution premium. Both of these restrictions would make the abuse clause ineffective, which is not intended.

b. Definition according to the German Enterprise Transformation Law

Another option could be the Enterprise Transformation Law. This law recognizes the division of legal entities under § 123 Umwandlungsgesetz – UmwG (Transformation Act). There are three ways for a split: the breakdown, the secession and the spin-off.[9] Splitting is a conversion process with the objective of total or partial distribution of the assets to one or more different (existing or newly founded) companies.[10] Here, it comes to a transfer of ownership shares (conceivable only where one of the individual properties in its substantial elements in the sub-category of outsourcing) is, by way of singular succession, without individual acts of trans-

---

7 Decision of the Federal Finance Court (BFH) of 8 November 1971 – GrS 2/71, BFHE 103, 440 (443 f.).

8 Ibid 444.

9 Arndt Stengel in Johannes Semler / Arndt Stengel (eds), *Umwandlungsgesetz, mit Spruchverfahrensgesetz* (3rd edn, C.H. Beck 2012) § 123 recital 11; Frank Wardenbach in Martin Henssler / Lutz Strohn, *Kommentar zum Gesellschaftsrecht* (2nd edn, C.H. Beck 2014) § 123 UmwG recital 4.

10 Arndt Stengel in Johannes Semler / Arndt Stengel (eds), *Umwandlungsgesetz, mit Spruchverfahrensgesetz* (3rd edn, C.H. Beck 2012) § 123 recital 12.

fer.[11] But that Transformation Law only allows certain entities as the transferor, transferee or the new legal entity in a fixed upper limit of split types (§§ 123 et seq. UmwG). The individual farmer and the civil code GbR partnership are not among them. These organizational forms for agriculture are, however, the most important.[12] A recourse to the conversion law does not help define "company split" within the meaning of the Direkt-ZahlDurchfG.

c. Independent definition of operating division within the meaning of the DirektZahlDurchfG

First, it needs to be considered in an independent definition that a definition must ensure the effectiveness of the scheme; nevertheless, it must not go beyond the wording. It makes sense, therefore, to first have the problematical cases in mind, which might be of importance. Problematical are mainly the following cases.

aa. Full preservation of the original company

The original company remains legally intact. A newly founded company gets only land on lease to cultivate. The land on lease is for the original company no longer available, and the company loses pecuniary claims for these areas. A loss of fixed assets is not connected to the lease, because the land has not been sold. The original company was not split, but continues to exist in its entirety. The new company is the owner of its own payment entitlements and it (in addition to the original company) receives the redistribution premium. If the leasing of land is not covered by the concept of company split, then this would mean that the abuse clause can be relatively easily circumvented.

---

11 Andreas Heidinger in Peter Limmer / Christian Hertel / Norbert Frenz / Jörg Mayer (eds), *Würzburger Notarhandbuch* (3rd edn, Carl-Heymanns Verlag 2012) 2693.
12 Rolf Steding, 'Die Rechtsnatur der GbR – ein aktuelles Streitthema' (2000) 7 BzAR 256.

bb. Shareholder in the newly founded company

Another issue is the extent to which the shareholders of the old company may or must be the same shareholders of a newly established company in order to establish an abuse, since the lease to a different company may lead to an increase of redistribution premium for that company if it has not yet fully exploited its total quota of 46 hectares It is undisputed that there will not be an abuse case if land is leased to someone to whom no business connection exists except for the leasing connections. The problem however arises already in the following case: The husband has run the company on his own. The wife now receives a partial area and produces on her area agricultural products. The wife cannot be denied the right to engage in agriculture. She then also has the right to the same agricultural subsidies as any other farmer. The family relationship or any other close relationship does not allow concluding that the wife got involved in agriculture only to increase the redistribution payment to her and her husband.

cc. Definition by Steffens

Steffens defines a company split as a division to at least two new separate farmers or to the original and at least one new separate farmer.[13] The problem with this definition is, first, that it is incomprehensible, because a company cannot be split into two independent farmers. It is true that after a company split, a new owner is required, and at least, for part of the pecuniary claims, otherwise the redistribution premium received for the pecuniary claims does not rise. The problem with the above-mentioned definition is that it is inaccurate and it is not possible to separate sharply between company splits, because a lot can be included under a company split. Does the company need to lose the ownership of the land? Is a lease possibly enough? Is it a company split if a parent company is established with two subsidiary companies? For all these questions, this definition does not give an answer, so there remains the need to try to answer these questions.

---

13 Wilfried Steffens, 'Erst prüfen, dann Anträge ausfüllen' (2014) 38 Land&Forst 86, 87.

dd. More thoughts on a definition

A company split must have as its objective, by definition, a division of the original assets of the company. The received payment entitlements cannot be looked at alone. Against this argumentation is the fact that, on the one hand, a company exists of much more wealth than just the payment entitlements. On the other hand, one could then use the concept of "payment entitlements" from the beginning for the abuse clause.[14] Additionally, occasional trading of the accompanying land area is possible under the CAP reform for only payment entitlements. If splitting is focused on the original assets of the operation, then the concept of a splitting of the operation, with a full retention of the original operation, cannot be relevant. If the company leases the operational land area and receives in return for the leasing of the area and the entitlement claim, lease rental income, then it has retained its assets.

The term company split contains no indication of who may be the shareholder of the new company, so that businesses with new shareholders or farmers can fall under the term company split. § 23 sentence 2 Direkt-ZahlDurchfG even assumes this. This leads to the conclusion that everyone is free to run a farm, and he may also, like any other company operator, receive direct payments in their entirety. To capture this case of abuse (see above) in a definition is difficult, because it has to tread a thin line because both the constitutional law under Article 3 GG and the GRC under Article 20 GRC[15] include equal treatment principles. Equivalent treatment might be violated if one tries to include the shareholder issues in the definition. Therefore, it is better to leave this problem completely out of the definition since this entails the risk that circumventing will then again take place. However, this will result in a significant administrative burden, because the Agricultural Chambers will have to examine whether a possible abuse may be present in every sale to strangers.

---

14 Ingo Glas, 'Zahlungsansprüche: 2015 wird neu verteilt' (2014) 7 top agrar 42, 44.
15 The GRC is relevant here, because it is performed with the DirektZahlDurchfG Union law and thus the scope of Article 51 GRC is opened.

3. Evidence for the sole purpose of obtaining the premium redistribution

This part is not unclear by its meaning, but it is difficult to prove this pre-requisite which shall be discussed below.

II. Requirements to meet the anti-abuse clause

1. The eligible farm

The maximum entitlement bonus that can be received by a farmer redistribution premium per year is ((30 hectares x 50 €) + (16 hectares x 30 €)) 1,980 €. Throughout the programme period until 2020 this can add up to a total of 9,900 €, which may be granted to a farm. So a farm with 92 hectares could get up to 9,900 € with a company split. For larger agricultural companies, which have a more hectares and rented land, this amount could be increased by not only splitting the farm once but also by doing several splits, thereby increasing the claim for the redistribution premium. However, a splitting is connected, especially for larger companies, with costs. Trading companies would be established by a notarial deed and entered into the commercial register.[16] For other forms of society, a social contract would have to be created, which must be created by a legally trained person in the case of absence of sufficient legal knowledge. This again leads to costs. If renting were not recognized as a company split, land would have to be transferred, which needs to be done by a deed and be registered in the land book. This in turn causes costs. Fixed assets, if wanted, would have to be split among the companies, which may lead to the discovery of hidden reserves and thus trigger chargeable tax events.[17] A company split for larger agricultural company with extensive surface equipment and appropriate fixed assets for the management of these, needs to be well thought out in tax law and civil law terms. The associated costs and risks could discourage abuse. The greater the number of companies resulting from the splitting, the greater is the risk that the redistribution bonus would not be paid.

---

16 See § 105 (2) HGB, § 161 (2) HGB, § 7 GmbHG.
17 Hans Günter Christoffel, 'Steuerfalle Stille Reserven, Folgen der Aufdeckung und Vermeidungsstrategien' (2012) 2 <http://www.datev.de/portal/ShowContent.do?pid=dpi&cid=204314> accessed 25 November 2014.

2. Company splitting proven to be only for the sole purpose to enjoy the premium redistribution

It remains to be clarified when it is proven that a company splitting took place for the sole purpose to enjoy the redistribution premium. The problem that arises here is the following: The federal states in the form of county units of the Chambers of Agriculture will be responsible for the examination of applications for the issue of the redistribution premium.[18] Under examination by these chambers, they would then safely conclude that a company split had only the purpose to increase the redistributive premium. This test will be difficult. In the previous collective applications for allocation of payment entitlements and the redistribution premium, the farmer had to give only information about the company and the date of establishment.[19] Inasmuch as a company foundation took place after 18/10/2011, he also has to affirm that the division is not made only for the purpose to benefit from the redistributive payment. Information on what purpose the company was founded for, or why the company split was carried out, the applicant must not give.[20] The redistribution premium that was granted in 2014 corresponds to the provisions for the years 2015-2020 redistribution premium,[21] so, therefore, it is assumed that the application forms will be, for this reason, similar to the one from 2014. The Chamber of Agriculture can use this information to first determine which companies have emerged through a company split after the date 18/10/2011 and could thus be candidates for potential abuse. The Member States are, in accordance with Article 41 (7) Regulation (EU) 1307/2013, obliged to take precautions to ensure that abuse does not take place. Of the applicants who are farmers of a company that was founded after the 18/10/2011, it is re-

---

18 See Landwirtschaftskammer Nordrhein-Westfalen, 'Antrag auf Betriebsprämie' (2014) <https://www.landwirtschaftskammer.de/foerderung/betriebspraemien/verfahren/antragsverfahren.htm> accessed 25 November 2014.
19 Sammelantrag Agrarförderung und Agrarumweltmaßnahmen 2014 des Landes Niedersachsen und des Landes Bremen <http://www.sla.niedersachsen.de/portal/live.php?navigation_id=34124&article_id=121197&_psmand=194> accessed 19 November 2014.
20 See Sammelantrag 2014, Anlage C, Umverteilungsprämie <http://www.landwirtschaftskammer.de/foerderung/formulare/sammelantrag-2014-anlage-c.pdf> accessed 18 November 2014.
21 See § 2 Umverteilungsprämiengesetz (UmvertPrämG) and § 21 Direktzahlungen-Durchführungsgesetz (DirektZahlDurchfG).

quired that they make a declaration in which they affirm that the establishment or splitting did not take place only for the purpose of obtaining the redistribution premium. This does not provide such an ensuring note. Whoever wants to act unlawfully, will also posses enough criminal energy to make a declaration with justification circumventing the law. The Chambers of Agriculture must therefore check for which purpose the company split was carried out.

First, it would be possible to refer to the registered corporate purpose or to the shareholders' agreement of a GbR. The commercial register identifies the corporate purpose.[22] However, no shareholder will register a company with an unlawful corporate purpose: "This company serves to benefit from the redistribution premium". So, the corporate purpose will have no reliable information for determining whether abuse took place. In agricultural enterprises, corporate purpose will regular be a form of production of agricultural products. So the corporate purpose does not help much.

Perhaps the purpose could be determined by other criteria. A first indication of an abuse may be, if from the original company, two companies are made, and by the new company formation, the same company form is selected and the same people are the shareholders. In addition, the number of hectares transferred can provide information on the purpose. A split that leads to an optimal allocation of obtaining the redistribution premium redistribution suggests, at least, that the redistribution premiums played a role. Also the management of land in a comparison before and after the company split would give an indication.

It will turn, however, on the question of when there are sufficient indications to ensure that the evidence of a misuse is present. During a presentation of lawyer Jens Haarstrich on the CAP reform on the German agricultural Rights Day in Goslar on 09/29/2014, he made clear that a legal advisor ought to be able to carry forward sufficient arguments for a company split that show it did not take place only for the purpose of obtaining the redistribution premium redistribution. This shows the difficulty associated with this restriction, and how easily this clause may lose its effectiveness. Because, literally, one further purpose for the splitting is already enough for no abuse to have taken place. Indisputably, arguments should only be relevant that can withstand a test on their traceability. Based on

---

22 Lutz Schade, *Handels- und Gesellschaftsrecht* (2nd edn, Verlagsgruppe Hüthig-Jehle-Rehm 2012) 44.

the abuse clause, an abuse has not taken place, if only one further reason for the chosen restructuring holds up.

3. Recourse to § 42 Tax Code (AO)

§ 42 AO (Abgabenordnung – AO (Tax Law)) regulates the abuse of legal designed possibilities to circumvent tax laws.[23] Pursuant to § 42 AO, an abuse exists, if an inappropriate legal form is chosen, not intended by law, which, in comparison to a taxable or third party appropriate form, would lead to an advantage. A tax is a cash payment without a right to individual return.[24] A subsidy is a public support with the help of public funds.[25] A subsidy is exactly the reverse of a tax. Therefore, § 42 AO is particularly interesting for the concretizing of the abuse facts. A misuse of the legally possible form can always be considered if a scheme is chosen which appears uneconomical, cumbersome, complicated, artificial, unnecessary, ineffective or nonsensical without considering the tax benefits.[26] These criteria can also be used for examining an abuse in the case of the redistribution premium. To apply § 42 AO, the prerequisites for an analogy need to be given. For that there needs to be a loophole. A loophole is already not present, since the abuse can be determined on the basis of subjective criteria (see above). However, even here the word "abuse" is used, so that nothing prevents using the above criteria according to § 42 AO for an additional support for an examination of an abuse under § 24 DirektZahl-DurchfG.

---

23 Eckart Ratschow in Franz Klein (ed), *Kommentar zur Abgabenordnung - AO* (12th edn, C.H. Beck 2014) § 42 recital 1; Ulrich Koenig in Armin Pahlke / Ulrich Koenig (eds), *Kommentar zur Abgabenordnung* (2nd edn, C.H. Beck 2009) § 42 recital 1.
24 Joachim Lang in Klaus Tipke / Joachim Lang (eds), *Steuerrecht* (21st edn, Otto Schmidt Verlag 2013) § 3 recital 13.
25 Ibid.
26 Eckart Ratschow in Franz Klein (ed), *Kommentar zur Abgabenordnung* (12th edn, C.H. Beck 2014) § 42 recital 48.

C. Conclusion

The application of the abuse clause will be an individual decision, which is difficult to predict, since it is difficult to predict the existence of the conditions based on predictable criteria. For the affected shareholder, it means legal uncertainty, and not security, where the abuse clause is relevant when the reason for the company division is to obtain the redistribution premium. The fact that the EU saw the need for the implementation of a mandatory abuse clause is understandable. The cases of abuse in the last funding period were notable. However, with this abuse clause, more problems are created than solved. For companies that are planning a company split, it represents a significant element of uncertainty. It was attempted to consider the entrepreneurial freedom under this scheme. However, there has been a failure to create an abuse clause which allows certainly beforehand to determine whether a company split is subject to the abuse clause or not. The potential cases will truly be limited, since the increased redistribution premium may outweigh the costs of operating splitting only for a few companies. This clause is also ineffective, as it can be relatively easily circumvented. In the agricultural chambers, this abuse clause will lead to considerable inspection expenses, which will not be outweighed by the abuse prevented. The decision not to follow the proposal by the EU to cut direct payments at 150,000 € to have yielded to the pressure of individual associations and a few agricultural corporations, by instead granting a distributing premium, is a political one and will not be discussed here. However, the configuration of the distribution premium with the abuse clause has not been successful. Whether cases of company splitting will increase in the future, will be seen as time passes.

To date, no regulations for the abuse clause have been adopted. This raises the concern that it may lead to a different application of the anti-abuse clause in the federal states, and it is up to the courts to contribute through individual decisions to concretize the abuse clause. Legislators will not take the trouble to clarify the abuse clause and use a different choice of words than those found in Regulation (EU) 1307/2013, because of the risk that the Commission could accuse Germany that the implementation has not been compliant with the EU Regulation act.

§ 15 Contractual relations on the EU agricultural market in the context of food security and production risk [1]

Izabela Lipińska

A. Introduction

This paper focuses on the relations between participants of the agricultural market in relation to acquiring resources for their further processing and the production of food products. It relates to contractual relations between, among others, agricultural producers, purchasing stations or processors. Their significant role was noticed by the legislator in the course of reforms of the Common Agricultural Policy, creating a new policy for the years 2014-2020. Due to the role that agricultural producers play in the face of liberalization of the European market, including limiting some market-orientated instruments, the legislator has noticed the need to give them special protection [2].

As a result of the reform, the agricultural market has started to become a complex system functioning as part of food supply chains. Its initial and, at the same time, one of the most important elements is an agricultural producer. It is the agricultural producer that has to take decisions about producing agricultural raw materials as well as obtaining their optimal quantity and quality. At the same time, the position of a farmer as a market participant is getting weaker and weaker. Depending on the production direction, the farmer is not always capable of keeping up with changes on the market and adjusting production to them. This results from a long and more and more complex production process, unstable state policy as well as from the production risk. The risk is connected mainly with agricultural producers being highly affected and not resistant to external factors which are beyond their control. These factors include, among other things,

---

1 The article was prepared under research grant OPUS n 2013/09/B/HS5/00683: Legal instruments of risk management in agriculture production, funded by the National Science Centre.
2 SAEPR/FAPA, *Wspólna Polityka Rolna jako europejska polityka żywnościowa, - Common Agricultural Policy as European Food Policy* (Warszawa 2011) 5 ff.

changing weather conditions (e.g. draught, hail, and flood) and animal and plant diseases. A farmer is becoming less and less independent in his actions. The production process is, to a vast extent, shaped by accepted obligations towards the agri-food industry. The obligations are laid down by legal regulations which shape the legal structure of the agricultural market.

The issue in question has been spotted by the European Union legislator who enacted specific regulations relating to concluding production contracts on the milk market during the reform in 2012[3]. Those regulations were supposed to enhance the sense of responsibility of commercial entities in the milk chain and to make them more aware of how important it is to respond to signals coming from the market as well as to improve the transmission of prices and to adapt supply to demand, and to help eliminate some unfair business practices[4]. Some legislative assumptions relating to organising the milk market have been transferred to other sectors.

The purpose of this paper is to indicate the role of the legislator in shaping production contracts on the EU market, in particular to show the scope of the act in question, its subject, typology, and function. The article also presents relevant legal and organizational solutions in Polish legislation in connection with the reform of the Common Agricultural Policy.

There are many reasons to raise that subject. To begin with, proper relations among market participants contribute to achieving one of the main goals of the EU policy, i.e. ensuring the safety of food. It is a very broad concept and may be analysed from many perspectives[5]. Firstly, it refers to securing a necessary amount of food on the internal market which fulfils food needs of consumers (safety of supplies). Secondly, it is closely connected with production capabilities of agricultural producers and the income they acquire (production safety). Thirdly, it is influenced by some legislative solutions the direct aim of which is to shape the agricultural market in such a way so that it is able to achieve its basic aims and be affected to the least possible extent by the production risk. The risk shapes both the safety of production and of supplies. As noted by Katarzyna Leśkiewicz, food safety in the legal context can be understood as an opti-

---

3 Regulation (EU) 261/2012 of the European Parliament and of the Council of 14 March 2012 amending Council Regulation (EC) 1234/2007 as regards contractual relations in the milk and milk products sector [2012] OJ L 94/38.

4 Ibid recital 8.

5 Kerstin Mechlem, 'Food Security and the Right to Food in the Discourse of the United Nations' (2004) 10 (5) European Law Journal 631.

mal state assumed by the legislator which should be achieved in compliance with relevant regulations of international, EU and domestic law[6].

Currently, food safety constitutes a key challenge for agriculture not only in the EU but all over the world[7]. According to the FAO, by 2050 the number of the world's population will have increased from 7 billion to 9 billion and the demand for food will have doubled. That is why the EU should keep contributing to the food supplies in the world and give special care to agricultural producers.

The main method applied in this work was a descriptive method and a dogmatic analysis of normative acts. Reference books and international analyses and reports were also used.

B. Contractual relations on the EU agricultural market

During many years of the functioning of the EU market, the legislator has not much interfered in the process of shaping contractual relations in the field of agricultural production. No classification has been made so far. The legal scope of these relations has not been specified either.

Legal acts which regulate the relations on the agricultural market usually use the term "delivery" which should be understood as a delivery contract of a particular raw material, for the production of e.g. sugar, made between a seller and an enterprise[8]. By defining a contract in such a brief way, the legislator gives the parties the freedom to shape their mutual relations. Its content does not even specify whether a seller should at the same time be an agricultural producer. The role of the legislator was limited mainly to point out the need to make contracts – delivery contract implied – and to prescribe a broad legal framework without introducing unified and, at the same time, compulsory provisions in that respect. A broader

---

6 Katarzyna Leśkiewicz, 'Bezpieczeństwo żywnościowe i bezpieczeństwo żywności – aspekty prawne - Food Safety and Food Security – legal aspects' (2012) 1 (10) Przegląd Prawa Rolnego 179.

7 European Commission, 'Communication from the Commission to the Council and the European Parliament of 31 March 2010 - An EU policy framework to assist developing countries in addressing food security challenges' COM (2010) 127 final.

8 Regulation (EU) 1308/2013 of the European Parliament and of the Council of 17 December 2013 establishing a common organisation of the markets in agricultural products and repealing Council Regulations (EEC) 922/72, (EEC) 234/79, (EC) 1037/2001 and (EC) 1234/2007 [2013] OJ L 347/671, appendix II.

definition of the delivery contract was used in economic and legal reference books[9]. They understand it as the whole system of production and supply of agricultural and horticultural produce by farmers or primary (initial) producers based on a so-called "advance contract". Under the advance contract the "recipient" provides a farmer with proper seed material, offers consulting and technical services and the possibility to get credit for the production. An agricultural producer, in turn, produces a pre-arranged amount of agricultural products of a pre-arranged quality which is to be "sold" to the recipient at a pre-arranged price. Although reference books use the term "sales", performing such a contract is actually about handing over the object of the contract.

According to the definition created by the Food and Agriculture Organisation of the United Nations (FAO), a production contract refers to a contract made between a farmer and a buyer which lays down both the terms and conditions of production and the marketing of agricultural products. That contract can also be defined as an agreement between a farmer and a manufacturing or especially marketing company in respect of the production and supply of agricultural produce at a pre-arranged price and the cooperation conditions in respect of acquiring the object of the contract[10].

Italian reference books, however, define the production contract as some "relations" between an agricultural producer and a business partner. The subject of these relations is the delivery of basic agricultural production to processing plants. The contract prescribes additional obligations which go further than a regular exchange of products for monetary com-

---

9 Antonio Iannarelli, 'Contractual Relationships and Inter-firm Co-operation in the Agri-food Sector' (2011) 4 Rivista di Diritto Alimentare 4 <http://www.rivistadirittoalimentare.it/rivista/2011-04/2011-04.pdf> accessed 28 September 2015; Martin Prowse, 'Contract Farming in Developing Countries - A Review' (A Savoir 2012) 12 <http://www.afd.fr/webdav/site/afd/shared/PUBLICATIONS/RECHERCHE/Scientifiques/A-savoir/12-VA-A-Savoir.pdf> accessed 28 September 2015; Caterina Pultrone, 'An Overview of Contract Farming: Legal Issues and Challenges' (2012) 17 Uniform Law Review, Revue de Droit Uniforme, UNIDROIT 263; Charles Eaton / Andrew W. Shepherd, 'Contract farming - Partnerships for growth' (2001) 145 FAO Agricultural Services Bulletin.
10 <www.fao.org/ag/ags/contract-farming/faq/en/> accessed 20 July 2015.

pensation and is covered by the exclusivity clause.[11] The clause includes a prohibition for a farmer to dispose of produced products except for "handing them over" to the other party.

Since the rules of contractual relations in civil law have not been included in the EU legal system, mutual relations between the parties to a production contract are shaped by legal regulations in particular countries. Particular provisions may impose a given contractual model or only suggest its use in specific cases, providing at the same time for the freedom of making contracts. For example, the Polish legislator included an agreement having production qualities in the civil code. It is a contract of delivery of pre-contracted agricultural produce under which an agricultural producer undertakes to produce and provide to a pre-contracting party, a specified amount of agricultural produce of a determined kind and the pre-contracting party undertakes to collect that produce within time limit agreed on, and performs specified additional performance if the contract or specific provisions provide for a duty to render such performance (Article 613 of Civil Code)[12]. That agreement was obligatory on the sugar and the poppy seed markets. Due to an unfavourable economic situation on some agricultural markets, however, farmers themselves are seeking to make that agreement more and more often – as it is happening on the fruit and vegetable markets. Pre-contracted deliveries of agricultural produce, being an industrial agreement, plays a significant role as it allows to spread risk of running production. As a so-called rule of shared risk says, pursuant to Article 622 of Civil Code, the consequences of failure to perform the agreement due to reasons which do not depend on a farmer, are shared by both parties.

Relations between a farmer and a purchaser of raw materials may be of various nature[13]. Reference books often present three main types – so-called spot transactions (spot markets), vertical integration contracts and quasi vertical integration contracts. Under spot transactions, the parties do

---

11 Antonio Iannarelli, 'Umowy w systemie rolno-spożywczym - Contracts in agri-food system' in Luigi Costato / Alberto Germanò / Eva Basile Rook (eds), *Trattato di Diritto Agrario* (vol. III Il diritto agroalimentare 2011) 423 ff.
12 Act of 23 April 1964 - Civil Code, Journal of Laws 1964 No 16, item 93, with latest amendments.
13 Izabela Lipińska, 'Contemporary Significance of the Cultivation Contract' (2013) 1 (27) Journal of Agribusiness and Rural Development 133 <http://www.jard.edu.pl/pub/12_1_2013.pdf> accessed 15 December 2015.

not regulate the rules of manufacturing a final product. A purchaser neither takes part in the production process nor is able to supervise it and an agricultural producer usually cannot count on any pre-production support. The opposite to spot transactions are vertical integration contracts. They include various cooperation processes between the parties. In extreme situations, an agricultural producer may at the same time be an owner of a manufacturing plant. As for quasi vertical integration contracts, the positions of parties are clearly defined and, thus, they are independent "players" but the production is organized based on pre-arranged rules. A purchaser has influence on the production process and can partially control it without the necessity to own or directly manage an agricultural farm.

In the course of the Common Agricultural Policy reform, the EU legislator modified the approach to the role of contractual relations on the agricultural market. It was noticed that in the case of some agricultural markets, those more sensitive, there is a need to introduce production contracts and to ensure their proper minimum standards. It refers, in particular, to the most protected markets so far, namely milk and sugar markets. Defined contractual relations are to contribute to a proper functioning of the internal market and common organization of the market, especially since production quotas are to be abolished – in case of milk in 2015 and sugar – 2017[14]. Moreover, the conclusion of contracts may also help to reinforce the responsibility of entities in other sectors and make them more aware of how important it is to respond to the signals from the market in order to improve the transmission of prices and adjust the supply to the demand as well as to avoid some unfair business practices. It is worth adding that terms and conditions of concluded contracts should be freely negotiated.

According to the preamble to Regulation 1308/2013, due to lack of the EU acts on formal written contracts, Member States may decide to introduce the obligation to apply such contracts under domestic law. It is a prerequisite, however, to ensure that the EU law is obeyed and the external market and common organisation of the market are not in any way interfered with. Adopted legislative solutions which leave member states a lot of freedom result from the assumption made by the European Parliament

---

14 Regulation (EU) 1308/2013 of the European Parliament and of the Council of 17 December 2013 establishing a common organisation of the markets in agricultural products and repealing Council Regulations (EEC) 922/72, (EEC) 234/79, (EC) 1037/2001 and (EC) 1234/2007 [2013] OJ L 347/671, art 124.

that in the EU there is huge diversity of economic and natural conditions which determine the agricultural production.

The first relevant legal solution was the setting of so-called "Milk Package", which was introduced under Regulation 261/2012 of 17 December 2013 establishing a common organisation of the markets of agricultural products and repealing Council Regulations (EEC) 922/72, (EEC) 234/79, (EC) 1037/2001 and (EC) 1234/2007[15]. Its aim was to guarantee a profitable production development and, consequently, ensure milk producers a proper level of living. The solutions included in the "package" are designed especially to reinforce their bargaining power against processors by giving them the possibility to collectively negotiate the milk supply contracts and to set up inter-branch organisations. Under current circumstances, with the milk quotas abolished, the contracts in question may constitute a "useful" tool for producers and processors when planning the size of the production. A debatable issue, however, is their impact on prices of raw milk in the face of global price decrease and the opening of the market.

Currently, contractual relations in the field of the agricultural production at the EU level are regulated by Council Regulation 1308/2013 of 17 December 2013 establishing a common organisation of the markets of agricultural products and repealing Council Regulations (EEC) 922/72, (EEC) 234/79, (EC) 1037/2001 and (EC) 1234/2007[16]. Thus, the legislator has confirmed the necessity to have written contracts and, at the same time, expressed the need to establish incentives for farmers to conclude contracts of common production.

As for the solutions adopted on particular markets, it needs to be noticed that, firstly, on the sugar market, pursuant to Article 125 Regulation 1308/2013, the conditions of purchasing sugar beets and sugar cane are regulated by written branch agreements. They are concluded between planters or organizations which associate planters and sugar plants or their organisations. The agreements drafted by the parties have to meet the re-

---

15 Regulation (EU) 261/2012 of the European Parliament and of the Council of 14 March 2012 amending Council Regulation (EC) 1234/2007 as regards contractual relations in the milk and milk products sector [2012] OJ L 94/38.

16 Regulation (EU) 1308/2013 of the European Parliament and of the Council of 17 December 2013 establishing a common organisation of the markets in agricultural products and repealing Council Regulations (EEC) 922/72, (EEC) 234/79, (EC) 1037/2001 and (EC) 1234/2007 [2013] OJ L 347/671.

quirements indicated in Attachment No. X and XI to the Regulation in question. First of all, they should be made in writing for a specified quantity of beet. They have to lay down the purchasing price for beet and the methods for calculating the price, the delivery manner together with the settlement for transport and collection. What is more, the agreements may be made for many years, which is obviously connected with some organisational and economic reasons. Such a solution resulted from the special nature of the sugar market and its legal organisation throughout the years.

As for the milk market, the rules of shaping contractual relations between farmers and a processor are laid down in Article 148 of Regulation 1308/2013. The legislator did not impose the obligation to conclude delivery contracts. It is left to the Member States to decide about that issue. Their obligatory nature at the level of states implies, however, that each delivery should be regulated by a written contract between the parties. In case of so-called first collectors, a Member State may stipulate that they need to submit a written offer to make a contract for raw milk delivery by farmers[17]. Both the contract and the offer must meet the requirements provided for in the Regulation in question. The EU legislator, however, does not intend to interfere with and modify the freedom of contract applicable in Member States. There is an exception to the rule concerning the deliveries to a cooperative to which a farmer belongs. In such case, a contract is not required if a statute or regulations of that cooperative include provisions of similar effects to those provided for in the contract.

If a fresh milk delivery is carried out through the agency of one or more purchasers, the domestic legislator has to determine which delivery stage or stages are covered by a contract. In order to meet legal assumptions, the contract has to be concluded prior to a delivery, be in writing, and contain specified elements which are prescribed in a quite detailed way by the EU legislator in Regulation 1308/2013. The basic element is the price for delivery or the way to establish it. The price arranged by the parties cannot be changed. It is calculated based on the combination of many factors, such as indicators reflecting the change to market conditions, the size and quality of production, composition of delivered raw milk, etc. The contract specifies the amount of milk which has to be produced, delivery dates, method of payment and other arrangements concerning the collection or

---

17 Julian T. Krzyżanowski, 'From Health Check to the Financial Perspective 2013-2020' (2013) 4 (30) 115 <http://www.jard.edu.pl/pub/9_4_2013_pl.pdf> accessed 15 December 2015.

delivery. The parties also have to decide on its duration. Since the agricultural production is characterized by high risk and uncertainty, the parties should include in the contract, clauses regulating *force majeure* or the situation where the contract is partially or fully impossible to be performed.

The manner of regulating mutual relations on the milk market leaves a lot of freedom to the parties. Normative solutions are definitely in the form of minimal standards and the parties to a contract can negotiate the particular elements. The legislator has left quite a lot of freedom to the parties to shape mutual relations on the milk market.

Providing a Member State with the possibility to decide about making obligatory written contracts under Article 168 Regulation 1308/2013, constitutes an attempt to unify some contractual rules. If delivery is carried out by one or more intermediaries it is obligatory to specify which stage or stages are covered by the contract[18]. Additionally, a Member State may establish a mediation mechanism for cases where there is no mutual agreement of the parties to conclude a contract. The contract content itself should meet general conditions which were specified in regulations on milk delivery and the minimum duration of the regulations is at least six months and cannot interfere with proper functioning of the internal market.

Pursuant to Article 168 Regulation 1308/2013, the object of a written delivery contract may cover all products produced on the EU agricultural market. If a Member State decides that it is obligatory to make contracts on a given market, it has to, at the same time, adjust its internal regulations so that it can meet the obligation to inform the Commission about adopted solutions.

C. Conclusion

In respect of securing a suitable amount of raw materials for industry and, consequently, ensuring food security – a production contract is a highly significant legal instrument. There are two levels of establishing its scope – namely the level of branch organisations and the state level. The first

---

18 A contract and/or an offer for a contract shall not be required where raw milk is delivered by a farmer to a co-operative of which the farmer is a member if the statutes of that cooperative or the rules and decisions provided for in or derived from these statutes contain provisions having similar effects.

case requires a proper balancing of the rights and leaving a specific scope of control on the part of the state.

A proper structure of a contract helps to carry out planned production, diversifies risk and guarantees a certain, pre-arranged level of income[19]. Its crucial aspects seem to include its duration and the possibility to renegotiate such elements as the price of a raw material when prices of particular production factors change. Proper formation of its elements influences the effectiveness of the actions taken by both a farmer and a processor. Making the contract, at the same time, makes it possible to implement, in the course of production, specified management mechanisms and, consequently, bring about higher effectiveness of the supply chain. It should result in the increase in cooperation between particular market participants – agricultural producers and "contracting parties".

The production contracts discussed may certainly be understood as agri-industrial contracts[20]. They, to a large extent, go beyond the applicable scope of a delivery contract. They combine a number of elements which are not only typical of the production of starting material for further processing but they also guarantee food safety. Based on the EU legal acts, it can be noticed that the legislator perceives the production contract as a very important factor in shaping the agricultural market. Thus, it seems that the role and significance of contracts in agri-business is going to increase. It helps to ensure certain stability of farming conditions for both parties, provided that negotiating powers are balanced.

19 Pavel Vavra, 'Role, Usage and Motivation for Contracting in Agriculture' (2009) 16 OECD Food, Agriculture and Fisheries Working Papers, doi: 10.1787/225036745705 <http://www.oecd.org/tad/agricultural-trade/43057136.pdf> accessed 15 December 2015.
20 Antonio Iannarelli, 'Contractual Relationships and Inter-firm Co-operation in the Agri-food Sector' (2011) 4 Rivista di Diritto Alimentare 4 <http://www.rivistadirittoalimentare.it/rivista/2011-04/2011-04.pdf> accessed 28 September 2015.

§ 16 The regulation of endocrine disruptors in plant protection products – a hazard for food safety?

Anne-Kristin Mayer

A. Introduction

Plant protection products play an important role in agriculture and society as they help to control pests and thus maintain current agriculture yields. But these products may cause harmful effects on animal or human health and may impair food safety via, for example, plant protection products residues in food. Keeping these effects in mind, the EU wants to ensure a high level of protection of both human and animal health as well as the environment, and at the same time aims to safeguard the competitiveness of community agriculture.[1] Plant protection products contain at least one active substance, which has to undergo a complex authorisation process. Nonetheless, especially representatives of civil society express concerns about the future authorisation process regarding endocrine active substances in plant protection products.[2] The European Food Safety Authority (EFSA) defines endocrine active substances as follows: "Endocrine active substances (EAS) are substances that can interact or interfere with normal hormonal action. When this leads to adverse effects, they are called endocrine disruptors."[3] Such adverse effects may be a change in the morphology, physiology, growth, development, reproduction, or life span of an organism, a system, or population that results in an impairment of func-

---

1 Regulation (EC) 1107/2009 of the European Parliament and of the Council of 21 October 2009 concerning the placing of plant protection products on the market and repealing Council Directives 79/117/EEC and 91/414/EEC [2003] OJ L 309/1 (Plant Protection Products Regulation / PPPR), Preamble.
2 Pesticide Action Network Europe, 'Endocrine disrupting pesticides' <http:// www.pan-europe.info/campaigns/pesticides/endocrine-disrupting-pesticides> gns/ pesticides/ed_pesticides.html> accessed 27 October 2015.
3 European Food Safety Authority (EFSA), 'Endocrine active substances' (20 May 2015) <http://www.efsa.europa.eu/en/topics/topic/eas.htm> accessed 20 June 2015.

tional capacity.[4] Thus, for example, exposure to endocrine substances in the womb can have life-long effects and may even have consequences for future generations.[5]

B. The legal framework concerning endocrine disruptors in plant protection products

In 2009, the EU passed legislation concerning the placing of plant protection products on the market and repealing Council Directives 79/117/EEC and 91/414/EEC.[6] This legislation introduced inter alia endocrine disrupting properties as a hazard-based "cut-off" criterion for the approval of active substances in pesticides.[7] The legal text of this Regulation states in Annex II, 3.6.5.:

> "3.6.5. An active substance, safener or synergist shall only be approved if, on the basis of the assessment of Community or internationally agreed test guidelines or other available data and information, including a review of the scientific literature, reviewed by the Authority, it is not considered to have endocrine disrupting properties that may cause adverse effect in humans, unless the exposure of humans to that active substance, safener or synergist in a plant protection product, under realistic proposed conditions of use, is negligible, that is, the product is used in closed systems or in other conditions excluding contact with humans and where residues of the active substance, safener or synergist concerned on food and feed do not exceed the default value set in accordance with point (b) of Article 18(1) of Regulation (EC) No 396/2005.
>
> By 14 December 2013, the Commission shall present to the Standing Committee on the Food Chain and Animal Health a draft of the measures concerning specific scientific criteria for the determination of endocrine disrupting

---

4 World Health Organization (WHO) / International Programme on Chemical Safety (ICPS), *IPCS Risk Assessment Terminology* (2004) 10.
5 European Commission, 'Endocrine disruptors' (22 April 2014) <http://ec.europa.eu/environment/chemicals/endocrine/index_en.htm> accessed 4 July 2015.
6 Regulation (EC) 1107/2009 of the European Parliament and of the Council of 21 October 2009 concerning the placing of plant protection products on the market and repealing Council Directives 79/117/EEC and 91/414/EEC [2003] OJ L 309/1 (Plant Protection Products Regulation / PPPR).
7 Philip Marx-Stoelting et al, 'Assessment of three approaches for regulatory decision making on pesticides with endocrine disrupting properties' (2014) 70 Regulatory Toxicology and Pharmacology 590.

properties to be adopted in accordance with the regulatory procedure with scrutiny referred to in Article 79(4)."

Due to a lot of political issues, e.g. the Transatlantic Trade and Investment Partnership (TTIP) negotiations[8] as well as practical issues[9] e.g. the time-consuming process concerning the definition of criteria for endocrine disruptors, the Commission has so far not agreed upon specific scientific criteria for the assessment of substances with endocrine disrupting properties. This delay is subject to court proceedings against the EU Commission brought by Sweden in 2014.[10] The European parliament and council joined the case in 2015.

As is apparent from the wording of Annex II 3.6.5 of the Plant Protection Products Regulation (PPPR), the current regulation is pursuing a hazard-based approach to regulating substances that interact with the endocrine system: Endocrine disrupting properties that may cause adverse effects in humans shall not be approved unless the exposure is negligible, or the substance is necessary to control a serious danger to plant health, which cannot be contained by other available means.[11] Thus active substances, synergists or safeners with endocrine disrupting properties to be used in plant protection products will not be authorised even if a risk assessment comes to the conclusion that there is no risk due to limited expo-

---

8   Zachary Davies Boren, 'TTIP controversy: EU drops pesticide laws because US says it should' *The Independent* (London, 22 May 2015) <http://www.independent.co.uk/news/world/europe/ttip-controversy-eu-drops-pesticide-laws-because-us-says-it-should-10270199.html> accessed 20 June 2015; Arthur Neslen, 'EU dropped pesticide laws due to US pressure over TTIP, documents reveal' *The Guardian* (London, 22 May 2015) <http://www.theguardian.com/environment/2015/may/22/eu-dropped-pesticide-laws-due-to-us-pressure-over-ttip-documents-reveal> accessed 20 June 2015.

9   European Commission, 'Defining criteria for identifying Endocrine Disruptors in the context of the implementation of the Plant Protection Product Regulation and Biocidal Products Regulation' (Roadmap June 2014) <http://ec.europa.eu/smart-regulation/impact/planned_ia/docs/2014_env_009_endocrine_disruptors_en.pdf> accessed 20 June 2015.

10 Case T-521/14 *Sweden v Commission* [2014] Case in progress.

11 European Commission, 'Defining criteria for identifying Endocrine Disruptors in the context of the implementation of the Plant Protection Product Regulation and Biocidal Products Regulation' (Roadmap June 2014) <http://ec.europa.eu/smart-regulation/impact/planned_ia/docs/2014_env_009_endocrine_disruptors_en.pdf> accessed 20 June 2015.

sure.[12] The pure potential hazard is sufficient not to authorise the active substance.

That is why scientists speak of "cut-off" criteria.[13] This provision shows the strong influence of the precautionary principle.[14] It is also an example of the fact that in recent years hazard classifications of chemicals within the environmental realm have become more popular in the EU as they are cost-effective and efficient.[15]

As the above indicates, it is generally important to distinguish between a hazard-based and a risk-based approach to regulating endocrine disrupting properties.

C. *Present situation and discussion regarding the handling of endocrine disrupting properties*

First of all, one has to define the terms hazard and risk since these terms often get mixed up. The International Code of Conduct on Pesticide Management 2014, published by the Food and Agriculture Organization of the United Nations (FAO) and the WHO, define these two terms as follows:

> "Hazard means the inherent property of a substance, agent or situation having the potential to cause undesirable consequences (e.g. properties that can cause adverse effects or damage to health, the environment or property)." [16.]
>
> "Risk is the probability and severity of an adverse health or environmental effect occurring as a function of a hazard and the likelihood and the extent of exposure to a pesticide."[17]

---

12 Philip Marx-Stoelting et al, 'Assessment of three approaches for regulatory decision making on pesticides with endocrine disrupting properties' (2014) 70 Regulatory Toxicology and Pharmacology 590, 591.

13 Jürgen Fluck / Kristian Fischer / Anja von Hahn (eds), *REACH + Stoffrecht Kommentar, Deutsches, Europäisches und Internationales Chemikalien-, Pflanzenschutz-, Biozid und sonstiges Stoffrecht* (lexxion 2012) 1001 recital 34 ff.; Philipp Henning / Kathrin Thiemann, 'Phase-Out und Cut-Off-Kriterien in den Zulassungsverfahren der REACH-, Biozid- und Pflanzenschutzmittel-Verordnungen' (2011) 8 Zeitschrift für Stoffrecht 142.

14 Steffen Pingen, 'Dünge- und Pflanzenschutzrecht' in Ines Härtel (ed), *Handbuch des Fachanwalts Agrarrecht* (Luchterhand 2012) ch 17 recital 77.

15 Ragnar E. Lofstedt, 'Risk versus Hazard – How to Regulate in the 21st Century' (2011) 2 European Journal of Risk Regulation 149, 153.

16 FAO/WHO, 'The International Code of Conduct on Pesticide Management' (2014) 4.

17 Ibid 7.

Ever since the formation of environmental, health and safety regulatory agencies in Europe in the 1970 s, there has been an ongoing debate about how to regulate chemicals[18]. Should regulatory decision-making be based on hazard classification alone or should there also be a full-risk assessment, meaning a scientifically based process consisting of 1) hazard identification, 2) hazard characterisation, 3) exposure assessment and 4) risk characterization[19], as well?[20] Thus far, this question cannot be answered unambiguously with regard to the handling of endocrine disruptors as there are still no uniform rules in the EU. The regulation of endocrine disruptors follows different approaches in different pieces of legislation. While the EU legislation on biocidal products (Biocidal Products Regulation (EU) No 528/2012 – "BPR")[21], on cosmetics (Cosmetics Regulation (EC) No 1223/2009)[22] and on plant protection products[23] adopt a hazard-based approach, the EU chemicals Regulation REACH (Regulation (EC) No 1907/2006 concerning the Registration, Evaluation, Authorisation and Restriction of Chemicals)[24] partly pursues a risk-based approach[25]. This

---

18   Ragnar E. Lofstedt, 'Risk versus Hazard – How to Regulate in the 21st Century' (2011) 2 European Journal of Risk Regulation 149.

19   FAO/WHO, *Principles and Methods for the Risk Assessment of Chemicals in Food, Chapter 2: Risk Assessment and its role in Risk analysis* (IPCS Environmental Health Criteria 240, 2009) 2-2.

20   Sweta Chakraborty, 'The Risk versus Hazard Debate: Reconciling Inconsistencies in Health and Safety Regulation within the UK and across the EU' (The Foundation of Law, Justice and Society 2012) <http://www.fljs.org/sites/www.fljs.org/files/publications/Chakraborty.pdf> accessed 31 July 2015.

21   Regulation (EU) 528/2012 of the European Parliament and of the Council of 22 May 2012 concerning the making available on the market and use of biocidal products [2012] OJ L 167/1.

22   Regulation (EC) 1223/2009 of the European Parliament and of the Council of 30 November 2009 on cosmetic products [2009] OJ L 342/59.

23   Plant Protection Products Regulation.

24   Regulation (EC) 1907/2006 of the European Parliament and of the Council of 18 December 2006 concerning the Registration, Evaluation, Authorisation and Restriction of Chemicals (REACH), establishing a European Chemicals Agency, amending Directive 1999/45/EC and repealing Council Regulation (EEC) 793/93 and Commission Regulation (EC) 1488/94 as well as Council Directive 76/769/EEC and Commission Directives 91/155/EEC, 93/67/EEC, 93/105/EC and 2000/21/EC [2006] OJ L 396/1.

25   European Commission, 'Defining criteria for identifying Endocrine Disruptors in the context of the implementation of the Plant Protection Product Regulation and Biocidal Products Regulation' (Roadmap June 2014) 3 <http://ec.europa.eu/smart-

becomes clear from the wording of Article 57 (f) REACH Regulation, which states:

> "The following substances may be included in Annex XIV[26] in accordance with the procedure laid down in Art. 58: substances – such as those having endocrine disrupting properties (…) – for which there is scientific evidence of probable serious effects to human health or the environment (…)".

The term "scientific evidence of probable serious effects" suggests a risk-based approach including a risk assessment. Thus, substances do not underlie the above mentioned "cut-off" criteria, but are subject to an authorisation procedure and may not be put on the market unless they have been authorised.[27] This shows that there are different approaches when dealing with endocrine disrupting properties.

To ensure a harmonised and coherent approach when dealing with endocrine disruptors in future, scientific criteria need to be established, which apply to all regulations dealing with endocrine substances. In this way, legal coherence and certainty can be achieved. A lot of work has already been done by the EFSA's scientific committee, which established an Endocrine Active Substances Task Force in 2010. In 2013, this committee published a scientific opinion on the hazard assessment of endocrine disruptors following a request from the European Commission.[28] In 2014, the European Commission launched an online consultation which was open until 16 January 2015. [29] A total of 22,411 contributions were received.[30] Nevertheless, no criteria have been agreed upon so far. Why this is the case is subject to several debates in the media. While some sources, such

---

regulation/impact/planned_ia/docs/2014_env_009_endocrine_disruptors_en.pdf> accessed 28 June 2015.

26 Annex XIV contains a list of substances subject to authorisation.
27 Philip Marx-Stoelting et al, 'Assessment of three approaches for regulatory decision making on pesticides with endocrine disrupting properties' (2014) 70 Regulatory Toxicology and Pharmacology 590, 591.
28 EFSA, 'Endocrine active substances' (20 May 2015) <http://www.efsa.europa.eu/en/topics/topic/eas.htm> accessed 28 June 2015.
29 European Commission, 'Commission consults the public on criteria to identify Endocrine Disruptors' (29 September 2014) <http://europa.eu/rapid/press-release_IP-14-1057_en.htm?locale=en> accessed 28 June 2015.
30 European Commission, 'Public consultation on defining criteria for identifying endocrine disruptors in the context of the implementation of the plant protection product regulation and the biocidal product regulation' <http://ec.europa.eu/dgs/health_food-safety/dgs_consultations/food/consultation_20150116_endocrine-disruptors_en.htm#CD> accessed 4 July 2015.

as The Guardian, quote commission officials, who say that under pressure from major chemical industry players stringent criteria were blocked[31], other sources, such as The Independent[32], make the TTIP negotiations responsible for the fact that the EU dropped criteria which could have banned 31 pesticides containing endocrine disrupting chemicals. However, a definition concerning specific scientific criteria for the determination of endocrine disrupting properties is not likely to be ready before 2017, which means a delay of four years.[33]

D. Future developments – a shift from a hazard-based to a risk-based approach?

As already mentioned above, a shift from the current hazard-based to a risk-based approach to regulate endocrine active substances may take place. In this regard, especially environmental non-governmental organisations (NGOs) argue for more hazard-based controls in the field of endocrine disrupting chemicals as they fear that "if the Commission gets the criteria 'wrong', many EDCs which can severely affect human health will slip through the regulatory net.[34] Getting the criteria "wrong" in this con-

---

31 Arthur Neslen, ' "Suppressed" EU report could have banned pesticides worth billions' *The Guardian* (London, 2 February 2015) <http://www.theguardian.com/environment/2015/feb/02/suppressed-eu-report-could-have-banned-pesticides-worth-billions> accessed 2 July 2015.

32 Zacharias Davies Boren, 'TTIP controversy: EU dropped pesticide laws because US says it should' *The Independent* (London, 22 May 2015) <http://www.independent.co.uk/news/world/europe/ttip-controversy-eu-drops-pesticide-laws-because-us-says-it-should-10270199.html> accessed 2 July 2015.

33 Henriette Jacobsen, 'EU health chief rejects "conspiracy theories" on hormone-affecting chemicals' *EurActiv* (1 June 2015) <http://www.euractiv.com/sections/science-policymaking/eu-health-chief-rejects-conspiracy-theories-hormone-affected-chemicals?__utma=1.831912285.1435912163.1435912163.1435912163.1&__utmb=1.3.9.1435912163&__utmc=1&__utmx=&__utmz=1.1435912163.1.1.utmcsr=google|utmccn=(organic)|utmcmd=organic|utmctr=(not%20provided)&__utmv=-&__utmk=100402590> accessed 3 July2015.

34 CHEMTrust (Chemicals, Health and Environment Monitoring Trust) / HEAL (Health and Environment Alliance), 'A CHEM Trust and HEAL Briefing: Challenges and solutions in the regulation of chemicals with endocrine disrupting properties' (2012) 3 <http://www.env-health.org/IMG/pdf/36-_heal_ct_edc_criteria_briefing_paper.pdf> accessed 28 June 2015.

text means to abandon the hazard-based approach and to introduce potency filters, which would introduce a risk assessment.[35] In the following, it
will be analysed whether a more risk-based approach complies with the
current wording of the Regulation and with WTO law. At the current stage
of development, the roadmap of the European Commission, which is still
subject to change, names three approaches to regulatory decision making[36]:

> "Option A: No policy change. The provisions in the BPR and the PPPR on
> regulatory consequences are not changed.
> Option B: Introduction of elements of further element of risk assessment into
> sectorial legislation where management measures for placing substances on
> the market are mainly based on hazard identification. This introduction
> should be done where necessary and desired to reduce potential socio-econo-
> mic impacts.
> Option C: Introduction of further socio-economic considerations, including
> risk-benefit analysis, into sectorial legislation, where necessary and desired,
> to allow the placing on the market of products in situations where an ED is
> essential to prevent adverse socio-economic impacts."

Option B and C, which are clearly more likely than Option A, introduce
some elements of risk assessment especially in order to reduce socio-economic impacts, such as exemptions from the ban for cases where not ap-
proving a substance would have a disproportionate negative impact on society.[37] Thus, due to the introduction of more risk elements, impacts on
the availability of substances on the market are expected to be reduced.
Nevertheless, it is not made clear whether the introduction of risk elements would lead to a full risk assessment or whether the basic approach
should still be a hazard one.[38] It seems like consideration of a risk assess-

---

35 CHEMTrust (Chemicals, Health and Environment Monitoring Trust) / HEAL
(Health and Environment Alliance), 'A CHEM Trust and HEAL Briefing: Challenges and solutions in the regulation of chemicals with endocrine disrupting properties' (2012) 7 <http://www.env-health.org/IMG/pdf/36-_heal_ct_edc_crite-
ria_briefing_paper.pdf> accessed 28 June 2015.
36 European Commission, 'Defining criteria for identifying Endocrine Disruptors in
the context of the implementation of the Plant Protection Product Regulation and
Biocidal Products Regulation' (Roadmap June 2014) 4 ff. <http://ec.europa.eu/
smart-regulation/impact/planned_ia/docs/2014_env_009_endocrine_disrup-
tors_en.pdf> accessed 20 June 2015.
37 Ibid 6.
38 See Comments of the U.S. Government, 'European Commission's Public Consultation on Defining Criteria for Identifying Endocrine Disruptors (ED's) in the

ment is limited to the derogation "whereby substances regarded as endocrine disruptors could be provided an exemption from the hazard based cut-offs by considering certain risk assessment elements."[39] This implies that there will not be a complete risk assessment. Scientists also warn that the options do not include a full risk assessment using all available data; the way the options are set out make the hazard characterisation option the preferred one.[40] This is also the view of the U.S. Government, which states that "the Commission is inclined to adopt a hazard-based approach (...), whereby endocrine active substances would be identified on the basis that they have a potential impact to the endocrine system or cause an impact on the endocrine system without further examination."[41] This approach is not only criticized by the U.S. Government, which fears the trade impacts of hazard-based "cut-off" criteria, but it is also contradictory to the opinion of the Scientific Committee (SC) of EFSA (European Food Safety Authority). The SC concurs that "uncertainties associated with the hazard-based approach for the management of an Endocrine Disruptor should be addressed by using a risk assessment approach".[42] It is also of the opinion that the future risk assessment should not only include potency as a criterion, but should also take into account the actual or predicted exposure to an endocrine disruptor.[43] As all these examples show, it is quite

---

Context of the Implementation of the Plant Protection Product Regulation and Biocidal Products Regulation' (16 January 2015) 3 f. The U.S. Government still thinks that the Commission is inclined to adopt a hazard-based approach to regulating endocrine disruptors.

39 European Crop Protection, 'ECPA statement on European Commission Roadmap document for development of criteria for endocrine disruptors' (2 July 2014) <http://www.ecpa.eu/information-page/human-health/endocrine-disruptors> accessed 4 July 2015.

40 Chris Harris, 'Endocrine Disruptors – Risk or Hazard?' *The Crop Site* (3 October 2014) <http://www.thecropsite.com/news/16859/endocrine-disruptors-risk-or-hazard/> accessed 4 July 2015.

41 Comments of the U.S. Government, 'European Commission's Public Consultation on Defining Criteria for Identifying Endocrine Disruptors (ED's) in the Context of the Implementation of the Plant Protection Product Regulation and Biocidal Products Regulation' (16 January 2015) 4.

42 EFSA Scientific Committee, 'Scientific Opinion on the hazard assessment of endocrine disruptors: Scientific criteria for identification of endocrine disruptors and appropriateness of existing test methods for assessing effects mediated by these substances on human health and the environment' (2013) 11 (3):3232 EFSA Journal 13 <http://www.efsa.europa.eu/en/search/doc/3132.pdf> accessed 4 July 2015.

43 Ibid 43.

difficult to foresee what the actual criteria will look like, and how far risk elements will be included in the definition of the criteria for identifying Endocrine Disruptors within the context of the implementation of the Plant Protection Product Regulation. At least, the wording of the Plant Protection Product Regulation leaves room for a more risk-based approach. The term "endocrine disrupting properties that may cause adverse effects" in Annex II, Section 3.6.5 of the PPPR can only be applied properly with the help of a risk assessment, which helps to find out whether there are adverse effects. Furthermore, a more comprehensive risk assessment would be in line with WTO law, especially with the SPS Agreement[44] (Agreement on the Application of Sanitary and Phytosanitary Measures).

Article 5 (1) of the SPS Agreement states that:

> "Members shall ensure that their sanitary and phytosanitary measures are based on an assessment, as appropriate to the circumstances, of the risk to human (...) life or health, taking into account risk assessment techniques developed by relevant international organizations."

Furthermore Article 2 (2) provides that:

> "Members shall ensure that any sanitary or phytosanitary measure is applied only to the extent necessary to protect human, animal or plant life or health, is based on scientific principles and is not maintained without sufficient scientific evidence, except as provided for in paragraph 7 of Article 5."

Undertaking a risk assessment can thus be seen as an integral part of a science based decision, as the WTO Appellate Body has found that the requirement for a risk assessment can be seen as a basic obligation contained in Article 2 (2), and that Article 2 (2) and Article 5 (1) should always be read together.[45] Furthermore, the risk assessment techniques developed by relevant international organizations, as referred to in Article 5 (1), all ask similar questions, such as[46]: What is the probability of an adverse effect occurring? What are the prerequisites for an adverse effect to occur? Thus, they contain elements of potency which could also be taken

---

44 Agreement on the Application of Sanitary and Phytosanitary Measures, entry into force: 1995.

45 Appellate Body Report, *EC Measures concerning meat and meat products (Hormones)* (AB-1997-4, 16 January 1998) recital 180.

46 EFSA Scientific Committee, 'Scientific Opinion on Risk Assessment Terminology' (2012) 10 (5):2664 EFSA Journal 9 <http://www.efsa.europa.eu/de/search/doc/2664.pdf> accessed 5 July 2015.

into consideration when looking for regulatory approaches concerning endocrine disruptors. The WTO Body has also found that "the existence of unknown or uncertain elements does not justify a departure from the requirements (…) for a risk assessment[47] Thus, WTO law follows a strong risk-based approach in order to make sure that sanitary or phytosanitary measures are not a disguised barrier to trade.

E. Conclusion

Although the hazard-based approach undoubtedly sets the highest level of food safety protection, it can be expected that, due to the international harmonisation of standards, more and more risk-assessment elements will find their way into the EU legislation regarding the regulation of endocrine disruptors. This development shows that harmonisation of protection standards and trade facilitation may entail a hazard for food safety.

---

47 Appellate Body Report, *Australia-Measures Affecting Importation of Salmon* (AB-2998-5, 20 October 1998) recital 130.

§ 17 Short food supply chains in the EU Law

Anna Kapała

A. Short food supply chains – a need to restore

Short food supply chains and local farming have always existed and before World War II they were the dominant system of agriculture and food, based on family farms and focusing on the regional provision of food.[1] However, it has never been the subject of the European Union rules that, instead, since its foundation as the European Communities in 1957[2], had focused on promoting the intensification of production to assure availability of supplies, which favoured monoculture, big and specialized farms.[3] It has been observed that this system of industrial agriculture, established to avoid hunger, is now, ironically, contributing to crises in food production.[4]

Recently, the EU has noticed the value of short food supply chains 'as a driver of change towards sustainability both in agro-food system and rural areas'.[5] In 2010, the European Parliament called the Commission to pro-

---

1 Harry Donkers, 'Sustainable Food Security. A Paradigm for Local and Regional Food Systems' (2014) 4 (12) International Journal of Humanities and Social Science 89. The Author observes that 'Though not formally certified or registered as such this system could best be described as a "natural" way of production (ie without input of chemical fertilizers and pesticides), mixed farming and short cycles of production'.

2 See the Treaty establishing the European Economic Community (TEEC) [1957].

3 See art 39 of TEEC and the Mansholt plan (later art 33 of consolidated version of the Treaty establishing the European Community (TEC) [2002] OJ C 325/33, now art 39 of consolidated version of the Treaty on the Functioning of the European Union (TFEU) [2012] OJ C 326/47).

4 Harry Donkers, 'Sustainable Food Security. A Paradigm for Local and Regional Food Systems' (2014) 4 (12) International Journal of Humanities and Social Science 89, 90.

5 Francesca Galli / Gianluca Brunori (eds), *Short Food Supply Chains as drivers of sustainable development. Evidence Document* (2013). Document developed in the framework of the FP7 project FOODLINKS (GA no 265287) <http://www.foodlinkscommunity.net/fileadmin/documents_organicresearch/foodlinks/CoPs/evidence-document-sfsc-cop.pdf> accessed 11 August 2015.

pose the adoption of instruments supporting farmer-managed food supply chains, short supply chains and farmers' markets in order to enable farmers to obtain a fairer share of the final sale price.[6] The potential of 'regional and local farming and regional and local markets' that 'is not currently being fully exploited' was recognized also in the Green Paper.[7] In the Communication on the 'CAP towards 2020' the Commission underlines the need to reverse the problem of a decreasing trend in the farmers' share of the value added generated by the food supply chain, and says that 'Support for developing direct sales and local markets should also be important.'[8] According to recent consumer surveys at national or regional scale, consumers are willing to participate in short food supply chains and local food production systems.[9] In fact, short supply chains are a phenomenon with a development potential, that "touches some of the most topical issues of the debate about food" [10], and is beneficial in many areas.[11]

---

6 European Parliament, 'Fair revenues for farmers: A better functioning food supply chain in Europe' Resolution of 7 September 2010 (2009/2237(INI)).

7 European Commission, 'Green Paper on promotion measures and information provision for agricultural products: a reinforced value-added European strategy for promoting the tastes of Europe' COM (2011) 436 final, 4, where the Commission states: 'Regional and local markets are an essential meeting place for producers and consumers. They enable the former to receive the rewards for their labours more efficiently and the latter to contribute to the development of their local areas, reduce the environmental impact of their consumption habits and access a wide variety of products rooted in their traditions and ways of life'.

8 European Commission, 'Communication from the Commission to the European Parliament, the Council, the European Economic and Social Committee and the Committee of the Regions of 18 November 2010 - The CAP towards 2020: Meeting the food, natural resources and territorial challenges of the future' COM (2010) 672 final.

9 'Recent consumer surveys at national or regional scale have shown, for example, that 70 % of British consumers want to buy local food and 72 % of French consumers consider it important', European Commission, 'Commission Staff Working Document of 6 December 2013 on various aspects of short food supply chains accompanying the document report from the Commission to the European Parliament and the Council on the case for a local farming and direct sales labelling scheme COM (2013) 866 final' SWD (2013) 501 final.

10 It touches such topics like: 'the question of the paradox of food; the problem of the relationship between global change, availability of natural resources and agricultural production; economic conflicts arising between different actors in the food chain; the question of the interaction between the city, the place of consumption, and the country, the place of production', cit Silvio Franco / Davide Marino, 'Il mercato della Filiera corta. I farmer's market come luogo di incontro di produttori

As regards its[11] benefits in the food safety area, it is worth mentioning that a close relationship between the producer and the consumer enables better identification with the producer, the production methods and the origin of the product, and assures better traceability.[12] Consumers are engaged in products quality control, and producers try to meet their demands. Local farming involved in short supply chains is charaterized by lower or no utilization of inputs[13], additives and preservatives or GMO.[14] In terms of food security, the focus on local resources contributes to the "paradigm of sustainable food security", which is specified in literature, and aims at providing 'sufficient and healthy food for all people, without exhausting our planet'.[15] The access to local products through short supply chains not only fits into the concept of food security intended by FAO as

---

e consumatori' (2012) Working Paper 19/2012 Gruppo 2013, 3 <http://www.gruppo2013.it/working-paper/Documents/WEB%20Working%20Paper%20 n.19%20-%20Gruppo%202013.pdf> accessed 12 August 2015. See also Francesco Adornato, 'Contratti e mercati di prossimità e di territorio dei prodotti agroalimentari' (2013) 1 Rivista di Diritto Alimentare 15 <http://www.rivistadirittoalimentare.it/rivista/2013-01/ADORNATO.pdf> accessed 12 August 2015

11 About benefits of short supply chains and local food system see: Committee of the Regions, 'Opinion of the Committee of the Regions on "Local food systems" (outlook opinion)' [2011] (2011/C 104/01) OJ C 104/1.

12 In the same way Harry Donkers, 'Sustainable Food Security. A Paradigm for Local and Regional Food Systems' (2014) 4 (12) International Journal of Humanities and Social Science 89, 100, who states that due to 'a direct connection between producers and consumers, large and complex tracking systems are not needed'.

13 'In local and regional food systems there is no urgency to use antibiotic compounds for preventative purposes'(...)'the starting-point for achieving resistance to diseases is the use, as far as possible, of natural production methods in a rich biodiversity setting' Harry Donkers, 'Sustainable Food Security. A Paradigm for Local and Regional Food Systems' (2014) 4 (12) International Journal of Humanities and Social Science 89, 100.

14 See Francesca Galli / Gianluca Brunori (eds), *Short Food Supply Chains as drivers of sustainable development. Evidence Document* (2013). Document developed in the framework of the FP7 project FOODLINKS (GA no 265287) 2 <http://www.foodlinkscommunity.net/fileadmin/documents_organicresearch/foodlinks/CoPs/evidence-document-sfsc-cop.pdf> accessed 11 August 2015.

15 Harry Donkers, 'Sustainable Food Security. A Paradigm for Local and Regional Food Systems' (2014) 4 (12) International Journal of Humanities and Social Science 89.

the physical access to food.[16] It seems to especially correspond to a broader concept of the 'Right to Food', understood as 'permanent and unrestricted access, (...) to quantitatively and qualitatively adequate and sufficient food corresponding to the cultural traditions of the people to which the consumer belongs'.[17]

Therefore the local food system and short food supply chains need a proper orientation and support, both at policy and legislation level. The aim of this study is to examine the current EU approach towards the short food supply chain and to indicate desirable directions of development of its regulation.

B. Short food supply chain in the EU Law

I. Definition of the short food supply chain in the EU Law

The first legal provision directly relating to short supply chains was included in the last Regulation (EU) 1305/2013 on support for rural development.[18] It provides the legal notion and special tools for their support. Among the instruments implementing one of the CAP priorities, which is 'improving competitiveness of primary producers by better integrating them into the agri-food chain', is the Regulation in Article 5 (3) (a) that indicates precisely 'promotion in local markets and short supply circuits', next to 'quality schemes, adding value to agricultural products, producer groups and organisations and inter-branch organizations'.

---

16 'Food security exists when all people, at all times, have physical and economic access to sufficient safe and nutritious food that meets their dietary needs and food preferences for an active and healthy life' (1996) World Food Summit.
17 Olivier de Schutter, UN Special Rapporteur on the Right to Food (2012) <http://www.srfood.org/en/official-reports> accessed 05 October 2015. His opinion appoints Harry Donkers, 'Sustainable Food Security. A Paradigm for Local and Regional Food Systems' (2014) 4 (12) International Journal of Humanities and Social Science 89, 98.
18 Regulation (EU) 1305/2013 of the European Parliament and of the Council of 17 December 2013 on support for rural development by the European Agricultural Fund for Rural Development (EAFRD) and repealing Council Regulation (EC) 1698/2005 [2013] OJ L 347/487.

Articel 2 of the Regulation legally defines the term 'short supply chain'.[19] Pursuant to it, the presence of intermediaries is allowed, whose number, though, should be 'limited' (without specifyng what number is considered as limited). Therefore, it not only refers to direct relations between producers and consumers, but requires 'geographical proximity' and also 'close social relations' between producers, processors and consumers. This indeterminate concept of proximity will probabily be interpreted variosly by Member States, but in any case it narrows the circle of participants in short chains, excluding those who are not connected by such relations.[20]

Short supply chains is a broader notion than direct sales and includes 'a multiplicity of commercial forms'[21], as the following examples show: farmers' market, direct sales from the manufacturer, "pick-your-own", 'box scheme', online sales, direct supply of products to catering and restaurants, local food area in supermarkets and community-based initiatives.[22]

---

19 Ibid art 2 (1) lit m): ' "short supply chain": means a supply chain involving a limited number of economic operators, committed to cooperation, local economic development, and close geographical and social relations between producers, processors and consumers'.

20 In the literature can be found another definition of short food chain: 'all those methods of marketing alternatives to large-scale distribution on a global scale that are characterized, on the one hand, by the reduction or elimination of intermediaries between agricultural producers and consumers and, secondly, by the local dimension of commercial transactions Clara Cicatiello / Davide Marino / Silvio Franco, 'Un focus sui consumatori che frequentano i farmers' market' in Domenico Cersosimo (ed), *I consumi alimentari evoluzione strutturale, nuove tendenze risposte alla crisi* (Gruppo 2013, Quaderni 2011) 140.

21 Francesco Adornato, 'Contratti e mercati di prossimità e di territorio dei prodotti agroalimentari' (2013) 1 Rivista di Diritto Alimentare 15 note 14 <http://www.rivistadirittoalimentare.it/rivista/2013-01/ADORNATO.pdf> accessed 12 August 2015.

22 See also in the litaruture various forms of local food chain in Sabrina Giuca, 'Conoscere la filiera corta' in Francesca Giarè / Sabrina Giuca (eds), *Agricoltori e filiera corta. Profili giuridici e dinamiche socio-economiche, Sistema di conoscenza* (Inea 2012) <http://dspace.inea.it/bitstream/inea/366/1/SE5-1156.pdf> accessed 11 August 2015 and Francesco Adornato, 'Contratti e mercati di prossimità e di territorio dei prodotti agroalimentari' (2013) 1 Rivista di Diritto Alimentare 15 <http://www.rivistadirittoalimentare.it/rivista/2013-01/ADORNATO.pdf> accessed 12 August 2015.

As regards the narrower phenomenon of 'direct supply', its legal notion was introduced in the Regulations (EC) 852/2004 and 853/2004 concerning food hygiene. It suggests that this activity is undertaken by the producer, it covers small quantities of primary products which can be supplied to the final consumer or to local retail establishments directly supplying the final consumer".[23] The establishment of rules governing this activity, as well as, rules ensuring the achievement of the objectives of the regulations is delegated to Member States competition.[24]

Nevertheless, it should be emphasized that this definition was provided by the EU legislator only for food hygiene purposes and did not refer to this activity in general. While the definition of 'short supply chains' in the Regulation 1305/2013 was necessary to determine which operations would be eligible for granting aid under measures provided by this act. However, the EU law did not establish a complex set of rules regarding short supply chains or local agriculture and local food systems.

The regulation of this phenomenon remains under Member States' initiative. Thus national rules in this area are very diverse. For example, the Italian legislator precisely and thouroughly regulates the activity of direct sales[25] and farmers' market.[26] Poland recently has adopted provisions enabling farmers to directly sell unprocessed and processed products deriving from their farms.[27]

---

23 See Regulation (EC) 852/2004 of the European Parliament and of the Council of 29 April 2004 on the hygiene of foodstuffs [2004] OJ L 139/1, art 1 (2) lit c) and Regulation (EC) 853/2004 of the European Parliament and of the Council of 29 April 2004 laying down specific hygiene rules for food of animal origin [2004] OJ L 139/55, art 1 (3) lit c), lit d) and lit e).

24 See Regulation (EC) 852/2004 of the European Parliament and of the Council of 29 April 2004 on the hygiene of foodstuffs [2004] OJ L 139/1, art 1 (3) and Regulation (EC) 853/2004 of the European Parliament and of the Council of 29 April 2004 laying down specific hygiene rules for food of animal origin [2004] OJ L 139/55, art 1 (4).

25 See decreto legislativo 18 maggio 228/2001, art 4 (G.U. 137/2001).

26 'Farmers' markets' are regulated in legge finanziaria per il 2007 no 296/2006 art 1 lit c) 1065 and implemented by decreto ministeriale 20 novembre 2007 (G.U. n 301/2007) sui mercati riservati all'esercizio della vendita diretta da parte degli imprenditori agricoli.

27 See art 3 ustawa z 2 lipca 2004 r. o swobodzie działalności gospodarczej (Dz.U. 2004 Nr 173 poz. 1807) as amended by ustawa z dnia 9 kwietnia 2015 r. o zmianie ustawy o podatku dochodowym od osób fizycznych oraz niektórych innych ustaw (Dz.U. z 2015 r., nr 0, poz. 699) in force from 1 January 2016.

II. Present EU support instruments for short supply chains

There are some tools of the EU rural development policy provided by Regulation 1305/2013 that support short supply chains. These are advisory services (advice for the development of short supply chains, Article 15), cooperation among supply chain actors for the establishment and the development of short supply chains and local markets and promotion activities in a local context relating to the development of short supply chains and local markets (Article 35). The novelty introduced by the Regulation is the possibility for Member States to create a thematic sub-programme within their rural development programmes, combining measures which could best address short food supply chains (Article 7 (1) (d)). It is also possible to get subsidies for investment linked with short food chains under the measure 'Investments in physical assets' (Article 17), 'Farm and business development' (Article 19), 'Leader' (Article 43-45).

III. Local farming and direct sales labelling

Since consumers may have difficulties to find local food or to distinguish it from other food, it is worth considering whether a new labelling scheme at the EU level should be created to ensure visibility and recognition of local food in order to help consumers to make informed choices and farmers to promote their products. Regulation (EU) 1151/2012 on quality schemes for agricultural products and foodstuffs recognised in Article 55 the importance of local food, by asking the Commission to present a report on the case for a new local farming and direct sales labelling scheme.[28] The legal provision cited expresses 'a new approach of European legislation' that consists 'of two important novelties: the first one is the autonomous consideration of the local market, the second is the admissibility of labelling that certifies origin from a restricted geographical area, but beyond a specific provision of particular qualities associated with the product.' This postulate assumes a need of distinction of local markets from other markets (national markets or the EU market) 'in particular as regards

---

28 Regulation (EU) 1151/2012 of the European Parliament and of the Council of 21 November 2012 on quality schemes for agricultural products and foodstuffs [2012] OJ L 343/1.

the aspects of labelling referring to the local origin of the agri-food product.'[29]

IV. Short supply chains and the food safety rules

The food sales carried out within short supply chains as well as within direct supply must comply with the provisions of Regulation (EC) 178/2002, which is the basis of the legal system of food safety[30]. Food business operators are subject to the obligations set out in Article 17 to ensure compliance of the food sold with the requirements of food law applicable to the activities at all stages of production, processing and distribution in the farms (enterprises) being under their control. In particular, any food business operator must ensure traceability of food[31] and any other substance intended to be added to food. He should be able to identify any person from whom he received foodstuff and the enterprise which he supplied his products (Article 18), i.e. the previous and subsequent "link" of the chain. In the context of short supply chains, it can be concluded that a limited number of intermediaries (or their absence in the case of direct supply) undoubtedly reduces the risk of difficulties in identifying successive links. In addition, there is a limited number of stages in the production chain that could potentially be a threat to food safety. These factors favor direct sales in the context of food safety.

---

29 Cit Irene Canfora, 'I marchi regionali di qualità e la correttezza dell'informazione dei consumatori: libera circolazione delle merci vs. tutela dell'agricoltura locale?' (2013) Rivista di Diritto Agrario 149, 151. The European Commission published a 'Report from the Commission to the European Parliament and the Council on the case for a local farming and direct sales labelling scheme' COM (2013) 866 final, exploring the possibilities of adopting a local farming and direct sales labelling scheme in the future.

30 Regulation (EC) 178/2002 of the European Parliament and of the Council of 28 January 2002 laying down the general principles and requirements of food law, establishing the European Food Safety Authority and laying down procedures in matters of food safety [2002] OJ L 31/1.

31 See the definition of 'traceability' in Regulation (EC) 178/2002 of the European Parliament and of the Council of 28 January 2002 laying down the general principles and requirements of food law, establishing the European Food Safety Authority and laying down procedures in matters of food safety [2002] OJ L 31/1, art 3 (15).

Food safety is closely related to food hygiene.[32] Regulation (EC) 852/2004[33] excludes from its scope direct supply by the producer of small quantities of primary products to the final consumer or to local retail establishments directly supplying the final consumer (Article 1 (2) (c)).[34] The Community legislator considered that in this specific case, characterized by a strong link between producer and consumer, public health should be guaranteed by national legislation.[35] This means that a farmer who directly sells small amounts of primary products to consumers is not subject to the obligations specified by the Community Regulation, but remains bound by national legislation in this area, which must, in any case, according to Article 1 (3), ensure the achievement of the objectives of Regulation 852/2004.

Sales within short chains which do not fit in the definition of direct supply, as well as the sale of processed products to the final consumer within the meaning of Regulation 178/2002, are considered a 'retail', which concept also applies under the Regulations of the hygiene package.[36] It means the working or processing of food and its storage at the point of sale or delivery to the final consumer. It refers to the act following the stage of primary production and is therefore subject to the requirements of Annex II of Regulation 852/2004, also if it relates to products of animal origin.

Food business operators participating in further stages following primary production, in addition to the requirements set out in Annex II, shall be

---

32 Pursunat to Regulation (EC) 852/2004 of the European Parliament and of the Council of 29 April 2004 on the hygiene of foodstuffs [2004] OJ L 139/1, art 2 (1) lit a) 'food hygiene' means the measures and conditions necessary to control hazards and to ensure fitness for human consumption of a foodstuff taking into account its intended use. In order to systematize the hygiene standards applicable to direct sales must be considered a package of normative acts issued during 2004-2005, forming the so called 'Hygiene package'.

33 Ibid. Pursunat to its art 1 'This Regulation lays down general rules for food business operators on the hygiene of foodstuffs (...); This Regulation shall apply to all stages of production, processing and distribution of food and to exports, and without prejudice to more specific requirements relating to food hygiene'.

34 Ibid art 2 (1) lit b): ' "primary products" means products of primary production including products of the soil, of stock farming, of hunting and fishing'.

35 Ibid recital 10.

36 'Retail' is defined in Regulation (EC) 178/2002 of the European Parliament and of the Council of 28 January 2002 laying down the general principles and requirements of food law, establishing the European Food Safety Authority and laying down procedures in matters of food safety [2002] OJ L 31/1, art 3 (7).

required to apply the principles of hazard analysis and critical control points (system of self-checking) HACCP pursuant to Article 5 of Regulation 852/2004. This requirement does not refer to agricultural producers who carry out direct supply. It applies however to producers selling directly processed products, and more generally to those who run retail sales within the meaning of Regulation 178/2002.

Holdings which carry out only primary production (and direct supply) should follow good practices in terms of production (particularly good hygiene practice and good agricultural practice). To facilitate the adoption of correct behaviour in the field of hygiene and maintenance under the control of possible risks, the Community legislator promotes development, both at national and Community level, manuals of proper hygiene practices.

Food businesses handling food of animal origin are required to meet, at every stage of the food chain, not only the general hygiene requirements laid down in Regulation 852/2004 but also those special hygiene requirements introduced by Regulation 853/2004.[37] This act applies only to unprocessed and processed food of animal origin. Direct supply of small quantities of primary products, and direct supply of small quantities of meat from poultry and lagomorphs slaughtered on the farm to the final consumer or to local retail establishments directly supplying such meat to the final consumer as fresh meat, are not subject to its rules.[38] Member States shall establish national rules to ensure the safety of such products.[39]

The act discussed does also not apply to retail sales of food of animal origin if the operations consist only of storage and transport or if the supply of food of animal origin from a retail establishment is carried out exclusively to other retail establishments and, in accordance with national law, is a marginal, localized and restricted activity (Article 1 (5) (ii)). Such supply should therefore be only a small part of the establishment; the establishment supplied should be in its immediate vicinity; and the supply

---

37 Regulation (EC) 853/2004 of the European Parliament and of the Council of 29 April 2004 laying down specific hygiene rules for food of animal origin [2004] OJ L 139/55.

38 Ibid art 1 (3) lit c), lit d), lit e). Pursunat to art 1 (3) lit e) also hunters who supply small quantities of wild game or wild game meat directly to the final consumer or to local retail establishments directly supplying the final consumer are not subject to this Regulation.

39 Ibid art 1 (3) lit d).

should concern only certain types of products or establishments.[40] In relation to these retail establishments, which are not subject to the Regulation
853/2004, Member States may adopt national measures to apply the requirements of this act. This means that the requirements of Regulation
852/2004 are sufficient to ensure food safety in establishments carrying
out retail activities involving the direct sale or supply of food of animal
origin to the final consumer (i.e. a marginal, localized and restricted activity). Regulation 853/2004 should generally apply to wholesale activities
(that is, when a retail establishment carries out operations with the supply
of food of animal origin to another establishment).[41]

Products of animal origin intended for human consumption are subject
to official control under Regulation (EC) 854/2004.[42] This Regulation
shall only apply for the activities and persons within the scope of Regulation 853/2004. Therefore, it does not refer to agricultural producers who
conduct direct supply of primary products, or to meat from poultry, or to a
marginal, localized and restricted activity.

C. Summary and outlook

Direct supplies of primary products are exempted from EU hygiene rules,
and Member States have an autonomy in defining appropriate provisions
in this regard. However, the sales of processed food (products of plant origin, products of animal origin or food containing both products) are not
exempted from the Regulation 852/2004. Retail of food of animal origin is
exempted from Regulation 853/2004 if it is a marginal, localized and restricted activity. It must be emphasized that Regulation 852/2004 in Article 5 (5) offers flexibility in implementing the rules regarding HACCP.
Therefore, it would be advisable for Member States to take advantage of
this possibility. It would help in creating optimal conditions, especially for
small farms which engage in short supply chains. The risk management

---

40 Regulation (EC) 853/2004 of the European Parliament and of the Council of 29
    April 2004 laying down specific hygiene rules for food of animal origin [2004] OJ
    L 139/55, recital 13.
41 Ibid recital 12.
42 Regulation (EC) 854/2004 of the European Parliament and of the Council of 29
    April 2004 laying down specific rules for the organisation of official controls on
    products of animal origin intended for human consumption [2004], OJ L 226/83.

towards short supply chains that 'have a lower level of complexity, involve a smaller number of nodes and often apply simplified methods' should be designed differently than those for bigger producers (...).[43] Certainly it is not about setting different hygiene standards for short supply chains, but about adopting 'a tailored design of risk management practices and control systems'.[44]

It can be concluded that the development of short chains in agriculture should be promoted, as this would help to reach the goals of agricultural policy set out in Article 33 of the TCE (now 39 TFEU).[45] 'The direct sale of agricultural products in short supply chains, in fact, guarantees an increase in agricultural productivity, improves the income of farmers, stabilises markets, guarantees security of supply and ultimately ensures reasonable prices for consumers.'[46] At the same time it contributes to more sustainable food systems and is a key element of, as denoted in the literature, "Food Democracy" the 'goal of which is a food system offering more opportunities for farmers and consumers, greater varieties of products, more information, more choices, more local involvement, as well as greater attention to health, the environment, animal welfare, and human values'.[47] There is therefore a need to exploit and to restore the local food

---

43 European Network for Rural Development, 'Local Food and Short Supply Chains' (2012) EU Rural Review 12 <http://enrd.ec.europa.eu/sites/enrd/files/fms/pdf/69D9962A-A9D5-5298-0AB7-C4B02470D0B5.pdf> accessed 13 August 2015, appointed by Francesca Galli / Gianluca Brunori (eds), *Short Food Supply Chains as drivers of sustainable development'. Evidence Document* (2013). Document developed in the framework of the FP7 project FOODLINKS (GA no 265287) 26 <http://www.foodlinkscommunity.net/fileadmin/documents_organicresearch/foodlinks/CoPs/evidence-document-sfsc-cop.pdf> accessed 11 August 2015.

44 Francesca Galli / Gianluca Brunori (eds), *Short Food Supply Chains as drivers of sustainable development. Evidence Document* (2013). Document developed in the framework of the FP7 project FOODLINKS (GA no 265287) 26 <http://www.foodlinkscommunity.net/fileadmin/documents_organicresearch/foodlinks/CoPs/evidence-document-sfsc-cop.pdf> accessed 11 August 2015.

45 Irene Canfora, 'Dalla terra al territorio: il ruolo dell'agricoltore nella filiera corta' in Francesca Giarè / Sabrina Giuca (eds), *Agricoltori e filiera corta. Profili giuridici e dinamiche socio-economiche* (INEA 2012) 31, 37f. <http://dspace.inea.it/bitstream/inea/366/1/SE5-1156.pdf> accessed 11 August 2015.

46 Ibid.

47 Neil D. Hamilton, 'Food Democracy II: Revolution or Restoration?' (2005) 13 Journal of Food Law & Policy 13, 41. The Author specifies 'it is not just a "revolution", it is also a restoration, an effort to restore democracy to our food system. It is about replacing the realities of industrialized Big Food with the democratic ide-

system, and it seems right to postulate definitions of 'Local Food Products' and 'Local Food Systems', and to introduce a simple EU label for local products.[48]

---

als of a more locally driven and human oriented food system, based on values other than mere economic efficiency'.

48 Committee of the Regions, 'Opinion of the Committee of the Regions on "Local food systems" (outlook opinion)' [2011] (2011/C 104/01) OJ C 104/1.

§ 18 Organic Farming 3.0 – towards a process of legal change

Mathias Olbrisch

A. Introduction

Food Change is the heading for a debate within politics and society on fundamental issues related to the future development of agriculture and nutrition economy.[1] The main question in this context is how to achieve global food security in a quantitative and qualitative manner.[2] *Conditio sine qua non* therefore is the sufficient availability of arable land for agricultural raw materials, which is called into question by the existing structures and circumstances in agriculture and nutrition economy.[3] For these reasons substantial changes are regarded as necessary that force an improvement of sustainability. Effects of sustainability are notably expected from organic production. However, organic production in its current form does not contribute sufficiently to the improvement of sustainability.[4] This is the reason why organic farming associations discuss, as is done in politics, the future direction and design of organic production under the key word of "organic 3.0".[5]

---

1 Bund Ökologische Lebensmittelwirtschaft, '100 % Bio - jetzt! - 5 Thesen zur Ernährungswende' (16 January 2013) <http://www.boelw.de/uploads/media/pdf/Do kumentation/Dossiers_und_Positionspapiere/BOELW_5_Thesen_zur_Ernaehrungs wende.pdf> accessed 19 September 2015.
2 Ibid.
3 'WWF fordert Ernährungswende' *DIE WELT Newsticker* (1 April 2015) <http:// www.welt.de/newsticker/dpa_nt/infoline_nt/brennpunkte_nt/article138996188/ WWF-fordert-Ernaehrungswende.html> accessed 19 September 2015.
4 Ulrike Eberle / Doris Hayn, 'Ernährungswende – Eine Herausforderung für Politik, Unternehmen und Gesellschaft' (Öko-Institut e.V. und Institut für sozial-ökologische Forschung 2007) 6.
5 Markus Arbenz / David Gould / Christopher Stopes, 'Organic 3.0 – for truly sustainable farming & consumption' (2015) IFOAM Organics International Discussion Paper <http://www.organic-israel.org.il/filesystem/Organic3.0_WEB.PDF> accessed 12 November 2015; Organic 3.0 was also the main topic of the exhibition for organic production Biofach in Nürnberg 2015.

The improvement of sustainability is one of the European Union´s central concerns. That is the reason why the EU aims to revise the legal framework for organic farming. This contribution evaluates the projected revision of the legal framework for organic farming that is embedded in a multi-level system from a legal point of view. In this respect the most important reform proposals on the EU level are introduced to the legal discussion.

B. *The reform proposals from a legal perspective*

From a legal point of view, the discussion about the reform occurs in the revision of the Basic Regulation (EC) 834/2007 on organic production and labelling of organic products and repealing Regulation (EEC) No 2029/91 [2007] OJ 189/1, that implies a high number of fundamental legal changes, which are however subject of serious criticism.[6]

I. *Contamination threshold*

The most significant political resistance is articulated against the planning of the EU-Commission to establish a contamination threshold for organic products, which refers to Directive 2006/125/EC on processed cereal-based foods and baby foods for infants and young children [2006] OJ L 339/16. COM (2014) 180 final, Article 20 final forbids organic labelling in cases of exceeding a limit value for substances that are not allowed. This is occasionally interpreted as an abandonment of the process-orientat-

---

6   The draft can be found in European Commission, 'Proposal for a Regulation of the European Parliament and of the Council of 24 March 2014 on organic production and labelling of organic products, amending Regulation (EU) XXX/XXX of the European Parliament and of the Council [Official controls Regulation] and repealing Council Regulation (EC) 834/2007' COM (2014) 180 final. The reform also affects the corresponding implementing of Commission Regulation (EC) 889/2008 of 5 September 2008 laying down detailed rules for the implementation of Council Regulation (EC) 834/2007 on organic production and labelling of organic products with regard to organic production, labelling and control [2007] OJ L 189/1 such as Commission Regulation 1235/2008 of 8 December 2008 laying down detailed rules for implementation of Council Regulation (EC) 834/2007 as regards the arrangements for imports of organic products from third countries [2008] OJ L 334/25.

ed regulative approach, which means that the organic quality depends on maintaining a certain way of production and not on maintaining particular threshold values.[7]

From a technical legal point of view, it is true that a threshold value is added, the exceeding of which causes a loss of organic quality. Nonetheless, the process-oriented regulative approach is not completely abandoned, because there are still many legal requirements for the production process, as for example, proven by COM (2014) 180 final, Article 5 (1) (c) and Article 6 (f).

The focus of the critique is obviously more the legal consequences of exceeding the threshold. In this way, the threshold burdens the wrong addressee because a farmer will be decertified if his products are contaminated, for example, with GMOs although it was not his fault.[8] In a paradigmatic assumption of a "polluter pays principle" this is regarded to be unjust and to endanger the social peace between conventional and organic farmers.[9] Furthermore, an unintentional, but quite possible, exceeding of a particular organic threshold value could potentially lead to decertification, even though the threshold values for conventional products would be able to ensure food safety sufficiently.[10]

These arguments seem to be reasonable and justify the assumption of an intrusion into the EU fundamental rights of the organic farmers. But this intrusion is mitigated by the compensation scheme in Article 20 no 3 COM (2014) 180 final, which entitles the concerned farmers to claim compensation payments.

Aside from these proportionality considerations, it seems to be problematic that COM (2014) 180 final, Article 20 no 2 leaves the Commis-

---

7 In so far the opinion of the Member of the European Parliament Martin Häusling <http://www.martin-haeusling.eu/images/150520_Pressebriefing_%C3%96ko-VO_Mai_2015.pdf> accessed 13 August 2015, also 'Agrarrat strebt erste Einigung über EU-Ökoreform an' *Agra-Europe* (Bonn, 11 May 2015) EU-Nachrichten 8.

8 Press briefing referring to the proposal for the rapporteur Martin Häusling for the parliament draft concerning the reform of the Council Regulation (EC) 834/2007 of 28 June 2007 on organic production and labelling of organic products and repealing Regulation (EEC) 2092/91 [2007] OJ L 189/1, 1 f. <http://www.martin-haeusling.eu/images/150520_Pressebriefing_%C3%96koVO_Mai_2015.pdf> accessed 13 August 2015.

9 'Agrarrat strebt erste Einigung über EU-Ökoreform an' *AgraEurope* (Bonn, 11 May 2015) EU-Nachrichten 8 f.

10 Ibid.

sion to define the threshold values. Firstly, this appears to be in contradiction to COM (2014) 180 final, Article 10 no 1 that regulates an orientation of the values of the Directive 2006/125/EC on baby foods and secondly the Commissions authority to define the threshold values comes into conflict with the Treaty on the Functioning of the European Union (TFEU), Article 290 whereupon all essential aspects have to be regulated by the legislative bodies of the European Union, which means by the Council and the European Parliament.[11] The regulation could eventually be interpreted to be in conformity with primary law if the threshold values are defined by taking into account the values of the Directive 2006/125/EC on baby foods. This aspect is related to general questions of the European rule of law. Consequently, this point makes a high legislative diligence appear necessary.

II. Environmental management systems

In future, environmental management systems should be a means to take into account the ecobalance of the processing sector. In this context the regulation in COM (2014) 180 final, Article 7 (1) (d) final is indefinite. It is partially made concrete by recital 15 of the Commission's proposal, whereby the food business operators have to "manage their environmental performance". How this management should work, is not defined by the Commission's proposal. According to Article 7 no 2 of the proposal, it is the Commission who has to lay down detailed provisions. This again conflicts with TFEU, Article 290, because – aside from the legislative purpose – all provisions can be regulated by the Commission. A new basic regulation for organic farming should regulate the essential provisions itself.

III. Modifications of the control system

Another big construction unit is the control system for the organic production.

---

11 In this way also Jörg Gundel, 'Gesetzgebung und delegierte Rechtsetzung im EU-Lebensmittelrecht: Welche Grenzen setzt der Wesentlichkeitsvorbehalt?' (2015) ZLR 143, who is extensively dealing with the question in how far essential aspects may be regulated by the Commission.

1. Risk based inspections

Organic farms are inspected *de lege lata* at least once a year in accordance with Regulation (EC) 834/2007, Article 27 (3) sentence 2. In cases of a higher risk of violation of law, the inspection intensity can be increased.

The Commission´s proposal abolishes the annual inspection, so that the inspection frequency would be determined by the risk of irregularities. From the pure risk based approach, the Commission expects a more proportionate distribution of the inspection burden such as a more effective use of the administrative resources.[12] As the inspections cause costs for the farmers, such a pure risk based approach would be a more proportionate legislative measure with regard to the farmer´s fundamental rights.[13] According to the current state of discussion, the previous annual inspection cycle should be kept.[14]

2. Extension of the compulsory certification

Since Regulation (EC) 834/2007, Article 28 (2) allows the Member States to exempt food retailing from the inspection system, a corresponding regulation is missing in COM (2014) 180 final, Article 24. As a result, the

---

12 European Commission, 'Proposal for a Regulation of the European Parliament and of the Council of 24 March 2014 on organic production and labelling of organic products, amending Regulation (EU) XXX/XXX of the European Parliament and of the Council [Official controls Regulation] and repealing Council Regulation (EC) 834/2007' COM (2014) 180 final, 6 f.

13 European Commission, 'Proposal for a Regulation of the European Parliament and of the Council of 6 May 2013 on official controls and other official activities performed to ensure the application of food and feed law, rules on animal health and welfare, plant health, plant reproductive material, plant protection products and amending Regulations (EC) 999/2001, 1829/2003, 1831/2003, 1/2005, 396/2005, 834/2007, 1099/2009, 1069/2009, 1107/2009, Regulations (EU) 1151/2012, [...]/ 2013, and Directives 98/58/EC, 1999/74/EC, 2007/43/EC, 2008/119/EC, 2008/120/EC and 2009/128/EC (Official controls Regulation)' COM (2013) 265 final, art 79 (1) lit b).

14 See German Federal Ministry for Food and Agriculture, 'Die Reform der EU-Ökoverordnung' (22 June 2015) <http://www.bmel.de/DE/Landwirtschaft/Nach-haltige-Landnutzung/Oekolandbau/_Texte/Reform-EU-Oekoverordnung.html> accessed 16 September 2015; see as well 'EU-Mitgliedstaaten gegen eigenen Bio-Schwellenwert für Pflanzenschutzmittel' *Agra-Europe* (Bonn, 9 February 2015) EU-Nachrichten 4 f.

compulsory certification would be extended to the whole value chain, which would be in accordance with the integrative regulative approach of the agriculture and nutrition economy law expressed paradigmatically in Regulation (EC) 178/2002 of the European Parliament and of the Council [2002] OJ L 031/1, Article 1 (3).

Whether this regulative change will be realised, is not sure at the moment.[15] An extension of the compulsory certification would at least increase the administrative workload. In addition to this, it is not clear how grocery stores would have to be certified, that do not exclusively sell only organic products. A legislative clarification is therefore necessary.

3. Group certification

A reduction in the inspection efforts is anticipated from the group certification system in Article 26 of the draft. This should enable especially small scale farmers to organize themselves in order to establish a system of reciprocal internal inspection. All in all, the legislative arrangement seems to be fragmented. A concretization should again be made by delegated acts, which again raises the question of the compatibility with TFEU, Article 290.

4. Outsourcing of inspection provisions

The inspection provisions shall, in future be transferred into a regulation for the inspection of food. COM (2013) 265 final is a draft, in Article 8 no. 1 (a), Article 9 (c) and Article 13 of which, the process orientation of the inspections is regulated, which is considered to be important.

The outsourcing of inspection provisions appears useful to avoid repetitions of equivalent regulations in a large number of legislative texts. In the same way, this technique supports a coherent legislative arrangement of the food inspection and provides a consistent basis for corresponding interpretations of the ECJ.

---

15 Against this extension see Martin Häusling, 'EU-Öko-Verordnung im Parlament' *Lebensmittelzeitung* (Frankfurt am Main, 18 May 2015) 28 <http://www.martin-haeusling.eu/images/150508_Lebensmittelzeitung_%C3%96ko-Verordnung.pdf> accessed 1 December 2015.

V. Adaptation of import rules

Legal changes are also planned concerning the import of third country goods. According to Regulation (EC) 834/2007, Article 32 and 33, there is a twin track approach, whereby an import as organic product is possible either in case of conformity or in case of equivalency. Conformity means that the Union´s regulations for organic production have to be kept, whereas equivalency is given when the third country´s provisions are recognised as adequate.[16] This equivalency check is *de lege lata* executed unilaterally by the Commission.

The draft departs in its Article 30 from unilateral equivalency recognition, which is instead dependant on trade agreements between the EU and third countries. Aside from this, the option of conformity coexists in a modified form.

VI. Restructuring of the legislative text

From a legal technical perspective the transfer of specific production rules into the annexes of the new regulation is notable. In this way, for example, exact production rules for the plant production are *de lege ferenda* located in annex II part I of the planned regulation.

Consequently, the operative part of the Regulation for organic production is relieved from containing detailed provisions. The resulting amelioration of readability of the legislative text corresponds to the Union´s general concern to simplify the EU law in the sense of the smart regulation approach, which is seems to be reasonable with reference to a better regulation.[17]

The far reaching authorizations of the Commission for the creation of delegated acts have to be considered as problematic, because on their basis it is possible to change and amend essential aspects of the specific production rules. An example is COM (2014) 180 final, Article 11 no 2 (b)

---

16 Kurt-Dietrich Rathke / Heinz-Joachim Kopp / Dietmar Betz, *Ökologischer Landbau und Bioprodukte* (2nd edn, C.H. Beck 2010) recital 1048 ff.

17 See European Commission, 'Communication from the Commission to the European Parliament, the Council, the European Economic and Social Committee and the Committee of the Regions – Better Regulation for better results – An EU agenda' COM (2015) 215 final.

whereby the Commission is empowered to define the maximum number of animals per hectare. Such provisions have a decisive influence on husbandry, and in this way, on the factual arrangement of core aspects of organic production. These essential provisions must - according to TFEU Article 290 - not be made by the Commission. This aspect should be taken into account in the further legislation process.

VII. Other changes

In order to prevent fraud in the context of organic labelling, COM (2014) 180 final forces the traceability of products. For this purpose, the draft empowers the Commission to adopt delegated acts, particularly concerning the specific production rules.[18]

Under the current legal situation, a farm may operate in a conventional and organic way simultaneously.[19] COM (2014) 180 final, Article 7 no 1 (a), no longer accepts this.

De lege lata Regulation (EC) 834/2007, Article 6 allows exemptions from the specific production rule, that organic products may only be produced from organic seeds and organic young animals. COM (2014) 180 final abolishes this exemption. Consequently, it seems as if this legal change has been put aside, so that a new regulation will also probably contain exemptions.[20]

In addition to COM (2014) 180 final, the establishment of an organic-agency or a clearing house was suggested.[21] Its major task shall be to har-

---

18 European Commission, 'Proposal for a Regulation of the European Parliament and of the Council of 24 March 2014 on organic production and labelling of organic products, amending Regulation (EU) XXX/XXX of the European Parliament and of the Council [Official controls Regulation] and repealing Council Regulation (EC) 834/2007' COM (2014) 180 final, art 10 (3), art 11 (2), art 12 (2), art 13 (2).

19 Kurt-Dietrich Rathke / Heinz-Joachim Kopp / Dietmar Betz, *Ökologischer Landbau und Bioprodukte* (2nd edn, C.H. Beck 2010) recital 485.

20 German Federal Ministry of Food and Agriculture, 'Die Reform der EU-Ökoverordnung' (22 June 2015) <http://www.bmel.de/DE/Landwirtschaft/Nach-haltige-Landnutzung/Oekolandbau/_Texte/Reform-EU-Oekoverordnung.html> accessed 11 September 2015.

21 See European Commission, 'Proposal for a Regulation of the European Parliament and of the Council of 24 March 2014 on organic production and labelling of organic products, amending Regulation (EU) XXX/XXX of the European Parliament and of the Council [Official controls Regulation] and repealing Council

monize the administration of the inspections as well as to provide data about the availability of organic seeds and young animals.[22]

C. Summary and conclusion

The planned reform of the law for organic farming seems to be quite appropriate to increase the sustainability of organic production. In terms of legal policy the reform presents itself as a plausible and suitable measure within the meaning of Organic 3.0. From a legal perspective some general aspects should be considered:

As the organic production primarily participates in the trade of food by a corresponding labelling, and as this form of facultative labelling depends on keeping certain "rules of the game", organic production can be seen as a factual phenomenon, which is not only shaped, but in general also established, by law.[23] From a legal point of view, its further existence, development and functionality are ensured, if the concerning regulations at least comply with the rule of law, particularly with TFEU, Article 290, which lets the far reaching empowerments of the commission appear problematic. For this reason it is important to take into account this aspect in the further reform process.

Regulation (EC) 834/2007' COM (2014) 180 final, Annex; see furthermore German Federal Ministry of Food and Agriculture, 'Bundesminister Christian Schmidt und EP-Berichterstatter Martin Häusling führen erste Abstimmungsgespräche zur Revision der EU-Ökoverordnung' (press release no 56, 12 February 2015) <https://www.bmel.de/SharedDocs/Pressemitteilungen/2015/056-SC-Gespraech-SchmidtHaeuslingOekoVO.html> accessed 19 September 2015.

22 Hanno Bender, 'Öko-Verordnung nimmt Form an' *Lebensmittelzeitung* (Frankfurt am Main, 13 February 2015) 28 <http://www.martin-haeusling.eu/images/150213_LZ_Lebensmittelzeitung_zu_%C3%96koVO_MH.JPG> accessed 1 December 2015; press briefing referring to the proposal for the rapporteur Martin Häusling for the parliament draft concerning the reform of the Council Regulation (EC) 834/2007 of 28 June 2007 on organic production and labelling of organic products and repealing Regulation (EEC) 2092/91 [2007] OJ L 189/1, 2 f. <http://www.martin-haeusling.eu/images/150520_Pressebriefing_%C3%96ko-VO_Mai_2015.pdf> accessed 13 August 2015.

23 Aside from the law-based organic production, IFOAM also considers such production as organic, which is not certified, but factually fulfils the requirements for organic quality, IFOAM, 'The full diversity of Organic Agriculture: What we call Organic' (2015) Position Paper <http://infohub.ifoam.bio/sites/default/files/page/files/full-diversity-organic-agriculture-en-web_0.pdf> accessed 31 October 2015.

§ 19 The participation and significance of cooperatives in food supply chains – selected legal issues

Aneta Suchoń

A. Introduction

The food supply chain connects three important sectors of the European economy: farming, food processing, and distribution[1]. One of the essential entities in this chain are, undoubtedly, cooperatives. Since they deal with agricultural production and sales of agricultural produce from their members' farms as well as with transporting, storing, packaging and purchasing the means of production and devices, processing and selling to consumers, they constitute a significant tool of the development of agro-logistics[2]. Co-operation of agricultural producers in the form of cooperatives is an expression of horizontal and vertical integration in agriculture. The former is based on the cooperation with all the entities belonging to the same stage of production or distribution. An example is the cooperative agricultural producers groups[3]. The latter is based on economic and production coop-eration among units which produce a given product (e.g. a dairy coopera-tive).

Working together helps farmers to increase their competitiveness, to play a fundamental role in the development of rural areas and to broaden

---

1 Sebastian Jarzębowski / Bogdan Klepacki, 'Łańcuchy dostaw w gospodarce żywnościowej' (2013) 103 Zeszyty Naukowe SGGW, Ekonomika i Organizacja Gospodarki Żywnościowej 107.
2 Bogdan Klepacki, 'Agrologistyka – nowe wyzwania dla nauki i praktyki' (2011) 3 Czasopismo Logistyka 12.
3 Jos Bijman / Roldan Muradian / Andrei Cechin, 'Agricultural cooperatives and val-ue chain coordination' in A.H.J. Bert Helmsing / Sietze Vellema (eds), *Value Chains, Inclusion and Endogenous Development: Contrasting Theories and Reali-ties* (Routledge Press 2011) 82; Jos Bijman, *Essays on Agricultural Co-operatives; Governance Structure in Fruit and Vegetable Chains* (2002) <http://repub.eur.nl/pub/867/EPS2002015ORG_9058920240_BIJMAN.pdf> accessed 27 July 2015.

consumers' knowledge of agricultural products[4]. Associating as agricultural producers and engaging in further stages of the food chain are also important in terms of ensuring food safety. The safety regulations cover the entire food chain, all stages of production, processing and distribution, ranging from primary production of food and feed, to the final consumer[5]. A vital issue is also monitoring the movement of foodstuffs, the early detection of at-risk food, which allows for its quick withdrawal from the market. According to D. Lambert and M. Cooper, the analysis of the structure of the food supply chain should consider, firstly, what participants there are in the chain, what their roles are and what the possible configurations of the chain are. Secondly, what the organisational structure is and the types of contracts. Thirdly, what resources (IT, people, and technologies) are involved and what the degree of integration among the participants of the chain is[6]. All these three aspects are essential for the maintenance of food safety. Cooperatives' participation and importance in the food chain depend upon many factors, among others, laws that may contribute to the development of cooperatives by means of increasing their participation in agricultural markets, processing and distribution.

The aim of this paper is to identify regulations that, firstly, encourage the agricultural producers to create cooperatives and promote participation of these entities in the supply chain and, secondly, reinforce the importance of agricultural cooperatives already existing in the context of food safety.

Due to the complexity of the issue, the paper refers to the EU laws and statistics, as well as to Polish regulations.

---

4 COPA-COGECA's memorandum on the future development of the European Model of Agriculture <http://copa-cogeca.be> accessed 20 July 2015.
5 Małgorzata Korzycka- Iwanow, *Prawo żywnościowe. Zarys prawa polskiego i wspólnotowego* (LexisNexis 2007).
6 Douglas Lambert / Martha Cooper, 'Issues in supply chain management' (2000) 29 (1) Industrial Marketing Management 65.

B. Cooperatives in the food supply chains

I. Agriculture Cooperatives in the European Union

According to statistical data, in the European Union there are about 22,000 agricultural cooperatives, and their total turnover exceeds 347 billion euros. They have more than a 50% share in the supply of means of production and over 60% in the processing and marketing of agricultural products[7].

The EU rules encourage agricultural producers to cooperate and build a stable organisational structure. First of all, it is necessary to mention the Regulations in regard to the agricultural markets, particularly the ones concerning milk, fruit and vegetables (Regulation (EU) 1308/2013).[8] The former allows cooperatives to act as purchasers and processing entities, groups and organisations of agricultural producers. The latter is dedicated to organisations of producers of fruit and vegetables, and in the new EU countries to initially recognised organisations of producers of fruit and vegetables. The farmers are encouraged to associate by the EU regulations relating not only to agricultural markets but also to finance and rural development (Regulation (EU) 1305/2013).[9]

Statistical data confirm that agricultural cooperatives play a significant role on European agricultural markets in terms of their stability, thus fitting in the treaty objective of the Common Agricultural Policy. In many regions of the European Union there is a relatively high share of coopera-

---

7 COGECA, 'Development of Agricultural Cooperatives in the EU 2014' (2014) <http://agricultura.gencat.cat/web/.content/de_departament/de02_estadis-tiques_observatoris/27_butlletins/02_butlletins_nd/documents_nd/fitxers_estat-ics_nd/2015/0152_2015_IA_Cooperatives_Cooperatives-UE.pdf> accessed 20 July 2015.

8 Regulation (EU) 1308/2013 of the European Parliament and of the Council of 17 December 2013 establishing a common organisation of the markets in agricultural products and repealing Council Regulations (EEC) 922/72, (EEC) 234/79, (EC) 1037/2001 and (EC) 1234/2007 [2013] OJ L 347/671.

9 Regulation (EU) 1305/2013 of the European Parliament and of the Council of 17 December 2013 on support for rural development by the European Agricultural Fund for Rural Development (EAFRD) and repealing Council Regulation (EC) 1698/2005 [2013] OJ L 347/487.

tives in the milk market, amounting to over 90%. This applies primarily to Austria, Denmark, Sweden and Finland[10].

In France, cooperatives actively support local farmers in developing their farms in a sustainable manner. In addition, they have recently taken over a number of important companies from the agri-food sector and created many subsidiaries which deal with processing and marketing. Currently, the farmers, through their cooperatives and their subsidiaries, control more than half of the processing industry of agricultural products[11]. In France, cooperatives deal with marketing and production, having a lot of various development options. It is also a real opportunity for them to improve their position on the great European market and compete with multinationals in the agro-food sector.

It is also worth emphasising the activities of cooperatives and their consortia in Italy for the benefit of products registered as a Protected Designation of Origin, Protected Geographical Indication and Traditional Specialty Guaranteed. Changes to the EU rules and the implementation of the Regulation (EU) 1151/2012[12] resulted in the implementation of a new act in Italy, namely the decree of 14 October 2013 concerning national rules on the implementation of the mentioned Ordinance (EU)[13]. Consortia safeguard production, inform consumers and promote interest in purchasing the protected products. They can create programmes aimed at improving the quality of production in the field of health, safety and hygiene,

---

10 Jos Bijman / Constantine Iliopoulos / Krijn J. Poppe / Caroline Gijselinckx / Konrad Hagedorn / Markus Hanisch / George W.J. Hendrikse / Rainer Kühl / Petri Ollila / Perttu Pyykkönen / Ger van der Sangen, 'EP pilot project: Support for Farmers' Cooperatives' (European Commission External Studies 2012) <http://ec.europa.eu/agriculture/external-studies/2012/support-farmers   coop/fulltext_en.pdf> accessed 7 July 2015.

11 French Ministry of Agriculture and Fisheries Edited, 'Agricultural Cooperation in France'   (2005)   <http://www.cooperation-agricole.coop/sites/CFCA/entreprisescoop/chiffres/20050725_presentation_anglais.pdf> accessed 11 July 2015.

12 Regulation (EU) 1151/2012 of the European Parliament and of the Council of 21 November 2012 on quality schemes for agricultural products and foodstuffs [2012] OJ L 343/1.

13 Decreto recante disposizioni nazionali per l'attuazione del Regolamento (UE) n. 1151/2012 del Parlamento europeo e del Consiglio del 21 novembre 2012 sui regimi di qualità dei prodotti agricoli e alimentary in materia di DOP, IGP e STG [2013] G.U.n. 251 del 25/10/2013 <https://www.politicheagricole.it/flex/cm/pages/ServeBLOB.php/L/IT/IDPagina/679> accessed 11 July 2015.

as well as chemical, physical, organoleptic and nutritional value of the product.

II. Cooperatives in Poland

The following cooperatives in Poland are of particular importance for the development of the food chain: a) cooperatives of agricultural producer groups – they associate producers of one or several products and are commonly called agricultural producer groups, which refer to branch cooperativeness, b) processing cooperatives, e.g. dairy cooperatives, c) supply and sale cooperatives, such as "Samopomoc Chłopska" cooperatives, d) agricultural production cooperatives, which deal with joint-farm management and work for the members' individual farms, according to the Cooperative Law Act of 16 September 1982[14].

The fundamental law which regulates the problem of cooperatives in Poland is the Cooperative Law Act of 16 September 1982[15]. According to it, a cooperative is a voluntary association of an unlimited number of persons, with variable personnel and participation fund, which runs a joint business activity in the members' interest. It may also run a social activity and an educational and cultural activity in the interest of its members and their milieu. The Cooperative Law Act of 16 September 1982 states that agricultural production cooperatives deal with joint farm management and work for the members' individual farms. The cooperatives may also be involved in another type of business activity. The regulations do not limit the types of business, and they do not define the proportions between the agricultural activity and another business. It should be noted that food law has recently started to cover the primary production of food. In order to ensure food safety, it is necessary to consider all aspects of the food chain, from primary production through its distribution after the sale or supply of food to the final consumer. Each aspect can have an impact on food safety. Primary production is the first part of the food chain regulated by law[16].

---

14 See more Aneta Suchoń, 'Legal and Economic Aspects of the Operation of Cooperatives in Polish Agriculture' (2012) 2 (7) Journal of Agricultural Science and Technology B 737.
15 Consolidated text Journal of Laws 2013, item 1443 as amended.
16 Małgorzata Korzycka-Iwanow, *Prawo żywnościowe. Zarys prawa polskiego i wspólnotowego* (LexisNexis 2007).

Some agricultural production cooperatives deal not only with plant activity but also with animals, processing and trade, following the farm-to-fork principle. A good example is Cooperative Agrofirma Witkowo. There are cooperatives engaged in running agricultural activities (primary production), not only in Poland but also in the Eastern states of Germany[17], in Bulgaria[18], and in Slovakia[19].

In Poland, social cooperatives are more and more popular. According to the Act on social cooperatives, the object of activity of a social cooperative is to run a joint enterprise based on individual work of its members. The operation of a cooperative is usually connected with the region where the cooperative conducts its activity[20]. Some of them are engaged in farming activities, more and more often in environmental activities, running an organic farm. Such cooperatives may benefit from the measures related to its agricultural activities. The basis is the Regulation of the Minister of Agriculture and Rural Development of 13 March 2015 on detailed conditions and procedures for the granting of financial assistance under the measure "Organic Farming" under the Rural Development Programme for 2014-2020. Some social cooperatives deal with processing of food or running agritourism farms which also offer food to tourists.

Milk cooperatives mainly purchase and process milk from their members. Under the membership contract, a member of the cooperative undertakes to produce and deliver to the cooperative a specified amount of agri-

---

17 Rolf Steding, *Die Produktivgenossenschaft im deutschen Genossenschaftsrecht* (Berliner Schriften zum Genossenschaftswesen, vol 6, Vandenhoeck & Ruprecht 1995); Rolf Steding, *Produktivgenossenschaften in der ostdeutschen Landwirtschaft - Ursprung und Anspruch* (2nd edn, Berliner Beiträge zum Genossenschaftswesen, vol 14, Institut für Genossenschaftswesen an der Humboldt-Universität zu Berlin 1994).

18 Iwan Boevsky, 'Support for Farmers' Cooperatives - Country Report Bulgaria' (2012) <http://edepot.wur.nl/244789> accessed 2 July 2015.

19 Agricultural cooperatives produce on an area of 52% of the agricultural land in Slovakia, ie app 1,268,000 ha; Ann Bandlerová / Pavol Schwarcz / Jarmila Lazíková / Ivan Takáč, 'Support for Farmers' Cooperatives - Country Report Slovakia' (2012) <http://edepot.wur.nl/244813> accessed 2 July 2015.

20 A social cooperative is a social economy entity offering support for the people at risk of social exclusion or who already are socially excluded. The operation of these entities and the concept of social economy are part of the EU actions. Aneta Suchoń, 'The principles of the organization and operations of social cooperatives for rural development in the light of the legal regulations in Poland' (2013) 3 (29) Journal of Agribusiness and Rural Development 179.

cultural product (e.g. milk) of a determined kind and the cooperatives undertake to collect and pay. Additionally, the contract may extend the obligations of a contracting party to provide instructional and advisory services so that a milk producer can get the "Extra" class grade, chargeable service of milking equipment and milk storage devices, washing and disinfectant products used in dairy industry or milking, and refrigeration equipment. Due to the fact that the object of collection can only be milk the quality of which has been determined by means of examination carried out by the authorised laboratory, the producer is obliged to subject the milk to such examination.

Besides these basic activities, some cooperatives take actions to develop dairy cattle breeding belonging to cooperative members, to increase milk production and improve its quality, to eliminate cattle diseases as well as to promote the principles of hygiene and disease prevention in cattle breeding. Additionally, cooperatives collaborate and help to organise farms specialising in milk production[21]. The milk products supply chain has a complicated structure which consists of various economic entities such as milk producers, dairies, distribution, commerce, consumers and existing between them economic and legal relations[22]. Additionally, the uniqueness of that chain results from the fact that milk is one of the staple foods for people. Therefore, there are, on the one hand, numerous requirements for milk production and, on the other, instruments intended to guarantee stability in terms of quantity[23].

The activity of cooperatives dealing with processing is highly affected by legislation on food law, particularly, for instance, by the Act of 25 August 2006 on Safety of Food and Nutrition[24], Regulation (EC) 178/2002[25],

---

21 See for example Statut spółdzielni <http://rokitnianka.pl/pliki/STATUT-28-XI-05.pdf > accessed 8 July 2015.

22 Michał Sznajder, 'Skutki likwidacji kwot mlecznych dla polskiego rolnictwa' (Kancelaria Senatu, Biuro Analiz i Dokumentacji 2010) <http://www.senat.pl/k7/dok/opinia/2010/oe-162.pdf> accessed 2 April 2011.

23 Monika Masalska / Adam Sosnowski, 'Zarządzanie kosztami logistycznymi w przedsiębiorstwie mleczarskim' *logistica.pl* <*http:// logistica.pl*> accessed 2 July 2015.

24 Consolidated text Journal of Laws *No 136, item 914* as amended.

25 Regulation (EC) 178/2002 of the European Parliament and of the Council of 28 January 2002 laying down the general principles and requirements of food law, establishing the European Food Authority and laying down procedures in matters of food safety [2002] OJ L 31/1.

Regulation (EC) 852/2004[26]. Each cooperative has introduced HACCP, which stands for Hazard Analysis and Critical Control Points. It is a system which gives a holistic approach to food safety. The HACCP system has been designed to recognise and control hazards that may appear at any stage of producing and storing food. Hazard refers to anything that may cause damage to a consumer[27].

Cooperatives associating agricultural producers which produce one or more products are commonly known as groups of agricultural producers. According to the Act on Groups of Agricultural Producers and their Associations of 15 September 2000[28], natural persons, organisational units without legal personality status and legal persons managing a farm, in accordance with the agricultural tax regulations, or running an agricultural business in special branches of agricultural production, may be organised into groups of agricultural producers in order to adjust agricultural production to market conditions, improve the effectiveness of management, plan production with special attention given to its quality and quantity, concentrate the supply, organise the sales of agricultural products, and protect the natural environment. In an attempt to encourage cooperation of agricultural producers and, simultaneously, taking into consideration the practical barriers encountered by the groups, the legislator amended the Regulations of the Act of 15 September 2000[29].

Apart from the agricultural producer groups, established according to the Act on agricultural producer groups of 15 September 2000, groups of fruit and vegetable producers, which operate by virtue of separate legal regulations, should also be noted. Above all, this concerns the Act on organisation of the fruit and vegetable markets, hop market, tobacco market and dried fodder market of 19 December 2003 and executive regulations. By meeting the requirements of the fruit and vegetable market these groups play a very significant role in the food chain. Group members provide agricultural products to the cooperative, which either keeps them

---

26 Regulation (EC) 852/2004 of the European Parliament and of the Council of 29 April 2004 on the hygiene of foodstuffs [2004] OJ L 139/1.

27 <http:// haccp-polska.pl/haccp_plan_haccp.html> accessed 2 July 2015.

28 Journal of Laws No 88, Pos 983 with amendments.

29 The amendments of 18 June 2004 (Journal of Laws 2004 No 162, Item 1694) and 15 December 2006 (Journal of Laws 2006 No 251, Item 1847) are particularly important. See more Aneta Suchoń / Jan Schürmann, 'Landwirtschaftliche Erzeugergemeinschaften in Polen - Rechtliche und wirtschaftliche Aspekte' (2012) 11 AUR 412.

(store) or directly sells them. The latter situation occurs primarily in relation to soft fruit such as cherries. As for some hard fruit, the groups more and more tend to make sales agreements, called trade agreements. Under these agreements a group or an organisation of producers undertakes to provide and transfer the ownership of fruit or vegetables to buyers. There are many requirements connected with the quality of products which are difficult to meet by individual producers. It is easier to achieve them while working together in cooperatives. As far as the rape oilseed is concerned, cooperative groups usually make a farming contract. Under farming contracts, agricultural producers undertake to produce and deliver to the contracting party (a dairy) a specified amount of milk of a determined kind and the contracting party, in turn, undertakes to collect that milk within the established time limit, pay the pre-arranged price and to perform specified additional performance if the contract or specific provisions provide for a duty to render such performance (Article 613 (1) of the Civil Code).

It is worth emphasising that agricultural cooperatives make farming contracts both as an agriculture producer (e.g. agricultural production cooperative, social cooperatives, agricultural producer group), and as the contracting party (e.g. dairy cooperatives). Furthermore, the mentioned membership agreement signed between a cooperative group or dairy cooperatives and agricultural producers contains elements of the farming contract.

One of the main factors encouraging farmers to cooperate and create cooperative agricultural producer groups are EU funds. According to Article 27 of Regulation (EU) 1305/2013 of the European Parliament and of the Council of 17 December 2013 on support for rural development by the European Agricultural Fund for Rural Development (EAFRD) and repealing Council Regulation (EC) 1698/2005, support under this measure shall be granted in order to facilitate the setting up of producer groups and organisations in the agriculture and forestry sectors for the purpose of adapting the production and output of producers who are members of such groups or organisations to market requirements; to jointly place goods on the market, including preparation for sale, centralisation of sales and supply to bulk buyers; to establish common rules on production information, with particular regard to harvesting and availability.

Cooperatives, agricultural producer groups and organisations are highly affected by the EU programme "quality schemes for agricultural products and foodstuffs" – action under the Rural Development Plan 2014-2020. Support to carry out information and promotion activities, including support actions in the field of information and promotion of high-quality products made by participants in quality systems, i.e. by promotional teams consisting of at least two manufacturers. The promotional team is an entity which integrates the participants of the quality system, such as a Group of Producers, a Producers Organisation, a Consortium, an Association, an Agricultural circle, an Agricultural trade association, or a cooperative.

C. Summary

The above analysis has shown that agricultural cooperatives, being present in many stages of the supply chain, are a significant instrument of the development of agro-logistics in the EU. It results from a diversified activity of such entities. On the one hand, it is possible to distinguish agricultural production cooperatives which run an agricultural activity, including an ecological one, that sell food products for further commercialisation or processing. Some cooperatives, however, do not sell processed food products to consumers, which makes them participants of a short supply chain. On the other hand, some cooperatives deal with selling agricultural products, providing agro-technical services or processing[30]. Both the EU legislation and the provisions contained in the national legal acts include instruments encouraging farmers to work together and effectively participate in further stages of the food supply chain. Cooperatives must comply with very comprehensive provisions relating to food safety.

After Poland's accession to the European Union more and more significance has been given to cooperative groups of agricultural producers and initially recognised groups or organisations of fruit and vegetables producers, which contributed to streamlining logistics management on that market. The purchase of professional transport equipment and devices, construction or renovation of storehouses, the purchase of assorting lines have contributed to the concentration of supply, enhancing the quality and attractiveness of Polish products. At the same time, such actions have influence on maintaining a proper level of production or safety. A cooperative as a legal form which associates milk producers is highly important for the

---

30 Aneta Suchoń, 'Cooperatives in food supply chains – selected legal and economic aspects' (2014) 6 Czasopismo Logistyka 13785.

stability and development of the milk market. However, the primary production and the sales of milk as the first stage of the supply chain, is regulated by numerous legal regulations connected with food safety. Even more obligations relate to milk processing, which is connected with HACCP and other quality systems not presently mandatory. More and more restricted requirements intend, primarily, to guarantee food safety for the consumer.

The safety of food is also impacted by the following factors: cooperatives are connected with a given region, have long tradition and have gained the trust of the residents. The stage of transportation is eliminated or reduced, which influences the quality of the food. Cooperatives are familiar with the needs of a given region and try to adapt their offer. An important factor is the cooperation between cooperatives in various stages of the food chain. It is also worth noting that the cooperative members and their families are also sometimes consumers of cooperatives, e.g. of dairy cooperatives, juice or meat, consumer cooperatives.

§ 20 The legal implementation of the principle of local residence in the Real Property Transactions Act

Hanna Schmelz

A. Concentration of agricultural soils in Europe

The final report of the 1996 World Food Summit states that food security "exists when all people, at all times, have physical and economic access to sufficient, safe and nutritious food to meet their dietary needs and food preferences for an active and healthy life".[1] Two important aspects of the guarantee of the food security are the ability of the local farmers to access agricultural soils and the general protection of the agricultural soils for reasons of food production. Especially in the developing countries of Africa, South America and Asia, the local farmers are prevented from accessing agricultural land by large scale foreign concerns which acquire entire areas of land, displacing whole local farmer families and indigenous peoples. These acquisitions through illegal conditions, constituted by violating human rights – in particular the human right to food[2] – are called land grabbing.[3] The phenomenon of land grabbing is accompanied by an-

---

1 Raj Patel, ' "Food sovereignty" is next big idea' *Financial Times* (20 November 2013); Food and Agriculture Organization (FAO), *Rome Declaration on Food Security and World Food Summit Plan of Action* (November 1996).
2 Ines Härtel, 'Ein (Menschen-)Recht auf Nahrung?' in Max-Emanuel Geis / Markus Winkler / Christian Bickenbach (eds), *Festschrift für Friedhelm Hufen zum 70. Geburtstag* (C.H. Beck 2015) 23 ff.
3 As of now, there has not been a universal definition, refer to the European Economic and Social Committee, 'Opinion of the European Economic and Social Committee of 21 January 2015 on Land grabbing – a warning for Europe and a threat to family farming' (NAT/632) 4 no 2.2; for more details about the term see Helmut Goeser, 'Land Grabbing – Ursachen, Wirkungen, Handlungsbedarf' (briefing WD 5-3010-204/11 of the Academic Research Service of the German parliament 2011) <https://www.bundestag.de/blob/192332/e135367c9c5de7bbfdf987adda71c606/land_grabbing-data.pdf> accessed 1 February 2016; German Federal Ministry of Economic Cooperation and Development, 'Investitionen in Land und das Phänomen des "Land Grabbing" – Herausforderungen für die Entwicklungspolitik' (2012) 2 BMZ-Strategiepapier <https://www.bmz.de/de/mediathek/publikationen/

other phenomenon: the land concentrations in the hands of a few.[4] Not only in the countries of the African or South American continent, but also in some member-states of the European Union, this kind of development of the agricultural structure is taking place.[5] Concerning the European cases of land transactions, some experts[6] are rejecting the term "land grabbing" because according to their views, the transactions of agricultural soils are not implemented by the violation of law and the displacement of local people. Nonetheless, these transactions involve land concentrations in the property of big companies like JLW Holding AG, KTG Agrar SE, AgroEnergy AG and realkapital KGaA.[7] The affected regions in the EU are the former Eastern bloc states like Romania, Bulgaria, the Republic of Hungary and Poland.[8] Furthermore, in the territory of the former German

---

archiv/reihen/strategiepapiere/Strategiepapier316_2_2012.pdf> accessed 1 February 2016.

4 Jennifer Franco / Saturnino M. Borras / Jan Douwe van der Ploeg, 'Land concentration, land grabbing and people's struggles in Europe: Introduction to the collection of studies' in Jennifer Franco / Saturnino M. Borras (eds), *Land concentration, land grabbing and people's struggles in Europe* (Transnational Institute for European Coordination / Via Campesina / Hands off the Land network June 2013) 6, 7.

5 Sylvia Kay / Jonathan Peuch / Jennifer Franco, 'Extent of Farmland Grabbing in the EU' (European Parliament Directorate-General for internal policies, policy department B: Agriculture and rural development, Study 2015) <http://www.europarl.europa.eu/RegData/etudes/STUD/2015/540369/IPOL_STU %282015%29540369_EN.pdf> accessed 1 February 2016.

6 Christine Chemnitz / Jes Weigelt, 'Bodenatlas 2015: Strukturwandel – Die neuen Großgrundbesitzer' (Heinrich-Böll-Stiftung / Institute for Advanced Sustainability Studies e.V. 2015) 29 <https://www.bund.net/fileadmin/bundnet/publikationen/ landwirtschaft/150108_bund_landwirtschaft_bodenatlas_2015.pdf> accessed 1 February 2016, according to whom land grabbing in Eastern Germany is detailed as a sellout of areas to external investors without displacement of local farmers and inhabitants, thus without the violation of a human right; opposing the term 'land grabbings' with regard to Eastern Germany is Werner Schwarz, 'Investoren in der Landwirtschaft – Chancen und Risiken für den Agrarstandort Deutschland' (2013) BzAR 402 ff.

7 A more in-depth perspective can be found at Bernhard Forstner / Andreas Tietz, 'Kapitalbeteiligung nichtlandwirtschaftlicher und überregional ausgerichteter Investoren an landwirtschaftlichen Unternehmen in Deutschland' Thünen Report 5 (Johann-Heinrich von Thünen-Insitut 2013) 38 <http://literatur.ti.bund.de/ digbib_extern/bitv/dn052170.pdf> accessed 1 February 2016.

8 Jennifer Franco / Saturnino M. Borras / Jan Douwe van der Ploeg, 'Land concentration, land grabbing and people's struggles in Europe: Introduction to the collection of studies' in Jennifer Franco / Saturnino M. Borras (eds), *Land concentration, land*

Democratic Republic (GDR), the phenomenon of land concentration can be recognized on a slowly increasing level, being constituted through new complex concern structures.[9] This development might very well be influenced by the German reunification process in 1990 s and the emergence of private agricultural transactions. As a matter of fact, the former state farms called agricultural productive cooperations (LPGs) possessed large amounts of hectares. In the 1990 s, the agricultural cooperatives' successors – constituted in the company structure of German limited companies (GmbHs) and cooperative societies (Genossenschaften) – became owners of these areas.[10] These historical facts make these agricultural enterprises and their large hectares of land appear to be very attractive for new company constructions and investors[11] of the (non-)agricultural sectors. These investors acquire loan capital especially due to their activities related to the stock exchange and the (inter-)nationally organised capital market.[12] They re-invest this capital in the agricultural soil by acquiring the soil or by virtue of purchasing (all) shares of companies operating in the agriculture market, their assets including agricultural soils. By purchasing a certain number of the company's shares, the investors gain both influence and control of the corporate management. In contrast, the local farmers are not able to keep up with this pace. With regard to agricultural enterprises that

---

grabbing and people's struggles in Europe (Transnational Institute for European Coordination / Via Campesina / Hands off the Land network June 2013) 17 – 20.

9 Christine Chemnitz / Jes Weigelt, 'Bodenatlas 2015: Strukturwandel – Die neuen Großgrundbesitzer' (Heinrich-Böll-Stiftung / Institute for Advanced Sustainability Studies e.V. 2015) 29 <https://www.bund.net/fileadmin/bundnet/publikationen/landwirtschaft/150108_bund_landwirtschaft_bodenatlas_2015.pdf> accessed 1 February 2016.

10 Rolf Steding, 'Von der LPG zur Agrargenossenschaft' (2004) NL-BzAR 274.

11 For further information on the term of investors on the non-agricultural sector refer to Lothar Schramm / Thomas Hahn, *Grundstückverkehrsrecht* (HLBS-Verlag 2014) 16; Closing report of the Federal Task Force from 20 March 2015, 24; Bernhard Forstner / Andreas Tietz / Klaus Klare / Werner Kleinhanss / Peter Weingarten, 'Aktivitäten von nichtlandwirtschaftlichen und überregional ausgerichteten Investoren auf dem landwirtschaftlichen Bodenmarkt in Deutschland' (2011) Final Report (Johann-Heinrich von Thünen-Institut 2011) 31 ff. <https://www.ti.bund.de/media/publikationen/landbauforschung-sonderhefte/lbf_sh352.pdf> accessed 8 February 2016.

12 Robert Fraunhoffer / Dirk Schiereck / Sergej Stimeier, 'Kapitalanlagen in Landwirtschaft – Rendite und Risiko' (2013) 91 Berichte über Landwirtschaft, Zeitschrift für Agrarpolitik und Landwirtschaft <http://buel.bmel.de/index.php/buel/article/view/26/schiereck-pdf> accessed 8 February 2016.

are both locally residing and family operated, there is concern that they may be almost entirely driven out of the marketplace. Against this background, the question arises as to whether the previous German regulatory instruments are still sufficient enough to guarantee the protection of the agricultural land and the ability for the local farmers to access the land.

One of the important regulatory instruments concerning the transaction of agricultural soil is the Real Property Transactions Act (Grundstück-verkehrsgesetz)[13]. By means of this law, transactions of real estate may be subject to the authorisation of an administrating bureau.[14] The official authorisation may only be denied under certain conditions.[15] Since 2006, farm land matters are to be regulated exclusively on a regional basis.[16] It remains to be seen whether the regional legislators will adopt a reform of their own.

B. Legal definition of the farmer with regard to Case Law of the ECJ

With regard to the Legal Multi-Level System of the European Union, one reform aspect[17] should be discussed. The aspect concerns the legal imple-

---

13 In the revised version published in the Federal Law Gazette part III, section 7810-1, last amended by art 108 of the statute of 17 December 2008 (German Federal Law Gazette 2008 I, 2586).

14 § 1 (1) GrdstVG: 'The provisions of this chapter are active for the agricultural soils (...).' § 2 (1) GrdstVG: 'The mutual transfer of property to real estate and its obligation require an official authorisation'.

15 § 9 (1) no 1 and (2) GrdstVG: '(1) Official authorisation may only be dismissed if there are facts that prove that 1. the transaction means an unhealthy proportioning of grounds and soils or 2. (...) 3. (...). (2) Regularly, an unhealthy proportioning of grounds and soils exists if the transaction is in contradiction to the improvement of the agricultural structure'.

16 For an instructive overview, refer to Ines Härtel, 'Der Föderalismus in der Bewährungsprobe des landwirtschaftlichen Bodenrechts' in Europäisches Zentrum für Föderalismus-Forschung Tübingen (ed), *Jahrbuch des Föderalismus 2015* (Nomos 2015) 228 ff.

17 Bauernbund Brandenburg e.V., 'Proposal of the farmers' association of Brandenburg to the real estate market task force Brandenburg' (January 2014): (1) A farmer with the right to acquire land is any natural person who is practicing the profession of a farmer (either as the owner of an agricultural enterprise or as a shareholder in a responsible position in an agricultural enterprise) and having their living and working residence within a thirty-kilometre-radius of the respective area or who is intending to fulfil these requirements within a short time frame or a

mentation of the principle of local residence by defining the term "farmer with the right to acquire land". There is tension between its legal structure and the decisions of the ECJ in the matter of legal restrictions concerning transactions relating to real estate.[18]

I. Effects and objectives

The definition affects the interpretation of the undetermined legal terms "unhealthy proportioning of grounds and soils" and "improvement of the agricultural structure" with regard to § 9 paragraph 1 no. 1 and paragraph 2 Real Property Transactions Act. According to consistent case law, a distribution is economically unhealthy and the authorisation has to be refused if the transaction is conducted towards a non-farmer despite the ability of a farmer or agricultural enterprise to acquire the real estate under the same conditions.[19] The provisions of the Real Property Transactions Act imply that there is competition between farmers and non-farmers. This competition should be decided in favour of the farmer who is both able and willing to increase his real estate capital. The definition of the term "farmer" influences the implied competition, established by the case law on § 9 paragraph 1 no. 1 and paragraph 2 Real Property Transactions Act, in favour of the person who is a farmer by the legal definition; that is, in favour of the person who will have his residence on the real estate that is to be acquired. This definition pursues the following aims: The incentive of foreign investors would be minimized, reducing the attractiveness of the areas to serve as mere capital and assets. The local positioning of the shareholders of legal persons may increase their overall awareness of the regional challenges involved with agricultural structure, social concerns

---

legal person if 75 percent of its shareholders fulfil the aforementioned requirements. (2) If the acquiring person is intending to fulfil the aforementioned requirements within a short time frame, the official authorisation is only granted under the condition that the acquiring person maintains their status for at least ten years and that they manage the area accordingly – otherwise, the official authorisation will be dismissed and the contract will be reversed.

18 For the individual renovation initiatives refer to the closing report of the Federal Task Force from 20 March 2015.

19 Consistent jurisdiction, most recently Decision of the Federal Court of Justice of 26 November 2010 – BLw 14/09 (2011) NJW-RR 521.

and economic influence. The capital of the local associations may empower the region as there are more re-investments to be expected.

II. Case Law of the ECJ relating to the acquisition of real estate

Whether the principle of residence is compatible with the provisions of the European law concerning the limitations of official authorisations, will be assessed in the conclusion (C.). The following part is about a judicial analysis of the holdings of the ECJ concerning the requirements for limitations of official authorisations (1. and 2.). Furthermore, the part gives a comparative analysis of the so called domestic models and the relevant case law (3.).

1. Official authorisations as limitations of the EU fundamental freedoms

The grounds of refusal relating to the acquisition of agricultural plots serve as limitations, especially to the unrestricted movement of capital.[20]

---

20 For the controversial differentiation of the freedom of unrestricted movement of capital and freedom of establishment refer to Benjamin Herz, *Unternehmenstransaktionen zwischen Niederlassungs- und Kapitalverkehrsfreiheit* (Nomos 2014); Christian Hubatsch, *Der Immobilienerwerb in der Europäischen Union* (Duncker & Humblot 2006) 141 f.; further referrals at Andreas Knapp, 'Diskriminierende Grunderwerbsbeschränkungen in der EU' (1999) 11 EWS 409, 412; Georg Ress / Jörg Ukrow in Eberhard Grabitz / Meinhard Hilf / Martin Nettesheim (eds), *Das Recht der Europäischen Union* (C.H. Beck 2014) TFEU, 152 a.d. 2014, art 65 recital 69; Christian Tietje in Hans von der Groeben / Jürgen Schwarze / Armin Hatje (eds), *Europäisches Unionsrecht* (7th edn, Nomos 2015) TFEU art 49 recital 23; with regard to the prior procedures, the ECJ has exclusively decided on the freedom of unlimited movement of capital. The reasoning was that limitations of the freedom of establishment were only an inevitable consequence to the limitations of unlimited movement of capital, thus insofar not warranting a dedicated ruling, this equals, Joined Cases C-515/99, C-519/99, C-520/99, C-521/99, C-522/99, C-523/99, C-524/99, C-526/99, C-527/99, C-528/99, C-529/99, C-530/99, C-531/99, C-532/99, C-533/99, C-534/99, C-535/99, C-536/99, C-537/99, C-538/99, C-539/99, C-540/99 *Reisch and others* [2002] ECR I-2192, para 28 f.; Case C-300/01 *Salzmann* [2003] ECR I-4899, para 41; Case C-370/05 *Festersen* [2007] ECR I-1129, paras 22, 24 f.; Georg Ress / Jörg Ukrow in Eberhard Grabitz / Meinhard Hilf / Martin Nettesheim (eds), *EU-Arbeitsweisevertrag* (C.H. Beck 2015) 55 a.d. 2015, art 63 recital 219.

The legal definition of the term "capital" is to be determined with respect to the Council Directive 88/361/EEC[21]. Annex I states, inter alia: investments in real estate and direct investments.

2. The justified requirements of the regulatory intervention in detail

The ECJ decided that limitations of official authorisations are justified under certain requirements that the national administrations' powers need to consider.

According to settled case law, national legal actions that are suited to restrict the exercise of the EU fundamental freedoms or to make exercising them less attractive, can be permitted if, first, they – in a non-discriminatory way – pursue an objective lying in the public interest and, second, if they are appropriate for ensuring that the aim pursued is achieved and does not go beyond what is necessary for the purpose.[22] A legal system of official authorisation can only be justified if such measures are based on objective criteria known in advance and allowing for all persons who are affected by a restrictive measure to have a legal remedy available to them.[23]

---

21 Council Directive 88/361/EEC of 24 June 1988 for the implementation of Article 67 of the Treaty [1988] OJ L 178/5; Council Directive 88/361/EEC of 24 June 1988, being a source of secondary law, cannot modify art 63 TFEU, which governs the free movement of capital. In its decision, the ECJ referred to the directive of details on the movement of capital: Case C-302/97 *Konle v Republic Austria* [1999] ECR I-3099 para 22; Case C-452/01 *Ospelt and Schlössle Weissenberg* [2003] ECR I-9743 para 7; refer to Andreas Haratsch / Christian Koenig / Matthias Pechstein, *Europarecht* (9th edn, Mohr Siebeck 2014) recital 1040.

22 Case C-452/01 *Ospelt and Schlössle Weissenberg* [2003] ECR I-9743 para 50 ff.; Case C-370/05 *Festersen* [2007] ECR I-1129 para 40; Joined Cases C-197/11 and C-203/11 *Libert and others* [2013] OJ C 225/4 para 49; Annette Göppert, 'Comment on the jurisdiction of the ECJ, Joined Cases C-197/11 and C-203/11' (2014) 7 BayVBl 203, 205.

23 Case C 452/01 *Ospelt and Schlössle Weissenberg* [2003] ECR I-9743 para 34.

a) The case of Ospelt

In the case of Ospelt, § 5 Vorarlberger GVG[24] of the Republic of Austria was ruled on. The ECJ decided that the limitation of authorisation was non-discriminating, pursuing a legitimate interest – e.g. support of an independent agricultural structure, maintenance of the rural population, decrease of the pressure on the real estate market – and setting up objectively foreseeable criteria while at the same time, it was crossing the line of the means necessary[25], violating the principle of proportionate government action. The ECJ decided that there was an unacceptable limitation of potential acquiring persons who were not managing the enterprise and who were not residing in the area even if those persons agreed to have the area leased to the same lessee under the same conditions as before. The chances of lease were further decreased for those farmers who did not have the capital to acquire real estate property.[26] In the view of the ECJ, an equally effective yet less stressful measure was tying the transaction of agricultural areas to a long term contract by virtue of which it is obligated to lease the area to another person. It was also possible for selling schemes to exist that benefit the lessors. Such schemes also allowed the non-managing persons to acquire areas if they obligated themselves to maintain the agricultural use of the soils.[27]

---

24 The law states: (1) The acquisition may only be authorized, a) – in case of an agricultural area – if the acquisition corresponds with the common interest of maintaining a proficient farmers society and if the acquiring person manages themselves within the means of an agricultural enterprise while also having their residence within the enterprise or if the acquisition does not contradict the maintenance and generation of an economically healthy, mid-size and small-size agricultural real estate.
25 Case C 452/01 *Ospelt and Schlössle Weissenberg* [2003] ECR I-9743 para 50 ff.
26 Ibid para 51.
27 Ibid para 52.

b) The case of Festersen

In the case of Festersen, § 16 of the Danish agricultural law[28] was ruled on. The ECJ states that the requirement of residence was not effective to obtain the aim of preventing the depopulation of the rural areas if the acquisition takes place by a farmer who has already been residing in the area of another enterprise.[29] Due to the consolidation of enterprises and hence their general decrease in numbers, this was, however, regularly the case. Furthermore, the ECJ ruled that the requirement of residence in the area was not necessary[30] to obtain the aim of decreased pressure on the real estate market. While the decrease of the pressure on the real estate market was a legitimate aim in order to avoid the acquisition of soils for mere capital reasons, the Danish government did not make a case as to whether there were no less stressful means to accomplish this. The ECJ clarified that the increased burden of proof concerning the necessity of the principle of residence lay on the national governments. This is due to the fact that the principle of residence restricts not only the free movement of capital, but also the right of the acquirer to choose his place of residence freely. In fact, he is guaranteed a right to do so by Article 2 (1) of Protocol No. 4 to the Convention for the Protection of Human Rights and Fundamental Freedoms, signed in Rome on 4 November 1950 (the ECHR). The duty to be continuously residing at a certain place turns out to be particularly restrictive.

Against this background, the ECJ stated that there were less stressful means of equal effectiveness: Provisions that constitute higher taxes if the area is re-sold after a short period of time, an outright minimum duration for an obligation to lease, price regulations by the state to establish a maximum price per hectare.[31]

---

28 The law states: (1) the property of an agricultural area which is within the borders of the agricultural zone and whose area does not exceed 30 hectares may be acquired if ... 4. within a six-week time frame, the acquiring person situates their residence in the respective area, 5. the acquiring person manages the area themselves.
29 Case C-370/05 *Festersen* [2007] ECR I-1129 para 32; refer to Dirk Buschle, 'Pflicht zur Begründung eines ständigen Wohnsitzes auf erworbenem Grund' (2007) 7 EuZW 215, 218 f.
30 Case C-370/05 *Festersen* [2007] ECR I-1129 para 40.
31 Ibid para 39.

3. Legal comparison: the compatibility of domestic models with European law

Comparable to the proposal to make the quality of a farmer and the authorisation for acquiring the agricultural soil dependent on the principle of residence are the so-called domestic models.[32] These models are intended to cover specific housing needs for residents, § 11 paragraph 1 sentence 2 no. 2 Federal Building Code[33]. Basically, these models can pursue urban development objectives. However, the ECJ made legal provisions for the implementation of these goals. Thus, with regard to a Flemish decree about the land and buildings policy from 27 March 2009, the ECJ decided that the domestic model laid down in this decree was not necessary in order to pursue the objectives. The domestic model required that the real estate should only be transferred to those acquirers who demonstrate a sufficient link to the municipality where the real estate is located. From the perspective of the ECJ, socio-economic objectives can constitute imperative reasons of general interest, justifying restrictions of the fundamental freedoms of the EU.[34] Such an objective could be the spatial planning intent invoked by the Flemish government to ensure sufficient residential space for socially disadvantaged sections of the population. However, the three alternative criteria of the decree[35] as conditions for the sufficient link represent a measure which is not necessary to pursue the objective. These criteria could be fulfilled not only by the poor sections of the population, but

---

32 Refer to Peter M. Huber / Ferdinand Wollenschläger, *Einheimischenmodelle - Städtebauliche Zielverwirklichung an der Schnittstelle von europäischem, nationalem, öffentlichem und privatem Recht* (Duncker & Humblot 2008); about the groups of cases refer to Martin Burgi, 'Die Legitimität von Einheimischenprivilegierungen im globalen Dorf' (1999) JZ 873, 874.
33 In German: Baugesetzbuch (BauGB) in the version of the announcement of 23 September 2004 (German Federal Law Gazette 2004 I, 2414), last amended by art 6 of the statute of 20 October 2015 (German Federal Law Gazette 2015 I, 1722).
34 Joined Cases C-197/11 and C-203/11 *Libert and others* [2013] OJ C 225/4 para 52.
35 According to the decree, there is only a sufficient bond to the municipality if the person who shall receive the real estate fulfils at least one of three following criteria: Having resided, without intermission, in the municipality or a directly bordering municipality for a period of at least six years. At the time of transfer, performing a job duty in the municipality, the job duty accounting for at least half of a working hour week. Due to significant and permanent community, family, social or economic reasons, having established a bond with the municipal.

also by those who do not have a particular demand for social protection on the real estate market.[36] Furthermore, less restrictive measures such as buyer's premium or subsidies for persons on low income would be conceivable.[37] The decision of the ECJ clarifies that domestic models can stand in accordance with the European law. However, the principle of residence and the duty of a rigid duration of stay are not sufficient criteria in order to pursue the objective *per se*.[38] In fact, further socio-economic criteria such as a certain income and a maximum net worth cap are required. Thus, the ECJ rejected a privileged treatment of the local population regardless of their need for protection.[39]

C. Summary and prospect

With regard to the ECJ holdings in the cases of Ospelt and Festersen, Brandenburg's idea to define the term "farmer with the right to acquire land" is canny in that the residential requirement is not an exclusive reason to dismiss the authorisation, unlike the cases of Ospelt and Festersen.

---

36 Joined Cases C-197/11 and C-203/11 *Libert and others* [2013] OJ C 225/4 para 55.
37 Ibid para 56.
38 Same as Martin Burgi, 'Die Legitimität von Einheimischenprivilegierungen im globalen Dorf' (1999) JZ 873, 879, according to whom a violation of art 3 (1) of the Basic Law and an illegitimacy by European law standards is established by inhabitant models that require a certain duration of local residence. In contrast, it is deemed legitimate to require that the acquiring person shall become a local inhabitant; also doubtful about the conformity to EU law Wolfgang Kahl / Angelika Röder, 'Subventionierung des örtlichen Gewerbes mittels Städtebaurecht? - VGH München, NVwZ 1999, 1008' (2001) 1 JuS 24, 28; dissenting view Peter M. Huber / Ferdinand Wollenschläger, *Einheimischenmodelle - Städtebauliche Zielverwirklichung an der Schnittstelle von europäischem, nationalem, öffentlichem und privatem Recht* (Duncker & Humblot 2008) recital 101, according to whom, as a means to the aim of proper structuring of cities and regions, even a residential obligation of up to 15 years is acceptable to prevent local inhabitants from being displaced; however, there is a differentiating comment to the case of Festersen as this case, according to Peter M. Huber / Ferdinand Wollenschläger, is about the directioning of the agricultural market, which does not justify a residential obligation of a 15 year time period.
39 Annette Göppert, 'Comment on the jurisdiction of the ECJ, Joined Cases C-197/11 and C-203/11' (2014) 7 BayVBl 203, 205; Joined Cases C-197/11, C-203/11 *Libert and others* [2013] OJ C 225/4.

This different legal instrument does, however, lead to the same result: The definition of the "farmer with the right to acquire land" strongly influences the authorisation decision in favour of the locally residing farmer. Only that farmer would be deemed a farmer in the legal sense, being privileged over a non-local farmer in the process. Most likely, this legal design would fail to fulfil the requirements that the ECJ rules to be within the necessary and proportionate dimension. Some guiding impulses can be gathered from the decision of the ECJ from 8 May 2013 as well. Whether local farmers and historically grown family operated companies of the region should be promoted depends, first of all, on their need for financial support, which has to be determined. This determination has to be made on the basis of their net worth and income. In particular, maximum caps of income and net worth on a year-to-year basis, as well as comparison groups of the income and net worth values of non-agricultural investors, should be established. If it were about the application of the provision to the individual case, the respective social conditions of each applicant would have to be made public to the granting authority. In any event, a denial of an official authorisation exclusively based on the fact that the applicant is not residing locally – thus deeming that he is not entitled to purchase as opposed to a local farmer who is capable and willing to increasing his capital – would most certainly be disproportionate.

Fourth Chapter:
Current Processes and Instruments in the Global Context

§ 21 Facilitations and difficulties in the development of common food safety standards – Codex Alimentarius and TTIP

Elisa Aust

A. Introduction

Genetically modified food will be sold in the EU without labelling, the obligation to label will be weakened, the admission procedure for new breeds will be less strict, more genetically modified food will be imported, the regional origin of products won't be traceable, and hormonally treated meat will be sold in the EU without labelling.[1] These are some of the negative visions and concerns of European consumer protectionists when thinking about the planned "Transatlantic Trade and Investment Partnership" (TTIP) that has been negotiated by the European Union and the United States of America since 7th of July 2013.

The two parties are presently bargaining for the vision of a common free trade area that would be the biggest economic area worldwide. This idea should be put into practice as soon as possible by a common and close Regulatory Cooperation in anticipation of strengthening influence on the global market. One aim is to dictate the European and American standards and values of food safety and food quality to other global players with less strict conceptions and regulations in the context of food safety and food quality, like Russia, India or China.

Another aim is to reduce 'unnecessary' costs for companies to strengthen the European and American economy in global competition.[2]

But what are the implications of the solutions to controversial questions that arise, such as the cultivation farming and consumption of genetically

---

1 Verbraucherzentrale Hamburg, 'Der "Worst Case" in Sachen Freihandelsabkommen TTIP: Das könnte beim Kauf und Verzehr von Lebensmitteln auf uns zukommen…' (August 2014) <http://www.vzhh.de/ernaehrung/347441/vzhh_TTIP_M%C3%B6gliche_Folgen.pdf> accessed 31 July 2015.
2 Directorate-General for Trade of the European Commission, *The Transatlantic Trade and Investment Partnership (TTIP) – Towards an EU-US trade deal – Inside TTIP – An overview and chapter-by-chapter guide in plain English* (2015) 5 f.

modified corn or the treatment of pigs with growth hormones, for the idea of a common valuation and standardization by a regulatory process? Both Unions and systems of food safety and food quality are based on different standards, which have frequently been the cause of lawsuits to the Appellate Body of the WTO by the United States of America, which argue that the different standards are an illegal barrier to trade.[3]

The parties plan to create a common Regulatory Cooperation Body called Regulatory Cooperation Council (RCC) or Regulatory Cooperation Body (RCB) in TTIP. The RCB should fuse these different points of view in favor of fast trade without any barriers by a wise and logical interconnection of both market and regulation systems into a common concept of food safety and food quality. On one hand, agricultural duties should be reduced in general. The sole exception should apply to sensitive products. Moreover, certificates of origin, exemption clauses, regulations and mechanisms to protect the commercial policy should be established.[4]

On the other hand, non-tariff trade barriers (NTBs) should be reduced, for example, by the mutual recognition of different product and food safety standards as equivalent, or by harmonization and creation of identical standards[5].

The European Union developed a textual proposal which gives a concrete idea of the embodiment of the RCB. This proposal is part of the European negotiation paper and will be examined critically hereafter.

Moreover, the textual proposal of sanitary and phytosanitary measures includes approaches to take into account the global role of the Codex Alimentarius Commission and the Food and Agriculture Organization of the United Nations (FAO). Initially, this article gives a short overview of the different basic market principles, taking into consideration the question of how the different markets balance the clashing interests of food safety and good food quality on one side, and a free-enterprise system on the other side.

---

3 Markus Krajewski, 'Stellungnahme für die 15. Sitzung des Ausschusses für Ernährung und Landwirtschaft zur öffentlichen Anhörung "Geplantes Freihandels- und Investitionsabkommen zwischen der EU und den USA: Transatlantic Trade and Investment Partnership – TTIP" ' (Ausschussdrucksache des Deutschen Bundestages 18(10)120-C, 30 June 2014) 5.
4 Ibid 1.
5 Bettina Rudloff, 'Lebensmittelstandards in Handelsabkommen – Unterschiedliche Regelungstraditionen von EU und USA und Tipps für TTIP' (2014) SWP-Aktuell 1, 2 f.

B. European and American basic principles of food safety and food quality

The major task of the Regulatory Cooperation is overcoming the differing European and American basic principles of food safety and food quality.

The food safety system of the European Union follows the precautionary principle, resulting in the replacement of risk taking, by risk aversion in Europe.[6] This means that the uncertainty of the existence and extent of risk, enables measures of hazard control, which do not require the explanation of the uncertainty by scientific evidence or clarification[7]. The term of risk requires that there be no risk of environmental damage or restriction of legal assets objectively, or rather that there be a conclusive scientific evaluation of the specific risk. From that point of view, the precautionary principle embodies the idea of avoidance[8]. The scientific evidence of the harmlessness of food is necessary for its admission to the European Market[9].

Contrary to this, the American system is characterized by the idea of 'aftercare' or a 'wait and see' approach[10]. Therefore, it is seen as a science-

---

6 Ragnar E. Löfstedt / David Vogel, 'The Changing Character of Regulation: A Comparison of Europe and the United States' (2001) 21 (3) Risk Analysis 399, 401.

7 Case C-284/95 *Safety Hi-Tech v S&T* [1998] ECR I-4301, para 48; Case C-236/01 *Monsanto v Presidenza del Consiglio dei Ministri* [2003] ECR I-8105; Case T-74/00, 76/00 *Artegodan v Commission* [2002] ECR II-327, para 184; Lucas Bergkamp / Laurence Kogan, 'Trade, the Precautionary Principle, and Post-Modern Regulatory Process – Regulatory Convergence in the Transatlantic Trade and Investement Partnership' (2013) 4 European Journal of Risk Regulation (EJRR) 493, 499 ff.; Johanna Monien, *Prinzipien als Wegbereiter eines globalen Umweltrechts? Das Nachhaltigkeits-, Vorsorge- und Verursacherprinzip im Mehrebenensystem* (Forum Umwelt-, Agrar- und Klimaschutzrecht, vol 4, Nomos 2014) 279; Arno Scherzberg, 'Risikoabschätzung unter Ungewissheit – Preliminary risk assessment im Kontext der Nanotechnologie' (2010) ZUR 303, 305.

8 Case C-127/02 *Landelijke Vereniging tot Behoud van de Waddenzee and Nederlandse Vereniging tot Bescherming van Vogels v Staatssecretaris van Landbouw, Natuurbeheer en Visserij* [2004] ECR I-7405; United States Chamber of Commerce, 'Precautionary principle' (4 August 2010) <https://www.uschamber.com/precautionary-principle> accessed 28 September 2015.

9 Rolf H. Weber / Urs Klemm / Tobias Baumgartner / Uebe Wesselina / Dirk Trüten, *Lebensmittelrecht EU-Schweiz* (2nd edn, Schulthess Verlag 2012) 65.

10 Ragnar E. Löfstedt / David Vogel, 'The Changing Character of Regulation: A Comparison of Europe and the United States' (2001) 21 (3) Risk Analysis, 399,

based approach[11] and built on a 'science-based risk assessment, cost-benefit analysis, and cost-effectiveness analysis'[12]. The American food market is generally open to the distribution of food as long as there is no scientific evidence of hazard for consumers that is emanating from the food[13]. The scientific evidence of hazard is a state-owned responsibility[14]. The American system is very often criticized because, for the most part, the evidence of hazard is provided after the entry into the market. Frequently, that leads to the situation that customers have already started to consume the food, thereby being exposed to the hazard. On these grounds, the American system is classified as more risk tolerant, as compared to the European system.[15] The US-Chamber of Commerce makes demands on a better consumer education, rather than on employing the precautionary principle[16].

In recent years, the differences between these basic principles of dealing with hazard in terms of the market access of food led to legal proceed-

---

404; Bill Durodie, 'Poisonous Dummies – European Risk Regulation after BSE' (1999) <http://www.durodie.net/pdf/PoisonousDummies.pdf> accessed 22 September 2015.

11 Roland Haines, 'Farm to Fork: A Strategy for Meat Safety' in Ontario – Ministry of the Attorney General (ed), *Report of the Meat Regulatory and Inspection Review* (2004) 112.

12 Lucas Bergkamp / Lawrence Kogan, 'Trade, the Precautionary Principle, and Post-Modern Regulatory Process – Regulatory Convergence in the Transatlantic Trade and Investment Partnership' (2013) 4 EJRR 493, 497; Ragnar E. Löfstedt / David Vogel, 'The Changing Character of Regulation: A Comparison of Europe and the United States' (2001) 21 (3) Risk Analysis 399.

13 Marcel Fricke, 'Genetisch veränderte Lebensmittel im Welthandelsrecht – Die welthandelsrechtliche Konformität der divergierenden Regulierungsansätze in den USA und der EU' in Thomas Bruha / Stefan Oeter (eds), *Europäisches und internationales Integrationsrecht, vol 5, Genetisch veränderte Lebensmittel im Welthandelsrecht* (LIT Verlag 2004) 104.

14 Bettina Rudloff, 'Lebensmittelstandards in Handelsabkommen – Unterschiedliche Regelungstraditionen von EU und USA und Tipps für TTIP' (2014) SWP-Aktuell 1, 5.

15 Arno Scherzberg, 'Risikoabschätzung unter Ungewissheit – Preliminary risk assessment im Kontext der Nanotechnologie' (2010) ZUR 303, 306.

16 United States Chamber of Commerce, 'Precautionary Principle' (4 August 2010) '[To] support a science-based approach to risk management, where risk is assessed based on scientifically sound and technically rigorous standards. [To] oppose the domestic and international adoption of the precautionary principle as a basis for regulatory decision making. [To] educate consumers, businesses, and federal policymakers about the implications of the precautionary principle' <https://www.uschamber.com/precautionary-principle> accessed 28 September 2015.

ings before the WTO. One such example was a dispute between the parties over market access of animals fed with growth hormones[17].

The food stuff control in the European Union and the United States of America is regulated in a contradictory manner. The European Union control is premised on the principle "from Farm to Fork", which means that every single step of the production chain is monitored. This way, it is possible to guarantee the customer food safety.[18]

Contrary to this, the USA focus on the final product, instead of the entire production chain, to guarantee the consumer a safe product. A well-known example is the chlorinated chicken – the symbol of the TTIP resistance. In USA, chicken is sterilized by chlorinated water, immediately prior to selling, to ensure that there are no hazardous bacteria present.[19] Therefore, it is not necessary to establish whether the chicken was certified – as safe in the steps of the production chain preceding this chlorination process.

Furthermore, the European and American risk assessment and risk management are organized differently.

The European Union separates the risk assessment and the risk management strictly[20]. Both the European Food Safety Authority (EFSA) and comparable national departments are independent scientific sources of consultancy and communication in questions of food safety. They are responsible only for science-based risk assessment through experts' reports and consultant recommendations[21]. The proper authority bases the political decision on these scientific experts' reports and consultant recommen-

---

17 Appellate Body Dispute DS26 *United States v European Communities (1998)* EC Measures Concerning Meat and Meat Products (Hormones), WT/DS26/AB/R, WT/DS48/AB/R, para 187.

18 Friedhelm Mühleib, 'Lebensmittelsicherheit und Prozessqualität von Lebensmitteln' *Agra-Europe* (Berlin, 2 March 2015) Dokumentation 1.

19 Bettina Rudloff, 'Lebensmittelstandards in Handelsabkommen – Unterschiedliche Regelungstraditionen von EU und USA und Tipps für TTIP' (2014) SWP-Aktuell 1, 6.

20 Jan-Erik Burchardi, *Die Vereinbarkeit der europäischen Vorschriften zur Kennzeichnung gentechnisch veränderter Lebensmittel mit dem Welthandelsrecht* (Duncker & Humblot 2007) 105 f.

21 European Food Safety Authority, 'About EFSA' <http://www.efsa.europa.eu/en/aboutefsa> accessed 28 September 2015; Jan-Erik Burchardi, *Die Vereinbarkeit der europäischen Vorschriften zur Kennzeichnung gentechnisch veränderter Lebensmittel mit dem Welthandelsrecht* (Duncker & Humblot 2007) 100.

dations.[22] 'So, where experts carry out a scientific risk assessment, the competent public authority must be given sufficiently reliable and cogent information to allow it to understand the ramifications of the scientific question raised, and decide upon a policy in full knowledge of the facts. Consequently, if it is not to adopt arbitrary measures, which cannot in any circumstances be rendered legitimate by the precautionary principle, the competent public authority must ensure that any measures that it takes, even preventive measures, are based on as thorough a scientific risk assessment as possible, account being taken of the particular circumstances of the case at issue.'[23] It is the duty of the European Commission and the Parliaments and the Member States as the most important risk managers to take appropriate measures[24]. The experts' reports and consultant recommendations are only guidelines, without the obligation to follow the scientific recommendations. Therefore, the risk managers reach decisions based on their own discretion[25].

In USA, the Food and Drug Administration (FDA) is the competent public authority in questions of food safety[26]. The sole competence depends on the product. There is no institutional separation between the risk assessment and the risk management. This leads to a greater concordance between the risk assessment and the political risk management.[27] The main emphasis of the risk management in terms of the market access is strongly linked with the scientific risk assessment[28].

---

22 Arno Scherzberg, 'Risikoabschätzung unter Ungewissheit – Preliminary risk assessment im Kontext der Nanotechnologie' (2010) ZUR 303, 305.
23 Case T-13/99 *Pfizer Animal v European Council* [2002] ECR II-3305, para 162.
24 European Food Safety Authority, 'Risk Managers' <http://www.efsa.europa.eu/en/ networks/riskmanagers> accessed 28 September 2015.
25 Stefan Leible / Felix Ortgies / Stephan Schäfer, 'Kapitel 3: Gesetzliche Anforderungen' in Brigitte Petersen / Manfred Nüssel (eds), *Qualitätsmanagement in der Agrar- und Ernährungswirtschaft* (Symposion 2013) 49, 57; Bettina Rudloff, 'Lebensmittelstandards in Handelsabkommen – Unterschiedliche Regelungstraditionen von EU und USA und Tipps für TTIP' (2014) SWP-Aktuell 1, 6 f.
26 U.S. Food and Drug Administration, 'What We Do' <http://www.fda.gov/AboutF-DA/WhatWeDo/default.htm> accessed 22 September 2015.
27 Bettina Rudloff, 'Lebensmittelstandards in Handelsabkommen – Unterschiedliche Regelungstraditionen von EU und USA und Tipps für TTIP' (2014) SWP-Aktuell 1, 7.
28 United States Chamber of Commerce, 'Precautionary Principle' (4 August 2010), '…science-based approach to risk management, where risk is assessed based on

C. The European SPS-Negotiation Paper (SPS-NP)

The idea to combine the differing approaches with the ambition of uniting food standards and the avoidance of needless regulation will be implemented the RCB. Furthermore, internationally accepted Standards and regulations of the Codex Alimentarius and the FAO, will form a basis for the regulatory process. The RCB should provide a more effective form of cooperation that identifies unnecessary regulatory trade barriers.[29] This type of instrument is relatively new and was first experienced in the North American Free Trade Agreement (NAFTA) of the USA, Mexico and Canada, where state government representatives are exclusively appointed to the positions of the RCB.[30]

I. The regulatory Cooperation Body

The European Textual Proposal in terms of Sanitary and Phytosanitary Measures is with regard to the Regulatory Cooperation the implementation of a Joint Management Committee - hereafter called 'the Committee' - in Article 18 SPS-NP.

The Committee may be seen as "the heart" of the Regulatory Cooperation and will be composed of regulatory and trade representatives of the EU and the USA who are responsible for SPS measures, Article 18 no. 1 SPS-NP. The main tasks of the Committee shall include the monitoring and controlling of the whole regulatory process relating to SPS measures by identification, prioritization, management and resolution of issues. In this context, the Commission makes it clear that the Committee shall not

---

scientifically sound and technically rigorous standards' <https://www.uschamber.com/precautionary-principle> accessed 28 September 2015.

29 'TTIP geht in die achte Verhandlungsrunde' *Lebensmittelzeitung* (6 February 2015) 30.

30 Markus Krajewski, 'Stellungnahme für die 15. Sitzung des Ausschusses für Ernährung und Landwirtschaft zur öffentlichen Anhörung "Geplantes Freihandels- und Investitionsabkommen zwischen der EU und den USA: Transatlantic Trade and Investment Partnership – TTIP" ' Ausschussdrucksache des Deutschen Bundestages 18(10)120-C (30 June 2014) 1.

be installed as a body with legislative authority, but as an administrative body[31].

Furthermore, the Committee shall be the relevant body in questions of import check modifications, to inform about the different regulatory systems of the parties and the status quo of the Common Regulatory Cooperation of specific SPS measures by a working paper. An additional function shall be the revision of the Annexes of the Agreement.

The planned Regulatory Cooperation can be separated into different types of cooperation. First, there is a horizontal cooperation, second there is a sectoral cooperation planned by the EU textual proposal.[32] The sectoral cooperation is planned in relation to chemicals, cosmetics, engineering, medical devices, motor vehicles, pharmaceuticals, services, textiles and clothing.

The horizontal cooperation will be realized by cooperative systems. These systems force the parties to create common regulations or to build bridges between the existing systems without taking over the other method. This will occur by a common cooperation "at an early stage" and the exchange of ideas and expertise. The European Commission suggests in Article 18 (4) SPS-NP the establishment of 'working groups consisting of expert-level representatives of the Parties.' Participants from non-governmental organisations may also be partly concluded to widen the circle of competence. Such a possible working group is planned by the commission in Article 17 no. 5 SPS-NP, who shall be entrusted with the development between the parties and international development as well as the cooperation in questions of animal welfare.

Furthermore, the European Commission proposes the involvement of stakeholders in Article 6 of the Initial Provisions for Regulatory Cooperation (RC). In particular, an impact assessment shall include the interested public as an integral part when preparing regulatory acts. The European Commission considers the use of internet platforms as an appropriate instrument to enable the participation of the interested populace.[33] In addi-

---

31 Directorate-General for Trade of the European Commission, *The Transatlantic Trade and Investment Partnership (TTIP) – Towards an EU-US trade deal – Inside TTIP – An overview and chapter-by-chapter guide in plain English* (2015) 19.

32 Ibid 17.

33 European Textual Proposal art 6 of the Initial Provisions for Regulatory Cooperation, 'When preparing regulatory acts…the regulating Party shall offer a reasonable opportunity…to provide input through a public consultation process…The

tion, the stakeholders shall meet with the RCB to discuss the main topics, Article 15 RC. But against considerable reservations of the general public, stakeholders shall not be part of the RCB.

II. The planned role of the Codex Alimentarius

The objectives of the Textual Proposal of Sanitary and Phytosanitary Measures are listed in Article 2 SPS-NP. Besides the reduction of unnecessary barriers to trade, Article 2 SPS-NP provides in no. 3 the implementation of the WTO Agreement on the Application of Sanitary and Phytosanitary Measures, and in no. 4 the entire integration of the Veterinary Agreement. In this context, Article 7 no. 7 SPS-NP mandates that tolerances and maximum residue levels enacted by the Codex Alimentarius Commission have to be applied for undue delay during 12 months after force and effect.

Article 19 SPS-Textual Proposal implements the international cooperation in the context of international bodies like the OIE, the Codex Alimentarius, the IPPC, etc. Furthermore, the parties shall re-establish the work on the Veterinary Agreement of the 21th of April 1998 and replace it with TTIP, Article 20 SPS-NP.

In Article 9 no. 2 SPS-NP, the principles set out in available guidance of international standards setting bodies recognized by the WTO SPS Agreement are consulted as a guideline to establish mechanisms for the determination, recognition and maintenance of equivalence. Also, the requirement of Import and Export Certifications shall be orientated to the principles and standards of the Codex Alimentarius, Article 12 no. 1 SPS-NP.

Article 4 SPS-NP prescribes that "the definitions in Annex A of the SPS Agreement apply as well as do those of Codex Alimentarius (Codex), the World Organization for Animal Health (OIE) and the International Plant Protection Convention (IPPC)". In doubt, the definition set out in the WTO SPS Agreement shall prevail. Against this background, the definitions of the WTO SPS Agreement are exposed and become "hard law" by implementation. Conversely, the parties want to use the Regulatory Cooperation, especially the Joint management committee, to improve a com-

---

regulatory Party should take use of electronic means of communication and seek to use dedicated single access web portals, where possible'.

mon basis to influence international standard-setting basis, Article 18 no. 3 c SPS-NP.

Condensed, the Codex Alimentarius shall be part of the TTIP as hard law by implementation, but in the same way, the parties try to seize the common power by the planned Regulatory Cooperation to influence the setting of international standards like the Codex Alimentarius. This idea of international collaboration is also written down in Article 19 SPS-NP: The Parties will collaborate in the international standard setting bodies (OIE, Codex Alimentarius, IPPC, etc.) with a view to reaching mutually satisfactory outcomes.

D. Conclusion

Every state and every union that shares a single market meets the challenge to bring into line, on one hand, the economy's need for a free and open market and, on the other hand, the consumer's protection against the hazards of a free and open market. And each individual state faces that big challenge differently. At first glance, the United States and European Union do not seem to be so far away from each other as market types of a mixed economy. But a closer look shows that the differences between the two systems run deep with regard to the guarantee of a high food safety by the European precautionary principle and the American science based approach. So, it will be a challenge to coordinate an appropriate integration of markets, especially in view of agricultural and food law, which is regarded generally as a litmus test[34]. This is because a change in the policy of food influences the 'health implications for consumers and for the welfare of farm animals' directly[35]. If the idea of the European Commission of the RCB is put to practice and becomes part of the final law of contracts, it will be the core of the regulatory cooperation. At present, the public debate appears to sooner revolve around subjects such as protection

---

34 Bettina Rudloff, 'Lebensmittelstandards in Handelsabkommen – Unterschiedliche Regelungstraditionen von EU und USA und Tipps für TTIP' (2014) SWP-Aktuell 1, 2.
35 Directorate-General for International Policies of the European Parliament, 'Risks and Opportunities for the EU Agri-Food Sector in a Possible EU-US Trade Agreement-Study' (2014) 13 <http://www.europarl.europa.eu/RegData/etudes/STUD/2014/514007/AGRI_IPOL_STU(2014)514007_EN.pdf> accessed 4 July 2016.

of investment and private arbitration tribunals when the focus of discussion should, at least to the same extent, be directed towards equipping the Regulatory Cooperation Body.

Another very important aspect in the European negotiation paper, in matters of food safety, is the implementation of internationally accepted standards. Initially, international standards should build a mutual basis for an easy interlinking of both systems. But in the long run both parties want to influence the global market with the newly developed standards and to tie down their own standards in the global market. This development could cause a displacement of the role of the WTO, the Codex Alimentarius Commission and the FAO.

Whether and, if so, how the ideas of the European Commission find expression in the final version of the contract remains to be seen.

§ 22 Corporate Social Responsibility (CSR) and the influence on food industry

Malte Wilhelm

A. Transparency in terms of food safety and quality

Numerous food scandals[1] in recent years have changed the expectations of consumers in terms of transparency within the nutrition industry, as well as in terms of the accompanying communication. The resulting social expectations forced companies, especially within the nutrition industry, to offer a product beyond the legal obligations. This is not only affecting the quality and price for purchase, but also the company's reputation. Such a sense of openness and transparency could improve the company's reputation and create valuable long term confidence in product safety.[2] One of the most popular methods used to precisely convey this form of product safety and quality is Corporate Social Responsibility (CSR). It is expected that companies work in a sustainable and transparent way and that they disclose certificates, such as MSC label[3], Bio-Siegel[4] or other organic certifications.[5]

---

1 Diethylene glycol wine scandal in 1985; Bovine spongiform encephalopathy (BSE) or mad cow disease in 1994; Food-and-mouth disease (FMD) in 2001; HUS or EHEC epidemic in 2011; Dioxin scandal in 2010 and 2011; Meat adulteration scandal in 2013; Animal feed scandal in 2013 and 2015.
2 European Commission, 'Communication from the Commission of 28 November 2008 on the European Competitiveness Report 2008' COM (2008) 774 final.
3 Eco-labeling of fish from sustainable fisheries.
4 German quality and test label, which indicates compliance with standards for organic farming according to EU.
5 Bibi van der Zee, *Green Business – Ressourcen, Klimawandel, Globalisierung, Grüne Strategien, Erneuerbare Energien* (GABAL Verlag 2011) 7 f.

B. *Summary of previous developments*

Due to the increasing globalisation of production chains, it is only logical that the European Union [previously European Community] has initiated early steps towards Europeanisation in CSR. Already in 2001 the European Community published a first Green Paper of CSR, which led in 2002 and 2006 to European Commissions (COM) communications. These communications already indicated that a new CSR strategy will be adopted. Finally in October 2011 a Europe-wide CSR strategy 2011-2014 was published. Following this strategy, the results were summarised in a public consultation with interested stakeholders and were published by the COM in November 2014. The lessons learned should lead to a new strategy, which will have a term from 2015 to 2020.[6]

Therefore, this article presents the current strategy, its evaluation as well as the expectations on the new strategy. In addition to this, the so-called CSR Directive 2014/95/EU is presented.

I. *CSR strategy 2011-2014*

The first important outcome of this strategy was a new definition of CSR. Before this strategy was announced, the COM defined CSR as a "concept whereby companies integrate social and environmental concerns in their business operations and in their interaction with their stakeholders on a voluntary basis".[7] By publishing the strategy 2011-2014 the primary strategic focus voluntarily changed into a mutual "respect for applicable legislation, and for collective agreements between social partners".[8] But the main aim of this strategy was to modify and implement social, ethical, en-

---

6   CSR Europe, 'News Release - CSR Europe calls for the new EU CSR strategy 2015-2019 to support a move from CSR compliance to innovation' (3 February 2015)   <http://www.csreurope.org/sites/default/files/MSF%20News%20release %2030%201%202015%20%283%29.pdf> accessed 27 January 2016.

7   European Commission, 'Promoting a European framework for Corporate Social Responsibility' (Green Paper) COM (2001) 366 final, no 20.

8   European Commission, 'Communication from the Commission to the European Parliament, the Council, the European Economic and Social Committee and the Committee of the Regions of 25 October 2011 – A renewed EU strategy 2011-14 for Corporate Social Responsibility' COM (2011) 681 final, no 3.1.

vironmental and stakeholder concerns into the core business operations of enterprises.

The EU declares several factors which demand to improve the political impact of CSR. Besides suggestions concerning self-regulation and co-regulation arrangements, transparency of all stakeholders is one of the most important factors. As already mentioned, the EU wanted to improve the communication, especially between enterprises and stakeholders, and wanted to support the possibility of getting more information legally provided for consumers. This aims at creating mutual confidence. Therefore, the strategy presented some international agreements[9] which already set up standards for transparency within multinational enterprises (MNE). The OECD Guidelines for Multinational Enterprises are one of these agreements. The current Guidelines state that transparency recently represents a part of consumer protection, which can be promoted by an enterprise.[10]

The legal nature of an OECD agreement is described as soft law. Soft law is characterised by the fact that it cannot exert any legally binding obligations. With the integration of soft law into legally sanctionable standards, known as hard law, a mandatory enforcement can be generated. However, soft law represents an excellent instrument in order to supplement hard law.[11] Participating States have to establish National Contact Points (NCP), which are checking infringements of the Guidelines and

---

9 OECD, 'Guidelines for Multinational Enterprises' (2011) <http://www.oecd.org/daf/inv/mne/48004323.pdf> accessed 1 February 2016; United Nations Global Compact, 'The ten principles of the UN Global Compact' <https://www.unglobalcompact.org/what-is-gc/mission/principles> accessed 1 February 2016; ISO 26000 Guidance Standard on Social Responsibility <https://www.iso.org/obp/ui/#iso:std:iso:26000:ed-1:v 1:en> accessed 1 February 2016; International Labour Organization (ILO), 'Tri-partite Declaration of Principles Concerning Multinational Enterprises and Social Policy' <http://www.ilo.org/wcmsp5/groups/public/---ed_emp/---emp_ent/---multi/documents/publication/wcms_094386.pdf> accessed 1 February 2016.
10 OECD, 'Guidelines for Multinational Enterprises' (2011) 30 <http://www.oecd.org/daf/inv/mne/48004323.pdf> accessed 1 February 2016.
11 Inga Hardeck, 'Die Empfehlungen der OECD-Leitsätze für multinationale Unternehmen im Bereich der Besteuerung – Inhalt, Risiken und Implikationen für international tätige Unternehmen' (2011) 24 IStR 936 f.

mediate between the disputing parties in order to find a compromise. The enforcement of the Guidelines is judicially impossible.[12]

The multidimensional character of CSR is shown by these international standards. 42 OECD and non-OECD states agreed to submit to these Guidelines and provided to change their national understanding of international businesses.[13] Within the strategy, the COM just describes a supporting function of public authorities. The main part of CSR should be created by the enterprises themselves. This support shall include a smart mix of voluntary and complementary regulation.[14] A result of this mix will be introduced in chapter III. This approach is comparable with the idea of the invisible hand of Adam Smith. This idea presupposes that the national government creates framework conditions to promote for instance, transparency and good accountability; in return, the industry is responsible for transparency and communication with the consumers.[15]

One of the most important aims of the European Council (EC) was to ensure transparency. The Green Paper of 2001 already focussed on increasing transparency in economic life, antagonizing corruption[16], enhancing the best practice of human resources management[17] and setting up higher standards for the screening of sensitive data[18]. Also, the Single Market Act I considered these objectives again and related them to more social and environmental themes, especially to environmental development and sustainable growth.[19]

---

12 Boris Kasolowsky / Thomas Voland, 'Die OECD-Leitsätze für multinationale Unternehmen und ihre Durchsetzung im Wege von Beschwerdeverfahren vor der Nationalen Kontaktstelle' (2014) 33 NZG 1288 f.

13 OECD, 'Guidelines for Multinational Enterprises' (2011) 3 <http://www.oecd.org/daf/inv/mne/48004323.pdf> accessed 1 February 2016.

14 European Commission, 'Communication from the Commission to the European Parliament, the Council, the European Economic and Social Committee and the Committee of the Regions of 25 October 2011 – A renewed EU strategy 2011-14 for Corporate Social Responsibility' COM (2011) 681 final, no 3.4.

15 Berrit Roth-Mingram, 'Corporate Social Responsibility (CSR) durch eine Ausweitung der nichtfinanziellen Informationen von Unternehmen' (2015) 34 NZG 1341 f.

16 European Commission, 'Promoting a European framework for Corporate Social Responsibility' (Green Paper) COM (2001) 366 final, 13 no 53.

17 Ibid 18 no 77.

18 Ibid 21 no 87.

19 European Commission, 'Communication from the Commission to the European Parliament, the Council, the Economic and Social Committee and the Committee

Against this background, the EC has committed itself to adopt legislative changes to create a framework for social and environmental transparency.[20] As a result, the EC and the EP (European Parliament) introduced Directive 2014/95/EU.

II. Results of the public consultation of CSR strategy 2011-2014

At the end of April 2014, the COM started a public consultation to assess the first CSR strategy and to gain some empirical value of a wide variety of stakeholders. The COM enabled two ways to participate in the assessment for the stakeholders. On the one hand, it was possible for anyone to fill out an online form to give individual feedback. Secondly, the COM arranged a multi-stakeholder forum to which around 450[21] people participated. The majority of the participants were mainly representatives from industry and non-governmental organisations.[22] Ninety[23] of them took the opportunity to express how their experiences with the strategy were and reported on their practical work.

In general, it can be noted that the respondents see the COM as one of the central actors in the field of CSR. 80% of the respondents confirm the importance of the role of the COM, but at the same time every second re-

---

of the Regions of 13 April 2011 – Single Market Act – Twelve levers to boost growth and strengthen confidence – "Working together to create new growth" ' COM (2011) 206 final, no 2.8.

20 European Commission, 'Communication from the Commission to the European Parliament, the Council, the European Economic and Social Committee and the Committee of the Regions of 25 October 2011 – A renewed EU strategy 2011-14 for Corporate Social Responsibility' COM (2011) 681 final, no 4.5.

21 Result of a request from the Europe Direct Contact Center, ID: 1086965/5061149 (21 August 2015).

22 European Commission / DG Enterprise & Industry, 'The Corporate Social Responsibility Strategy of the European Commission: Results of the Public Consultation carried out between 30 April and 15 August 2014' (November 2014) 7 <https://www.google.de/url?sa=t&rct=j&q=&esrc=s&source=web&cd=1&ved=0ahUKEwj-qMHKp9bKAhVIiCwKHRjnCkoQFggjMAA&url=http%3A%2F%2Fec.europa.eu%2FDocsRoom%2Fdocuments%2F8021%2Fattachments%2F1%2Ftranslations%2Fen%2Frenditions%2Fnative&usg=AFQjCNH2jSJZamzDSu_Lb_EBnbOlaXhdrA&bvm=bv.113034660,d.bGg&cad=rja> accessed 1 February 2016.

23 Result of a request from the Europe Direct Contact Center, ID: 1086965/5061149 (21 August 2015).

spondent highlighted that there could be more potential for dedication. Overall private actors are regarded as the key figure within CSR. The COM's work is assessed by around two-thirds of the respondents as at least useful. In particular, the results highlighted the inter-relationship between industry and society. The adoption of Directive 2014/95/EU is also mentioned.[24]

As a central task for the future, the paper presents the enhancement of transparency.[25] In the form of product traceability from the origin, through processing to the consumer, the transparency creates a unique sense of product safety, which can mean a product be consumed without hesitation. It is not surprising that measures of CSR by 79% of respondents are considered as important for medium-term and long-term competitiveness.[26]

Another point of this consultation was to identify why CSR is important for companies. The respondents indicated that even if the economy is more trustful than authorities, consumers distrust the economic world because they see an excessive imbalance between their own distinct power and the power of the business world. CSR can therefore change this perception and can strengthen the confidence of consumers in industry.[27]

III. Directive 2014/95/EU as regards disclosure of non-financial and diversity information by certain large undertakings and groups

Directive 2014/95/EU, also known as the CSR-Directive, became legally valid at the end of 2014. Member States of the EU have until the end of 2016 to implement this Directive into national law, so that the report requirements will be compulsory for the first time in the fiscal year 2017.

---

24 European Commission / DG Enterprise & Industry, 'The Corporate Social Responsibility Strategy of the European Commission: Results of the Public Consultation carried out between 30 April and 15 August 2014' (November 2014) 12 <https://www.google.de/url?sa=t&rct=j&q=&esrc=s&source=web&cd=1&ved=0ahUKEwj-qMHKp9bKAhVIiCwKHRjnCko-QFggjMAA&url=http%3A%2F%2Fec.europa.eu%2FDocsRoom%2Fdocuments%2F8021%2Fattachments%2F1%2Ftranslations%2Fen%2Frenditions%2Fnative&usg=AFQjCNH2jSJZamzDSu_Lb_EBnbOlaXh-drA&bvm=bv.113034660,d.bGg&cad=rja> accessed 1 February 2016.
25 Ibid 3.
26 Ibid 33.
27 Ibid 34.

As already mentioned, the COM sets itself the task to spread transparency between enterprises and consumers. In addition to the efforts to structure the financial system to be more transparent and responsible, the non-financial aspects, at least regarding enterprises with an average number of 500 employees during the fiscal year, become more important. These enterprises should also report about social, environmental and employee matters. This includes, for example, a description of the business model and an exposition of applied due diligence processes which permit an evaluation of the results of the business model, as well as non-financial indicators that are significant for the business purpose.[28] It is expected that approximately 6,000 enterprises in Europe will be affected.[29]. In Germany, MNE have to expect fines up to 50,000 € for infringements of reporting obligations.[30] This disclosure should increase the confidence of consumers in the industry and in product safety.

For several times, Nestlé published a comprehensive sustainability report, setting up a presentable example for the nutrition industry. The latest report was published in 2014. The reports describe Nestlé by different indicators like the number of employees and annual revenues. Subsequently it lists individual business units such as "food and nutrition security" or "supporting nutrition and health". The presentation of single units is a good example to show how transparency could improve the communication with consumers. For example, Nestlé describes its cooperations with authorities such as the WHO, EFSA and other organisations. Aim of the cooperations is to create standards for the certification of products within the Nestlé Nutritional Profiling System (NNPS). Every Nestlé product

---

28 Directive 2014/95/EU of the European Parliament and of the Council of 22 October 2014 amending Directive 2013/34/EU as regards disclosure of non-financial and diversity information by certain large undertakings and groups [2014] OJ L 330/1, art 19 a (1).

29 Ibid art 19 a (1) lit a) – c); Andreas Glaser, 'Corporate Social Responsibility (CSR): Erweiterung der (Lage-) Berichterstattung um nicht-finanzielle Informationen zur Erhöhung der Unternehmenstransparenz in Umwelt- und Sozialbelangen' (2015) 2 IRZ 55.

30 § 341 x (2) HGB (Provision inserted by the law transposing Directive 2013/34/EU of the European Parliament and of the Council of 26 June 2013 on the annual financial statements, consolidated financial statements and related reports of certain types of undertakings and amending Directive 2006/43/EC of the European Parliament and of the Council and repealing Council Directives 78/660/EEC and 83/349/EEC [2013] OJ L 182/19 (Accounts Directive implementation Act - BilRUG) of 17 July 2015, German Federal Law Gazette 2015 I, 1245).

needs to have this certificate to reach the highest level of quality and safety standards. Simultaneously, existing products are critically examined. As a result of this consideration, Nestlé proclaims the aim to reduce salt, sugar and fat in their products.[31]

It should be noted that subsidiaries are seen as independent units and are therefore not covered by the reporting requirements of large enterprises, if the parent enterprise is reporting about them in a consolidated management report. This also applies to subsidiaries that would otherwise be defined as a large enterprise in accordance with the Directive.[32] Such an exception presupposes that the interested consumer is dealing with the corporate structures in order to get the information, provided that they are covered by the Directive.

A critical point are the exceptions which Member States may make to exempt undertakings from the mandatory reporting requirement. The Member States have the possibility to take measures to exempt from the reporting requirement under the Directive, provided that the undertaking concerned makes a report corresponding to national requirements.[33] If 28 Member States will create their own guidelines for reporting, the result will be a diverse mix of different reporting standards which will not be comparable. It will be difficult to reach the goal of using transparency as an indicator of the safety of products, especially in the case of cross-border operating enterprises.

The original idea of the voluntary nature of CSR is adopted explicitly with this Directive, but it does not contain any substantive requirements

---

31 Nestlé, 'Nestlé in society – Creating Shared Value and meeting our commitments 2014' (2014) 10 ff., 51 f. <https://www.nestle.com/asset-library/documents/library/documents/corporate_social_responsibility/nestle-in-society-summary-report-2014-en.pdf> accessed 1 February 2016.
32 Directive 2014/95/EU of the European Parliament and of the Council of 22 October 2014 amending Directive 2013/34/EU as regards disclosure of non-financial and diversity information by certain large undertakings and groups [2014] OJ L 330/1, art 19 a (3), art 29 a (1) lit a), (2), (3).
33 Ibid art 19 a (4) and Directive 2013/34/EU of the European Parliament and of the Council of 26 June 2013 on the annual financial statements, consolidated financial statements and related reports of certain types of undertakings, amending Directive 2006/43/EC of the European Parliament and of the Council and repealing Council Directives 78/660/EEC and 83/349/EEC [2013] OJ L 182/19 art 30 (1), art 34.

for CSR, it only defines an obligation to increase transparency.[34] This Directive should represent a positive composition between the expectations of a legislative framework, and the individual liberty of industry to be self-determined within business. With an exception for Small and Medium-sized Enterprises (SMEs), the EC and the EP made a smart move to create no bureaucratic burdens at the expense of the middle class. It remains to be seen whether the additional burden for reporting obligations and the sanctions for breaches of the requirements will lead to a disproportionate burden of large enterprises, or whether the consumers will appreciate the information.

IV. Expectations of the strategy 2015-2019

The president of the European network for CSR, Étienne Davignon, chose prudent words to describe the expectations and further developments desired for the CSR strategy. He demanded to "unleash the full potential of CSR as it is already defined. European CSR Strategy 2020 should not only focus on a common understanding of CSR to minimise risk, compliance and transparency but also to support companies to take advantage of opportunities to innovate of products and services that create shared value and sustainable living for all".[35]

The results of the public consultation affirm the statement of Étienne Davignon. Accordingly, 80% of the respondents desire a further commitment on CSR of the COM. How this exactly should be implemented is not discernible from the published document. However, enhancing the transparency plays a crucial role (cf. chapter II). It is of utmost importance that the COM establishes a standard, modelled similar to the Global Reporting

---

34 Stefanie Deinert, 'Die CSR-Richtlinie und die Belange der Arbeitnehmer und sonstigen Erwerbstätigen in der Liefer- und Wertschöpfungskette' in Stefanie Deinert / Christian Schrader / Bettina Stoll (eds), *Corporate Social Responsibility – Die Richtlinie 2014/95/EU – Chancen und Herausforderungen* (Kassel University Press 2015) 60.

35 CSR Europe, 'CSR Europe calls for the new EU CSR strategy 2015-2019 to support a move from CSR compliance to innovation' (3 Feburary 2015) <http://www.csreurope.org/csr-europe-calls-new-eu-csr-strategy-2015-2019-support-move-csr-compliance-innovation> accessed 28 January 2016.

Initiative (GRI)[36] benchmarks, in order to make things more comparable with each other. If the comparability stays at the previous level, then the reader will only be able to draw a conclusion when great effort is expended.

A groundbreaking change to the current strategy can thus be achieved keeping in mind that the reporting requirements are expanded. For example, it is only partly understandable why subsidiaries may profit from their parent enterprise's trade, so that they can built up secure trading relations, but in contrast to independent companies, are not taken into the obligation when it concerns the reporting requirements. Here, structures of MNEs are strengthened rather than to promote healthy competition. Similarly, the threshold of reporting must be reduced to a level where more companies are affected by the regulation. Obviously, SMEs will carry a heavier burden than before, but here it has to be expected that political instruments will be created which just absorb those extra burdens. This can be done through compensation or through direct involvement of suppliers in the reports of reportable enterprises. Such involvement of SME makes particular sense, if the economic importance of this is significant for the preservation of prosperity. In Germany, more than 60%[37] of all employees are salaried by SME and this number of SME is responsible for around 55%[38] of GDP.

Finally, the new strategy needs to have a stronger effect on harmonising national rules as of yet. The degree of harmonisation is, with numerous exceptions which MS can make through individual exceptions, very low. Again, establishing comparative figures, as it claims the GRI can be helpful to reduce the national solo attempts

---

36 Global Reporting Initiative (GRI), 'G4 Sustainability Reporting Guidelines' (2013) section 4 - standard disclosures <https://www.globalreporting.org/resourcelibrary/GRIG4-Part2-Implementation-Manual.pdf.> accessed 28 January 2016.
37 German Federal Office of Statistics, 'Mehr als 60% der tätigen Personen arbeiten in kleinen und mittleren Unternehmen' (2013) <https://www.destatis.de/DE/ZahlenFakten/GesamtwirtschaftUmwelt/UnternehmenHandwerk/KleineMittlereUnternehmenMittelstand/Aktuell_.html> accessed 28 January 2016.
38 German Federal Ministry for Economic Affairs and Energy, 'German Mittelstand: Motor der deutschen Wirtschaft' (May 2014) <https://www.bmwi.de/BMWi/Redaktion/PDF/Publikationen/factbook-german-mittelstand,property=pdf,bereich=bmwi2012,sprache=de,rwb=true.pdf.> accessed 28 January 2016.

C. Summary

So far, the main purpose of the COM was to raise awareness for Corporate Social Responsibility. Initially set heavily on self-binding instruments, this area is now regulated more and more. In particular, Directive 2014/95/EU put it in the public eye. The guiding principle of this Directive is the comparability and disclosure of sustainable and responsible corporate governance. The public consultation has shown here how high the acceptance and the importance of such a commitment are. Especially the area of transparency can be found in all stages of development of CSR in Europe. Those times where companies could exclusively seek to dedicate to classic marketing instruments for sales promotion operations, seem to be over. The serious respect for environmental and social responsibility of a company influences the purchase decision of consumers increasingly. Despite everything, the Directive grants a degree of latitude through numerous exceptions and the necessary implementation into 28 diverse Member State laws. This makes an intensive scientific comparison of the reported data appear impossible. A much better handling of the reporting would have been possible through an initiative which would have evaluated reportable factors regarding their durability beforehand. Only with such a basis, is a reporting that is to combine the interests of 28 Member States comparable and usable for further purposes. The Directive therefore promises a new era of transparency of MNE. Certainly, the Directive helps to make known more about specific processes, but the future will show whether this will help to understand the globalised value chains through not completely comparable standards. That future food crises can be prevented due to the Reporting Directive is unlikely. It is hoped that future scandals can be rapidly and extensively clarified. In the area of food quality, the obligation to disclose can probably make a greater progress. An illustration of sustainable economic activity and an increasing recognition by the consumer may be a step forward. Again, the future development will provide more clarity.